Development Research in Practice

Development Research in Practice

The DIME Analytics Data Handbook

Kristoffer Bjärkefur
Luíza Cardoso de Andrade
Benjamin Daniels
Maria Ruth Jones

 **WORLD BANK GROUP**

Contents

Boxes

Figures

Foreword

For most of our history, data have been scarce and expensive to obtain, and economic research has advanced at a slow pace, especially in data-poor countries. The high cost of impact evaluations, for example, has mainly been determined by the cost of collecting data. This is rapidly changing because of recent advances in technology (see the World Bank's *World Development Report 2021*). Technology, like smartphones, mobile networks, e-services, and e-government, has changed the process through which data are generated and has created massive amounts of real-time transaction-level data, with more data being generated in the last two years than in all human history combined.

Yet most data are unused, especially in the public sector and in low-capacity environments. The scarcity we now face is of a different nature: we are limited by high-quality research skills and institutional capabilities for making sense of all the data and turning them into a resource for human progress.

Building knowledge takes time, and evidence, especially in development economics, is scarce and difficult to generate. Realistically, evidence informs only a tiny proportion of the policy decisions being made every day. Making steady progress toward bridging the knowledge gap requires taking research from a microentrepreneurial to a corporate mode of delivery. At Development Impact Evaluation (DIME), we have invested in a research production function and workflows that capitalize on scale and specialization in the delivery of research. In so doing, we have lowered the costs of research while optimizing the quantity and quality of research output. We set up the DIME Analytics team as an institutional solution to increase the quality of data collection and analysis for our research portfolio. This has been a high-return investment. The team has helped transform the way we work and, in the process, created a host of open-source resources like the DIME Wiki, toolkits, and reproducibility protocols that have been made available to the wider community of development economics researchers and practitioners.

The provision of tools and innovations that help improve the global production of development economics research is, we feel, part and parcel of the responsibility of institutions like the World Bank and other academic centers of excellence that have the organization and resources to create and deliver public knowledge goods. In so doing, we hope to contribute to building capacities both internally and in the rest of the global research community, especially for those that may not operate with the same level of organization and resources as we do.

Although research is a great organizing principle for creating and extracting value from data, it is very rare for data to be ready for use. Identifying sources, obtaining permissions, integrating data from different sources, and triangulating and ground-truthing to understand biases in coverage and representativeness are all necessary steps to developing an understanding of how data quality can be improved, what the data can be used for, and how results should interpreted. A high level of technical specialization and the right combination of disciplines brought into a research team can significantly increase the quality of data and economic research.

At DIME, as we have been making consistent advancements in the great puzzle of creating and using data responsibly, investing in the quality of data and research for development, we have made those tools available and open source. Now we feel we should go one step further. The idea behind this handbook is to provide a step-by-step guide to high-quality, reproducible data work over the full life cycle of an empirical research project. The book is directed to development researchers all over the world, to be read cover to cover or as a desk reference as needs arise.

Arianna Legovini
Adviser, Development Impact Evaluation (DIME)
World Bank

Acknowledgments

This book is dedicated to all the Development Impact Evaluation (DIME) team members who have wrangled data without being taught how, hustled to get projects done on time, wondered if they really should get their PhD after all, and in doing so made this knowledge necessary and possible.

We thank all the people who helped us get here, especially Arianna Legovini, for her leadership at DIME, unending support of our work, and detailed comments on this book, and Florence Kondylis, for her leadership in founding and growing DIME Analytics and supporting this project from the very first. We also thank the following members of DIME Analytics for their contributions to the ideas in this book and their help organizing them: Roshni Khincha, Avnish Singh, Patricia Paskov, Radhika Kaul, Mizuhiro Suzuki, Yifan Powers, and Maria Arnal Canudo. This work has been financially supported by the United Kingdom Foreign, Commonwealth & Development Office (FCDO) through the DIME i2i Umbrella Facility for Impact Evaluation at the World Bank.

Our gratitude to the many people who read and offered feedback as the book took shape: Stephanie Annijas, Maria Camila Ayala Guerrero, Kaustubh Chahande, Thomas Escande, Aram Gassama, Steven Glover, Nausheen Khan, Robert Norling, Michael Orevba, Caio Piza, Francesco Raffaelli, Daniel Rogger, Ankriti Singh, Ravi Somani, and Leonardo Viotti. Although they number far too many to name individually, we also thank all the members of DIME and its teams over the years for the innovative work they have done, the lessons learned, and the team spirit that makes our work so fruitful and rewarding.

This published version of the book has been revised repeatedly since its internal release in June 2019, with extensive feedback from readers and experts. We additionally thank Vincenzo di Maro (manager, DIME3) for his support throughout this process, as well as peer reviewers David McKenzie (lead economist, World Bank), Holly Krambeck (program manager, World Bank), Alaka Holla (program manager, World Bank), Jim Shen (senior manager, Abdul Latif Jameel Poverty Action Lab), Federica di Battista (trialling lead, FCDO), and Gabriel Vicente, Rajee Kanagavel, and Maksim Pecherskiy from the Development Data Partnership team.

This book is a living product that is written and maintained publicly. For the code and edit history, see https://github.com/worldbank/dime -data-handbook; for online and PDF copies, visit https://worldbank.github .io/dime-data-handbook/. The website includes updated instructions

for providing feedback as well as notes on updates to the content.
Whether you work with DIME, the World Bank, or another organization
or university, we ask that you read the contents of this book critically.
We welcome feedback and corrections to improve the book. Please visit
https://worldbank.github.io/dime-data-handbook/feedback to provide
feedback. You can also email us at dimeanalytics@worldbank.org, and we
will be very thankful. We hope that you enjoy *Development Research in
Practice*!

About the Authors

Kristoffer Bjärkefur

Kristoffer Bjärkefur is a data scientist consultant with Development Impact Evaluation (DIME). As a member of the DIME Analytics team, he works to improve the reproducibility, transparency, and credibility of development research. He combines his backgrounds in development economics research and computer programming to make tools and best practices from the world of computer science more easily available to practitioners in development data. He supports teams at all stages in the life cycle of data and particularly enjoys planning data workflows. In DIME Analytics, he leads the work on data security and privacy.

Luíza Cardoso de Andrade

Luíza Cardoso de Andrade is a junior data scientist with DIME. Her work on the DIME Analytics team focuses on promoting research transparency and reproducibility practices through trainings and code review. She also works across DIME's portfolio of impact evaluations to incorporate nontraditional data sources such as high-frequency crowdsourced and web-scraped data. She has developed original software tools for research, including web-based data interfaces and the `ietoolkit` and `iefieldkit` Stata packages. Her research work has focused on agriculture, gender, and environmental policy.

Benjamin Daniels

Benjamin Daniels is a fellow at the Georgetown University Initiative on Innovation, Development, and Evaluation. His research focuses on the delivery of quality primary health care in developing contexts. His work has highlighted the importance of direct measurement of provider knowledge, effort, and practice. He has supported some of the largest research studies to date using clinical vignettes, provider observation, and standardized patients. He works with DIME Analytics to improve the transparency and credibility of development research. This work comprises research training and resources like the DIME Wiki and software products like `iefieldkit` and `ietoolkit`, among other Stata code tools.

Maria Ruth Jones

Maria Ruth Jones cofounded and now leads DIME Analytics, an initiative to improve the quality, transparency, and reproducibility of empirical research. Her research interests center on survey methods, innovations in measurement, and technology adoption. She created and manages public goods to benefit the global research community, such as Development Research in Practice, the DIME Wiki, and the Manage Successful Impact Evaluations course. She joined the World Bank in 2009. Previous roles include coordination of the Global Agriculture and Food Security Program impact evaluation portfolio (2012–16) and a program of impact evaluations with the government of Malawi (2009–11).

Abbreviations

3ie	International Initiative for Impact Evaluations
AEA	American Economic Association
API	application programming interface
ATE	average treatment effect
AWS	Amazon Web Services
CAPI	computer-assisted personal interview
CSL	Citation Styles Library
DIME	Development Impact Evaluation
DOI	digital object identifier
EGAP	Evidence in Governance and Politics
EPS	encapsulated PostScript
FDE	full disk encryption
FSE	file system encryption
GPS	global positioning system
HFC	high-frequency check
IAT	implicit association test
ID	identifier or identification
IPA	Innovations for Poverty Action
IRB	institutional review board
IV	instrumental variables
J-PAL	Abdul Latif Jameel Poverty Action Lab
MDE	minimum detectable effect
MSIE	Manage Successful Impact Evaluations
MSIES	Manage Successful Impact Evaluation Surveys
ODK	Open Data Kit
OSF	Open Science Framework
PAP	preanalysis plan
PDF	portable document format
PII	personally identifying information
PNG	portable network graphic
RCT	randomized control trial
RD	regression discontinuity

RIDIE	Registry for International Development Impact Evaluations
SSC	Statistical Software Components
URL	uniform resource locator
USB	universal serial bus
VPN	virtual private network

Introduction

Development Research in Practice: The DIME Analytics Data Handbook is intended to teach all users of development data how to handle data effectively, efficiently, and ethically. An empirical revolution has changed the face of development research over the last decade. Increasingly, researchers are working not just with complex data, but with *original* data—data sets collected by the research team itself or acquired through a unique agreement with a project partner. Research teams must carefully document how original data are created, handled, and analyzed. These tasks now contribute as much weight to the quality of the evidence as the research design and the statistical approaches do. At the same time, empirical research projects are expanding in scope and scale: more people are working on the same data over longer time frames. For that reason, the central premise of this book is that data work is a "social process," which means that the many people on a team need to have the same ideas about what is to be done, when, where, and by whom so that they can collaborate effectively on a large, long-term research project.

Despite the growing importance of managing data work, little practical guidance is available for practitioners. There are few guides to the conventions, standards, and best practices that are fast becoming a necessity for empirical research. *Development Research in Practice* aims to fill that gap. It covers the full data workflow for a complex research project using original data, sharing the lessons, tools, and processes developed within the World Bank's Development Impact Evaluation (DIME) department, and compiling them into a single narrative of best practices for data work. This book is not sector specific; it does not teach econometrics or how to design an impact evaluation. Many excellent resources address those topics. Instead, it teaches how to think about all aspects of research from a data perspective, how to structure research projects to ensure high-quality data, and how to institute transparent and reproducible workflows. Adopting these workflows may have significant up-front learning costs, but these investments pay off quickly, saving time and improving the quality of research going forward.

How to read this book

This book aims to be a highly practical resource so that readers can immediately begin to collaborate more effectively on large, long-term research projects using the methods and tools discussed. This introduction outlines the basic philosophies that motivate this book and the approach taken to research data. The central message is that research data work is primarily about communicating effectively within a team and that effective collaboration is enabled by standardization and simplification of data tasks. This book provides a narrative outline of the data workflow at each stage of an empirical research project, from design to publication, as visualized in figure I.1. Chapters 1 and 2 contextualize the workflow and set the stage for the hands-on data tasks described in detail in chapters 3 to 7.

FIGURE I.1 Overview of the tasks involved in development research data work

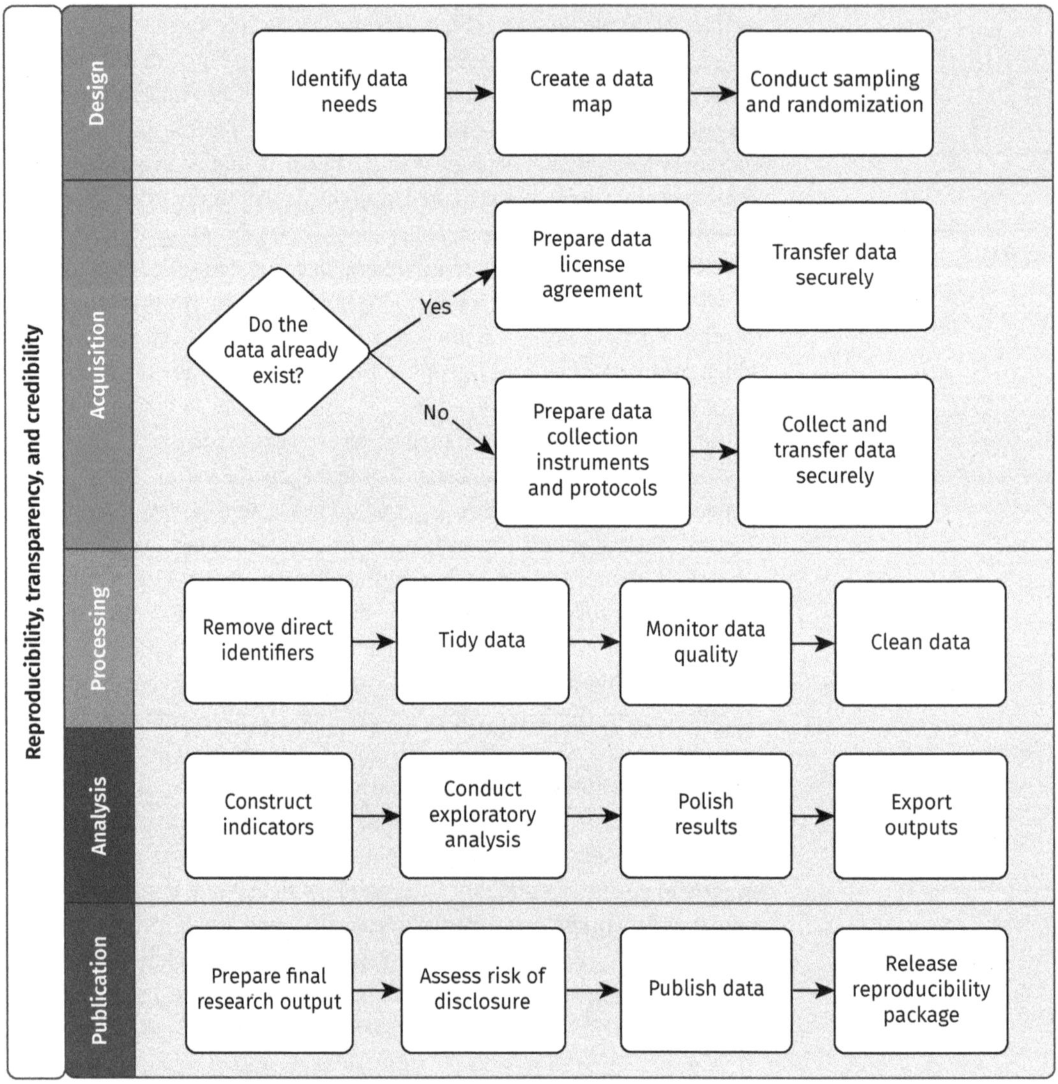

Source: DIME (Development Impact Evaluation), World Bank.

Chapter 1 outlines the principles and practices that help consumers of research to be confident in the conclusions reached and describes the three pillars of a high-quality empirical research project: credibility, transparency, and reproducibility. It presents three popular methods of committing to the use of particular research questions or methods, discusses how to apply principles of transparency to all research processes, and provides guidance on how to make research fully reproducible.

Chapter 2 teaches readers how to structure data work for collaborative research while ensuring the privacy and security of research participants. It discusses the importance of planning data work and associated tools in advance, long before any data are acquired. It also describes ethical concerns common to development data, common pitfalls in legal and practical management of data, and how to respect the rights of research participants at all stages of data work.

Chapter 3 turns to the measurement framework, describing how to translate research design into a data work plan. It details DIME's data map template, a set of tools to communicate the project's data requirements both across the team and across time. It also discusses how to implement random sampling and random assignment in a reproducible and credible manner.

Chapter 4 covers data acquisition. It starts with the legal and institutional frameworks for data ownership and licensing, examining the rights and responsibilities of using data collected by the research team or by others. It provides a deep dive on collecting high-quality primary electronic survey data, including developing and deploying survey instruments. Finally, it discusses how to handle data securely during transfer, sharing, and storage, because secure data handling is essential to protecting respondent privacy.

Chapter 5 describes data-processing tasks. It details how to construct "tidy" data at the appropriate units of analysis, how to ensure uniquely identified data sets, and how to incorporate data quality checks routinely into the workflow. It also provides guidance on the process of de-identifying and cleaning personally identifying data, focusing on how to understand and structure data in preparation for constructing indicators and performing analytical work.

Chapter 6 discusses data analysis tasks. It begins with data construction, which is the creation of new variables from the original data. It introduces core principles for writing analytical code and creating, exporting, and storing research outputs such as figures and tables reproducibly, using dynamic documents.

Chapter 7 outlines the publication of research outputs, including manuscripts, code, and data. It discusses how to collaborate effectively on technical writing using dynamic documents. It also covers how and why to publish data sets in an accessible, citable, and safe fashion. Finally, it provides guidelines for preparing functional and informative reproducibility packages that contain all of the code, data, and metadata needed for others to evaluate and reproduce the work.

Each chapter starts with a box summarizing the most important points, takeaways for different types of readers, and a list of key tools and resources for implementing the recommended practices. Each chapter provides an understanding of which tasks will be performed at every stage of the workflow and how to implement them according to best practices. Each also provides an understanding of how the various stages of the workflow tie together and what inputs and outputs are required and produced from each. The references and links contained in each chapter lead to detailed descriptions of individual ideas, tools, and processes that will be useful when implementing the tasks. Box I.1 describes the Demand for Safe Spaces project, which is the basis for the examples given throughout this handbook.

BOX I.1 THE DEMAND FOR SAFE SPACES CASE STUDY

A completed project, Demand for Safe Spaces: Avoiding Harassment and Stigma, is used to illustrate the empirical research tasks described throughout this handbook. Each chapter contains boxes with examples of how the practices and workflows described in it were applied in this real-life example. All of the examples of code and diagrams referenced in the case study can be accessed directly through this book's GitHub repository. Minor adaptations were made to the original study materials for function and clarity. All of the original materials are included in the project's reproducibility package. The Demand for Safe Spaces study is summarized in its abstract as follows:

What are the costs to women of harassment on public transit? This study randomizes the price of a women-reserved "safe space" in Rio de Janeiro and crowdsources information on 22,000 rides. Women in the public space experience harassment once a week. A fifth of riders are willing to forgo 20 percent of the fare to ride in the "safe space." Randomly assigning riders to the "safe space" reduces physical harassment by 50 percent, implying a cost of $1.45 per incident. Implicit association tests show that women face a stigma for riding in the public space that may outweigh the benefits of the safe space.

The Demand for Safe Spaces study used novel original data from three sources. It collected information on 22,000 metro rides from a crowdsourcing app (referred to as crowdsourced ride data in the case study examples), a survey of randomly sampled commuters on the platform (referred to as the platform survey), and data from an implicit association test. The research team first elicited revealed preferences for the women-reserved cars and then randomly assigned riders across the reserved and nonreserved cars to measure differences in the incidence of harassment. Researchers used a customized app to assign data collection tasks and to vary assigned ride spaces (women-reserved cars vs. public cars) and the associated payout across rides. In addition, the team administered social norm surveys and implicit association tests on a random sample of men and women commuters to document a potential side effect of reserved spaces: stigma against women who choose to ride in the public space.

This handbook focuses on the protocols, methods, and data used in the Demand for Safe Spaces study rather than on the results. A working paper by Kondylis et al. (2020) provides more information about the findings from this study and how it was conducted.

For materials for all of the examples in the book, see https://github.com/worldbank/dime-data-handbook/tree/main/code. For access to the Demand for Safe Spaces study repository, see https://github.com/worldbank/rio-safe-space. For the working paper, see https://openknowledge.worldbank.org/handle/10986/33853.

The DIME Wiki: A complementary resource

The handbook contains many references to the DIME Wiki, a free online collection of impact evaluation resources and best practices. This handbook and the DIME Wiki are meant to go hand in hand: the handbook provides the narrative structure and workflow, and the DIME Wiki offers specific implementation details, detailed code examples, and a more exhaustive set of references for each topic. The DIME Wiki is a living resource that is continuously updated and improved, both by the authors of this book and by external contributors. All readers are welcome to register as DIME Wiki users and contribute directly to it at https://dimewiki .worldbank.org.

Standardizing data work

In the past, data work was often treated as a "black box" in research. A published manuscript might exhaustively detail research designs, estimation strategies, and theoretical frameworks, but typically reserved very little space for detailed descriptions of how data were collected and handled. It is almost impossible to assess the quality of the data in such a paper and whether the results could be reproduced. This situation is changing, in part because more publishers and funders are requiring researchers to release their code and data (Swanson et al. 2020).

Handling data and producing documentation are key skills for researchers and research staff. Standard data processes and documentation practices are important throughout the research process to convey and implement the intended research design accurately (Vilhuber 2020) and to minimize security risks: better protocols and processes lower the probability of data leakages, security breaches, and loss of personal information. When data work has been done in an ad hoc manner, it is very difficult for others to understand what has been done—readers simply have to trust that the researchers have performed these tasks correctly. Most important, if any part of the data pipeline breaks down, research results become unreliable (McCullough, McGeary, and Harrison 2008) and cannot be accepted at face value according to the intended research design (Goldstein 2016). Because "laboratory" settings almost never exist in this type of research, such a failure has a very high cost (for an example, see Baldwin and Mvukiyehe 2015): failure wastes the investments made in knowledge generation and wastes the research opportunity itself (Camerer et al. 2016).

Accurate and reproducible data management and analysis are essential to the success and credibility of modern research. Data-handling processes need to be standardized and documented for the data work to be evaluated and understood alongside any final research outputs. *Process standardization* is an important component of this effort. Process standardization is an agreement within a research team about how all tasks of a specific type will be approached. It means that there is little ambiguity about how something ought to be done and therefore that the tools to do it can be set in advance. Standard processes help other people to understand the work and make the work easier to document. Process standardization and documentation allow readers of code to (1) understand quickly what a particular process or output is supposed to be doing, (2) evaluate whether or not it does that task correctly, and (3) modify it either to test alternative hypotheses or to adapt it in their own work. This book discusses specific standards recommended by DIME Analytics, but the goal is to convince readers to discuss the adoption of a standard within research teams rather than necessarily to use the particular standards recommended here.

Standardizing coding practices

Modern quantitative research relies heavily on statistical software tools, written with various coding languages, to standardize analytical work. Outputs like regression tables and data visualizations are created using code in statistical software for two primary reasons. Using a standard command or package ensures that the work is done right and that the procedure can be confirmed or checked using the same data at a later date or implemented again using different data. Keeping a clear, human-readable record of these code and data structures is critical. Although it is often possible to perform nearly all of the relevant tasks through an interactive user interface or even through software such as Excel, this practice is strongly discouraged. In the context of statistical analysis, the practice of writing all work using standard code is widely accepted. To support this practice, DIME now maintains portfolio-wide standards about how analytical code should be maintained and made accessible before, during, and after release or publication.

Over the last few years, DIME has extended the same principles to preparing data for analysis, which often constitutes just as much (or more) of the manipulation done to data over the life cycle of a research project. This book encourages research teams to think about the tools and processes they use for designing, collecting, and handling data just as they do for conducting analysis. To this end, DIME Analytics has contributed tools and standard practices for implementing these tasks using statistical software.

Although most researchers do nearly all data work using code, many come from economics and statistics backgrounds rather than computer science backgrounds, and they often understand code to be a means to an end rather than an output itself. This attitude needs to change: in particular, development practitioners must think about their code and programming workflows just as methodically as they think about their research workflows; they need to think of code and data as research outputs, similar to manuscripts and briefs.

This approach arises because code is the "recipe" for the analysis. The code tells others exactly what was done, explains how they can do it again in the future, and provides a road map and knowledge base for further original work (Hamermesh 2007). Performing tasks through written code creates a record of every task performed (Ozier 2019). It also prevents direct interaction with the data files that could lead to nonreproducible processes (Chang and Li 2015). DIME Analytics has invested a lot of time in developing code as a learning tool: the examples written and the commands provided in this book are designed to provide a framework for common practice, so that everyone working on these tasks in DIME is able to read, review, and provide feedback on the work of others, starting from the same basic ideas about how various tasks are done.

Most specific code tools have a learning and adaptation process, meaning that researchers will become most comfortable with each tool only by using it in the real world. To support the process of learning to create and use reproducible tools and workflows, this handbook references free and open-source tools wherever possible and points to more detailed instructions when relevant. Stata, a proprietary software, is the notable exception because of its persistent popularity in development economics and econometrics (StataCorp 2021). Appendix A presents two guides: the DIME Analytics Coding Guide, which provides instructions on how to write good code and how to use the examples of code in this book, and the DIME Analytics Stata Style Guide. DIME project teams are strongly encouraged to adopt and follow coding style guides explicitly in their work. Style guides harmonize code practices within and across teams, making it easier to understand and reuse code, which ultimately helps teams to build on each other's best practices. Some of the programming languages used at DIME already have well-established and commonly used style guides, such as the *Tidyverse Style Guide* for R and PEP-8 for Python (see van Rossum, Warsaw, and Coghlan 2013; Wickham, n.d.). Relatively few resources of this type are available for Stata, which is why DIME Analytics has created and included one here. For the complete DIME Analytics Coding Standards, see the GitHub repository at https://github.com/worldbank/dime-standards.

The team behind this book

DIME generates high-quality, operationally relevant data and research to transform development policy and support the World Bank's mission of reducing extreme poverty and securing shared prosperity (Legovini, Di Maro, and Piza 2015). DIME develops customized data and evidence ecosystems to produce actionable information and recommend specific policy pathways to maximize impact. DIME conducts research in 60 countries with 200 agencies, leveraging a US$180 million research budget to shape the design and implementation of US$18 billion in development finance. DIME also provides advisory services to 30 multilateral and bilateral development agencies (Legovini et al. 2019). DIME research is organized into four primary topics: economic transformation and growth; gender, economic opportunity, and fragility; governance and institution building; and infrastructure and climate change. Over the years, DIME has employed dozens of research economists and hundreds of full-time research assistants, field coordinators, and other staff. The team has conducted more than 325 impact evaluations. *Development Research in Practice* takes advantage of the concentration and scale of this research to synthesize many resources for data collection and research and make DIME tools available to the larger community of development researchers. (For more information, see https://www.worldbank.org/en/research/dime.)

As part of its broader mission, DIME invests in public goods to improve the quality and reproducibility of development research around the world. DIME Analytics, the team responsible for writing and maintaining this book, is a centralized unit that develops and ensures the adoption of high-quality research practices across the DIME portfolio. It works through an intensive, collaborative innovation cycle: DIME Analytics trains and supports research assistants and field coordinators, provides standard tools and workflows to all teams, delivers hands-on support when new tasks or challenges arise, and then develops and integrates lessons from those engagements to bring to the full team. Resources developed and tested in DIME are converted into public goods for the global research community through open-access trainings and open-source tools. Appendix B, the DIME Analytics resource directory, provides an introduction to public materials.

DIME Analytics has devoted many hours to learning from data work across DIME's portfolio, identifying inefficiencies and barriers to success, developing tools and trainings, and standardizing best-practice workflows adopted in DIME projects. It has invested significant energy in the language and materials used to teach these workflows to new team members and, in many cases, in software tools that support these workflows explicitly. DIME team members often work on diverse portfolios of projects with a wide range of teammates and have found that standardizing core processes across all projects results in higher-quality work, with fewer opportunities to make mistakes. In that way, the DIME Analytics team has institutionalized, developed, and refined tools and practices over time and given the department a common base of knowledge and practice. In 2018, for example, DIME adopted universal reproducibility checks for publications; the lessons from this practice helped to move the DIME team from having 50 percent of the papers assessed for reproducibility in 2018 require significant revision to having 64 percent of the papers submitted in 2019 pass without any revision.

Looking ahead

Although adopting the workflows and mind-sets described in this book requires an up-front cost, it will save research teams a lot of time and hassle very quickly. In part this is because readers will learn how to implement essential practices directly, in part because they will find new tools for more advanced practices, and, most important, because they will acquire the mind-set of doing research with a focus on high-quality data.

Some readers may find the number of new tools and practices recommended in this book to be daunting (see figure I.1). The experience at DIME has shown that full-scale adoption is possible; in the last few years, the full DIME portfolio has transitioned to transparent and reproducible workflows, with a fair share of hiccups along the way. The authors of this book were involved in supporting that at-scale transition and hope that, by sharing the resources and lessons learned, the learning curve for readers will be less steep. The summary boxes at the beginning of each chapter provide a list of the key tools and resources to help readers to prioritize. The handbook also offers "second-best" practices in many cases, suggesting easy-to-implement ways to increase transparency and reproducibility in cases when full-scale adoption of the recommended workflow is not immediately feasible. In fact, teams are encouraged to adopt one new practice at a time rather than to rebuild their whole workflow from scratch right away. It is hoped that, by the end of the book, all readers will have learned how to handle data more efficiently, effectively, and ethically at all stages of the research process.

References

Baldwin, Kate, and Eric Mvukiyehe. 2015. "Elections and Collective Action: Evidence from Changes in Traditional Institutions in Liberia." *World Politics* 67 (4): 690–725.

Camerer, Colin F., Anna Draber, Eskel Forsell, Teck-Hua Ho, Jürgen Hube, Magnus Johannesson, Michael K. Kirchler, et al. 2016. "Evaluating Replicability of Laboratory Experiments in Economics." *Science* 351 (6280): 1433–36.

Chang, Andrew C., and Phillip Li. 2015. "Is Economics Research Replicable? Sixty Published Papers from Thirteen Journals Say 'Usually Not.'" Board of Governors of the Federal Reserve System, Washington, DC.

Goldstein, Markus. 2016. "More Replication in Economics?" *Development Impact* (blog), October 26, 2016. https://blogs.worldbank.org/impactevaluations /more-replication-economics.

Hamermesh, Daniel S. 2007. "Replication in Economics." *Canadian Journal of Economics/Revue Canadienne d'Économique* 40 (3): 715–33.

Kondylis, Florence, Arianna Legovini, Kate Vyborny, Astrid Zwager, and Luíza Andrade. 2020. "Demand for 'Safe Spaces': Avoiding Harassment and Stigma." Policy Research Working Paper 9269, World Bank, Washington, DC. https:// openknowledge.worldbank.org/handle/10986/33853.

Legovini, Arianna, Vincenzo Di Maro, and Caio Piza. 2015. "Impact Evaluation Helps Deliver Development Projects." Policy Research Working Paper 7157, World Bank, Washington, DC.

Legovini, Arianna, Serge Guigonan, Guadalupe Bedoya Arguelles, Theophile Bougna Lonla, Kayleigh Bierman Campbell, Paul J. Christian, Aidan Coville, et al. 2019. *Science for Impact: Better Evidence for Better Decisions— the Dime Experience.* Washington, DC: World Bank Group. http:// documents.worldbank.org/curated/en/942491550779087507/Science -for-Impact-Better-Evidence-for-Better-Decisions-The-Dime-Experience.

McCullough, Bruce D., Kerry Anne McGeary, and Teresa D. Harrison. 2008. "Do Economics Journal Archives Promote Replicable Research?" *Canadian Journal of Economics/Revue Canadienne d'Économique* 41 (4): 1406–20.

Ozier, Owen. 2019. "Replication Redux: The Reproducibility Crisis and the Case of Deworming." Policy Research Working Paper 8835, World Bank, Washington, DC.

StataCorp. 2021. Stata Statistical Software: Release 17. StataCorp, College Station, TX.

Swanson, Nicholas, Garret Christensen, Rebecca Littman, David Birke, Edward Miguel, Elizabeth Levy Paluck, and Zenan Wang. 2020. "Research Transparency Is on the Rise in Economics." *AEA Papers and Proceedings* 110 (May): 61–65.

Van Rossum, Guido, Barry Warsaw, and Nick Coghlan. 2013. "PEP8: Style Guide for Python Code." Python. https://www.python.org/dev/peps/pep-0008/.

Vilhuber, Lars. 2020. "Implementing Increased Transparency and Reproducibility in Economics." Cornell University, Ithaca, NY. https://doi.org/10.5281/zenodo.3911311.

Wickham, Hadley. n.d. *The Tidyverse Style Guide*. Tydyverse. https://style.tidyverse.org/index.html

Chapter 1

Conducting reproducible, transparent, and credible research

Policy decisions are made every day using the results of development research, and these decisions have wide-reaching effects on the lives of millions. As the emphasis on evidence-informed policy grows, so too does the scrutiny placed on research methods and results. Three major components make up this scrutiny: credibility, transparency, and reproducibility. These three components contribute to one simple idea: research should be high quality and well documented. Research consumers, including policy makers who use the evidence to make decisions, should be able to examine and recreate it easily. In this framework, it is useful to think of research as a public service that requires researchers as a group to be accountable for their methods. Accountability means acting collectively to protect the credibility of development research by following modern practices for research planning and documentation.

Across the social sciences, the open science movement has been fueled by concerns regarding the proliferation of low-quality research practices; data and code that are inaccessible to the public; analytical errors in major research papers; and, in some cases, even outright fraud. Although the development research community has not yet experienced major scandals, improvements clearly are needed in how code and data are handled as part of research. Moreover, having common standards and practices for creating and sharing materials, code, and data with others will improve the value of the work that researchers do.

This chapter outlines principles and practices that help research consumers to have confidence in the conclusions reached. Each of the three components—credibility, transparency, and reproducibility—is discussed in turn. The first section covers research credibility. It presents three popular methods of committing to the use of particular research questions or methods and avoiding potential criticisms of cherry-picking results: study registration, preanalysis plans, and registered reports. The second section discusses how to apply principles of transparency to all research processes, which allows research teams to be more efficient and research consumers to understand thoroughly and evaluate the quality of research. The final section provides guidance on how to make research fully reproducible and explains why replication materials are an important research contribution in their own right. Box 1.1 summarizes the main points, lists the responsibilities of different members of the research team, and supplies a list of key tools and resources for implementing the recommended practices.

BOX 1.1 SUMMARY: CONDUCTING REPRODUCIBLE, TRANSPARENT, AND CREDIBLE RESEARCH

Credibility, transparency, and reproducibility are three pillars of a high-quality empirical research project. The steps and outputs discussed in this chapter should be prepared at the beginning of a project and revisited through the publication process.

1. *Credibility.* To enhance credibility, researchers need to make as many research decisions as possible before beginning data work. These decisions can be precommitted publicly through the following mechanisms:

   - Register research studies to provide a record of every project, so that all evidence about a topic can be maintained; preregister studies to protect design choices from later criticism.
   - Write preanalysis plans both to strengthen the conclusions drawn from those analyses and to increase efficiency by creating a road map for project data work.
   - Publish a registered report to combine the benefits of the first two steps with a formal peer review process and conditional acceptance of the results of the specified research.

2. *Transparency.* All data acquisition and analysis decisions made during the project life cycle should be documented, including details on what information will be released publicly and a plan for how it will be published:

   - Develop and publish comprehensive project documentation, especially instruments for data collection or acquisition that may be needed to prove ownership rights and facilitate the reuse of data.
   - Retain the original data in an unaltered form and archive data appropriately, in preparation for de-identification and publication at the appropriate times.
   - Write all data-processing and analysis code with public release in mind.

3. *Reproducibility.* Analytical work needs to be prepared so that it can be verified and reproduced by others. To do so, the research team should do the following:

   - Understand what archives and repositories are appropriate for various materials.
   - Prepare for legal documentation and licensing of data, code, and research products.
   - Initiate reproducible workflows that will transfer easily within and outside of the research team, and provide the necessary documentation for others to understand and use all materials.

(Box continues on next page)

DEVELOPMENT RESEARCH IN PRACTICE: THE DIME ANALYTICS DATA HANDBOOK

Key responsibilities for task team leaders and principal investigators

- Develop and document the research design and the corresponding data required to execute it.
- Guide the research team in structuring and completing project registration.
- Understand the team's future rights and responsibilities regarding data, code, and research publication.
- Determine what methods of precommitment are appropriate, and lead the team in preparing them.

Key responsibilities for research assistants

- Adjust outputs and documentation to meet the specific technical requirements of registries, funders, publishers, or other governing bodies.
- Inform the team leadership whenever methodologies, data strategies, or planned executions are not sufficiently clear or not appropriately documented or communicated.
- Become familiar with best practices for carrying out reproducible and transparent research, and initiate those practices within the research team.

Key resources

- Registering a research study at https://dimewiki.worldbank.org/Study_Registration
- Creating a preanalysis plan at https://dimewiki.worldbank.org/Preanalysis_Plan
- Preparing to document research decisions at https://dimewiki.worldbank.org/Data_Documentation
- Publishing data in a trusted repository at https://dimewiki.worldbank.org/Publishing_Data
- Preparing and publishing a reproducibility package at https://dimewiki.worldbank.org/Reproducible_Research

Developing a credible research project

Research design is the process of planning a scientific study so that data can be generated, collected, and used to accurately estimate specific parameters in the population of interest. For more details, see the DIME Wiki at https://dimewiki.worldbank.org/Experimental_Methods and https://dimewiki.worldbank.org/Quasi-Experimental_Methods.

The evidentiary value of research is traditionally a function of *research design* choices, such as *sampling*, *randomization*, and robustness to alternative specifications and definitions (Angrist and Pischke 2010; Ioannidis 2005). A frequent target for critics of research is the fact that researchers often have a lot of leeway in choosing projects or in selecting results or outcomes *after* they have implemented projects or collected data in the field (Ioannidis, Stanley, and Doucouliagos 2017). Such leeway increases the likelihood of finding "false positive" results that are not true outside of carefully selected data (Simmons, Nelson, and Simonsohn 2011). Credible methods of research design are key to maintaining credibility in these choices and avoiding serious errors. They are especially relevant for research that relies on original data sources, from innovative big data sources to unique surveys. Development researchers should take these concerns seriously. Such flexibility can be a significant issue

Sampling is the process of selecting units from the population of interest to observe such that statistical properties appropriate to the research design are present in the observed group. For more details, see the DIME Wiki at https://dimewiki .worldbank.org/Sampling.

Randomization is the process of generating a sequence of unrelated numbers, typically for the purpose of implementing a research design that requires a key element to exhibit zero correlation with all other variables. For more details, see the DIME Wiki at https:// dimewiki.worldbank.org /Randomization.

Study registration is the process of recording the existence, intention, and design of a research study in a third-party database. For more details, see the DIME Wiki at https:// dimewiki.worldbank.org /Study_Registration.

for the quality of evidence overall, particularly if researchers believe that certain types of results are substantially better for their careers or their publication chances.

This section presents three popular methods of committing to particular research questions or methods and avoiding potential criticisms of cherry-picking results for publication: registration, preanalysis plans, and registered reports. Each method involves documenting specific components of research design, ideally before analyzing or extensively exploring the data. Study registration provides formal notice that a study is being attempted and creates a hub for materials and updates about the study results. Preanalysis plans constitute a more formal commitment to use specific methods on particular questions. Writing and releasing a preanalysis plan in advance of working with data help to protect the credibility of approaches that have a high likelihood of producing false results (Wicherts et al. 2016). Finally, registered reports allow researchers to approach research design as a process subject to full peer review. Registered reports enable close scrutiny of a research design, provide an opportunity for feedback and improvement, and often result in a commitment to publish based on the credibility of the design rather than on the specific results.

Registering research

Registration of research studies is an increasingly common practice, and more journals are beginning to require registration of the studies they publish (Vilhuber, Turrito, and Welch 2020). *Study registration* is intended to ensure that a complete record of research inquiry is readily available. Registering research ensures that future scholars can quickly discover what work has been carried out on a given question, even if some or all of the work done is never formally published. Registration can be done before, during, or after a study is completed, providing essential information about its purpose. Some currently popular registries are operated by the American Economic Association (AEA; at https://www .socialscienceregistry.org), the International Initiative for Impact Evaluation (3ie; at https://ridie.3ieimpact.org), Evidence in Governance and Politics (EGAP; at https://egap.org/content/registration), and the Open Science Framework (OSF; at https://osf.io/registries). Each registry has a different target audience and different features, so researchers can select one that is appropriate to their work. Study registration should be feasible for all projects, because registries are typically free to access and initial registration can be submitted with minimal information. A generally accepted practice is to revise and expand the level of detail gradually over time, adding more information to the registry as the project progresses.

Preregistration of studies before they begin is an extension of this principle (Nosek et al. 2018). Registration of a study before implementation or data acquisition starts provides a simple and low-effort way for researchers to demonstrate that a particular line of inquiry was not generated by the process of data collection or analysis itself, particularly when specific hypotheses are included in the registration. Preregistrations need not provide exhaustive details about how a particular hypothesis will be approached, only that it will be. Preregistering individual elements of research design or analysis can further strengthen the credibility of the research and requires only a minor investment of time or administrative effort. For this reason, DIME requires all studies to be preregistered in a public database and to specify at least some primary hypotheses before providing funding for impact evaluation research. See box 1.2 for a description of how the Demand for Safe Spaces project was registered.

BOX 1.2 REGISTERING STUDIES: A CASE STUDY FROM THE DEMAND FOR SAFE SPACES PROJECT

The experimental component of the Demand for Safe Spaces study was registered at the Registry for International Development Impact Evaluations (RIDIE) under identifier 5a125fecae423. The following are highlights from the registration:

- *Evaluation method.* Both a primary evaluation method (randomized control trial) and additional methods (difference-in-differences and fixed effects regressions) were included.
- *Key outcome variables.* Key variables were take-up of rides in women-only car (binary), occurrence of harassment or crime during ride (binary), self-reported well-being after each ride, overall subjective well-being, and implicit association test D-score.
- *Primary hypotheses to be tested.* Riding in the women-only car reduces harassment experienced by women; riding in the women-only car improves psychological well-being; women are willing to forgo income to ride in the women-only car.
- *Secondary research question and methods.* Supplementary research methods (implicit association test and platform survey) were used to examine an additional hypothesis: the women-only car is associated with a social norm that assigns responsibility to women for avoiding harassment.
- *Sample size for each study arm.* The registration indicates the number of individual participants, number of baseline rides, number of rides during the price experiment, number of car-assigned rides, and number of expected participants in the implicit association test.
- *Data sources.* The study relied on data previously collected (through the mobile app) and data to be collected (through platform surveys and implicit association tests).
- *Registration status.* The project was categorized as a nonprospective entry, because the crowdsourced data had already been received and processed. The team sought to ensure the credibility of additional data collection and secondary research questions by registering the study.

For the project's registration on RIDIE, see https://ridie.3ieimpact.org/index.php?r=search /detailView&id=588.

Writing preanalysis plans

If a research team has a large amount of flexibility to define how it will approach a particular hypothesis, study registration may not be sufficient to avoid the criticism of "hypothesizing after the results are known," also known as HARKing (Kerr 1998). Examples of such flexibility include a broad range of concrete measures that could each be argued to measure an abstract concept, choices about sample inclusion or exclusion, or decisions about how to construct derived indicators (Huntington-Klein et al. 2021). When researchers are collecting a large amount of information and have leverage over even a moderate number of these options, it is often possible to obtain almost any desired result (Gelman and Loken 2013).

A *preanalysis plan* (PAP) can be used to assuage these concerns by specifying in advance a set of analyses that the researchers intend to conduct. The PAP should be written up in detail for areas that are known to provide a large amount of leeway for researchers to make decisions later, particularly for areas such as interaction effects or subgroup analysis (for an example, see Cusolito, Dautovic, and McKenzie 2018). PAPs should not, however, be viewed as binding the researcher's hands (Olken 2015). Depending on what is known about the study at the time of writing, PAPs can vary widely in the amount of detail they include (McKenzie and Özler 2020). Various templates and checklists provide details of what information to include (for a recommended checklist, see McKenzie 2012). See box 1.3 for an example of how to prepare a PAP.

A **preanalysis plan** (PAP) is a document containing extensive details about a study's analytical approach, which is archived or published using a third-party repository in advance of data acquisition. For more details, see the DIME Wiki at https://dimewiki.worldbank.org/Preanalysis_Plan.

BOX 1.3 WRITING PREANALYSIS PLANS: A CASE STUDY FROM THE DEMAND FOR SAFE SPACES PROJECT

Although the Demand for Safe Spaces study did not publish a formal preanalysis plan, it did publish a concept note in 2015, which included much of the same information as a typical preanalysis plan. Prepared before fieldwork began, the note was subject to review and approval within the World Bank and from a technical committee, including blinded feedback from external academics. The concept note was updated in May 2017 to include new secondary research questions. The concept note specified the planned study along the following dimensions:

- *Theory of change,* including the main elements of the intervention and the hypothesized causal chain from inputs, through activities and outputs, to outcomes
- *Hypotheses* derived from the theory of change
- *Main evaluation question(s)* to be addressed by the study
- *List of main outcomes of interest,* including name, definition, and level of measurement of each of the outcome variables
- *Evaluation design,* including a precise description of the identification strategy for each research question and a description of the treatment and control groups
- *Sampling strategy and sample size calculation,* detailing the assumptions made

(Box continues on next page)

- *Description of all quantitative data collection instruments*
- *Data processing and analysis,* describing the statistical methods to be used, the exact specification(s) to be run, including clustering of standard errors, key groups for heterogeneity analysis, adjustments for testing multiple hypotheses, and a strategy to test (and correct) for bias

For a version of the study's concept note, see https://git.io/JYatw.

The core function of a PAP is to describe carefully and explicitly one or more specific data-driven inquiries, because specific formulations are often very hard to justify retrospectively with data or projects that potentially provide many avenues to approach a single theoretical question (for an example, see Bedoya et al. 2019). Anything outside of the original plan is just as interesting and valuable as it would have been if the plan had never been published, but having precommitted to the details of a particular inquiry makes its results immune to a wide range of criticisms of specification searching or multiple testing (Banerjee et al. 2020).

Publishing registered reports

A **registered report** is a manuscript category offered by some publishers; it includes peer review and publication of a research design, often accompanied by a conditional commitment to accept a manuscript detailing the results of the study.

A *registered report* takes the process of prespecifying a complex research design to the level of a formal publication. In a registered report, a journal or other publisher will peer review and conditionally accept a specific study for publication, typically guaranteeing the acceptance of a later publication that carries out the analysis described in the registered report. Although far stricter and more complex to carry out than ordinary study registration or preanalysis planning, the registered report has the added benefit of encouraging peer review and expert feedback on the design and structure of the proposed study (Foster, Karlan, and Miguel 2018). Registered reports are never required, but they are designed to reward researchers who are able to provide a large amount of advance detail for their project, want to secure publication interest regardless of results, or want to use methods that may be novel or unusual.

Registered reports are meant to combat the "file-drawer problem" and ensure that researchers are transparent in the sense that all of the promised results obtained from registered-report studies are actually published (Simonsohn, Nelson, and Simmons 2014). This approach has the advantage of specifying in detail the project's complete research and analytical design and securing a commitment for publication regardless of the outcome. This may be of special interest for researchers studying events or programs for which there is a substantial risk that they will not be able to publish a null or negative result (for an example, see Coville et al. 2019) or when they wish to avoid any pressure toward finding a particular result—for example, when the program or event is the subject of substantial social or political pressures. As with preregistration and preanalysis, nothing in a registered report should be understood to prevent a researcher from pursuing additional avenues of inquiry once the study is complete, either in the same or in separate research outputs.

Conducting research transparently

Transparent research exposes not only the code but also also all the research processes involved in developing the analytical approach. Such transparency means that readers can judge for themselves whether the research was done well and the decision-making process was sound. If the research is well structured and all relevant *research documentation* is shared, readers will be able to understand the analysis fully. Researchers who expect the process to be transparent also have an incentive to make better decisions and to be skeptical and thorough about their assumptions. They will also save themselves time, because transparent research methods make coding more efficient and prevent teams from having the same discussion multiple times.

Clearly documenting research work is necessary to allow others to evaluate exactly what data were acquired and how the information was used to obtain a particular result. Many development research projects are designed to address specific questions and often use unique data, novel methods, or small samples. These approaches can yield new insights into essential academic questions, but they need to be documented transparently so they can be reviewed or replicated by others in the future (Duvendack, Palmer-Jones, and Reed 2017). Unlike disciplines in which data are more standardized or research is more oriented toward secondary data, the exact data used in a development research project often have not been observed by anyone else in the past and may be impossible to collect again in the future.

Regardless of the novelty of study data, transparent documentation methods help to ensure that data were collected and handled appropriately and that studies and interventions were implemented correctly. As with study registrations, project and data documentation should be released on external *archival repositories* so that they can always be accessed and verified.

Documenting data acquisition and analysis

Documenting a project in detail greatly increases transparency. Many disciplines have a tradition of keeping a "lab notebook" (Pain 2019); adapting and expanding this process to create a lab-style workflow in the development field are critical steps toward more transparent practices. Transparency requires explicitly noting decisions as they are made and explaining the process behind the decision-making. Careful documentation also saves the research team a lot of time; it avoids the need to have the

Research documentation is the collection of all written records and materials needed for a third party to understand and evaluate the design and results of a given study. For more details, see the DIME Wiki at https://dimewiki.worldbank.org/Research_Documentation.

An **archival repository** is a third-party service for storing information that guarantees the permanent availability of current and prior versions of materials.

same discussion twice (or more!), because a record exists of why something was done in a particular way. Several tools are available for producing documentation, and documenting a project should be an active, ongoing process, not a one-time requirement or retrospective task. New decisions are always being made as the plan becomes a reality, and there is nothing wrong with sensible adaptation so long as it is recorded and disclosed.

Email, however, is *not* a documentation service, because communications are rarely well ordered, can be easily deleted, and are not available for future team members. At the very least, emails and other decision-making communications need to be archived and preserved in an organized manner so that they can be easily accessed and read by others in the future. Various software solutions are available for building proper documentation over time. Some solutions work better for keeping field records such as implementation decisions, research design, and survey development; others work better for recording data work and code development. The Open Science Framework (OSF; https://osf.io) provides one such solution, with integrated file storage, version histories, and collaborative wiki pages. GitHub (https://github.com) provides a transparent documentation system through commit messages, issues, README.md files, and pull requests, in addition to version histories and wiki pages. Such services offer multiple ways to record the decision-making process leading to changes and additions, to track and register discussions, and to manage tasks. (For more details on how to use Git and GitHub and for links to all DIME Analytics resources on best practices and how to get started, see the DIME Wiki at https://dimewiki.worldbank.org /Getting_started_with_GitHub.)

These flexible tools can be adapted to different team and project dynamics. Services that log the research process can show modifications made in response to referee comments, by having tagged version histories at each major revision. They also allow the use of issue trackers to document the research paths and questions that the project tried to answer as a resource for others who have similar questions. Each project has specific requirements for managing data, code, and documentation; and the exact transparency tools to use will depend on the team's needs. In all cases, the tools should be chosen before project launch, and a project's documentation should begin as soon as decisions are made.

Cataloging and archiving data

Data and data collection methods should be fully cataloged, archived, and documented, whether the data are collected by the project itself or received from an outside partner. In some cases, this process is as simple as uploading a survey instrument or an index of data sets and a codebook to an archive. In other cases, the process is more complex. Proper documentation of data collection often requires a detailed description of the overall sampling procedure (for an example, see Yishay et al. 2016). Settings with many overlapping strata, treatment arms, excluded observations, or resampling protocols might require extensive additional documentation. This documentation should be continuously updated and kept with the other study materials; it is often necessary to collate these materials for publication in an appendix.

When data are received from partners or collected in the field, the *original data* (including field corrections) should be placed immediately in a secure permanent storage system. Before analytical work begins, it is necessary to create a "for-publication" copy of the acquired data set by removing all personally identifying information. This copy will be the public version of the original data set and must be placed in an archival repository where it can be cited (Vilhuber, Turrito, and Welch 2020). This type of data depositing or archiving precedes publishing or releasing any data: data at this stage may still need to be embargoed or have other, potentially permanent, access restrictions, so the archive can be instructed formally to release the data later. If the planned analysis requires the use of confidential data, those data should be stored separately (and most likely remain encrypted) so that it is clear what portions of the code will work with and without the restricted-access data.

Some institutions have their own dedicated data repositories, such as the World Bank Microdata Library (https://microdata.worldbank.org) and the World Bank Data Catalog (https://datacatalog.worldbank.org). Some project funders, such as the U.S. Agency for International Development (https://data.usaid.gov), provide specific repositories in which they require the deposit of data they have funded. Researchers should take advantage of these repositories when possible. If no such service is provided, researchers must be aware of privacy issues regarding directly identifying data and questions of data ownership before uploading original data to any third-party server, whether public or not. This is a legal question for the institutions affiliated with the principal investigators. If the data required for analysis must be placed under restricted use or restricted access, including data that can never be distributed directly to third parties, a plan is needed for storing these data separately from publishable data. Making such a plan maximizes transparency by having a clear release package as well as by providing instructions or developing a protocol for allowing access in the future for replicators or reviewers under appropriate access agreements (for details on how to document this type of material, see Vilhuber et al. 2020).

Regardless of restricted-access and confidentiality considerations, the selected data repository should create a record of the data's existence and provide instructions for how another researcher might obtain access. More information on the steps required to prepare and publish a de-identified data set are presented in chapters 6 and 7. Data publication should create a data citation and a *digital object identifier* (DOI) or some other persistent index that can be used in future work to indicate unambiguously the exact location of the data. The data publication package should also include methodological documentation and complete human-readable codebooks for all of the variables located there.

Original data constitute a new data set, as obtained and corrected, that becomes the functional basis for research work.

A **digital object identifier** (DOI) is a permanent reference for electronic information that persistently updates to a URL or other location if the information is moved.

Analyzing data reproducibly and preparing a reproducibility package

Reproducible research is the class of research studies for which individuals not involved in the research can examine and recreate the results from the raw study materials by following the research documentation. For more details, see the DIME Wiki at https://dimewiki .worldbank.org/Reproducible _Research. See also pillar 3 of the DIME Research Standards at https://github.com /worldbank/dime-standards.

Data publication is the process of releasing research data so they can be located, accessed, and cited. For more details, see the DIME Wiki at https://dimewiki.worldbank .org/Publishing_Data. See also pillar 5 of the DIME Research Standards at https:// github.com/worldbank /dime-standards.

Computational reproducibility is the ability of another individual to reuse the same code and data and obtain the exact same results. For more details, see the DIME Wiki at https://dimewiki.worldbank .org/Reproducible_Research. See also pillar 3 of the DIME Research Standards at https://github.com /worldbank/dime-standards.

Reproducible research makes it easy for others to apply the techniques used in the project to new data or to implement a similar research design in a different context. Development research is moving rapidly in the direction of requiring adherence to specific reproducibility guidelines (Christensen and Miguel 2018). Major publishers and funders, most notably the American Economic Association, have taken steps to require code and data to be reported accurately, cited, and preserved as research outputs that can be accessed and verified by others. Making research reproducible in this way is a public good. It enables other researchers to reuse code and processes to do their own work more easily and effectively in the future. Regardless of what is formally required, code should be written neatly, with clear instructions. It should be easy to read and understand. The corresponding analysis data also should be made accessible to the greatest legal and ethical extent possible through *data publication*.

Common research standards from journals and funders feature both regulation and verification policies (Stodden, Guo, and Ma 2013). Regulation policies require authors to provide reproducibility packages before publication, which the journal then reviews for completeness. Verification policies require authors to make certain materials available to the public, but their completeness is not a precondition for publication. Other journals provide guidance with checklists for reporting on whether and how various practices were implemented, but do not require any specific practices (Nosek et al. 2015). Producing these kinds of resources also has the advantage of creating additional opportunities for citations. Even if privacy considerations mean that some or no data or results will be published, these practices are still valuable for project organization.

Regardless of external requirements, it is important to prepare to release all data that can be published. When data cannot be published, it is important to publish as much metadata as allowed, including information on how the data were obtained, what fields the data contain, and aggregations or descriptive statistics. Even if the data cannot be published, code files rarely contain restricted information, so the code should still be made available, with clear instructions for obtaining usable data. Additionally, reproducibility demands should be considered when designing the informed consent protocols or data license agreement for sensitive data. Such efforts could include establishing acceptable conditions (such as a secure transfer or cold room) under which third parties may access data for the purpose of independently reproducing results.

At DIME, all published research outputs are required to satisfy *computational reproducibility*. Before releasing a working paper, the research team submits a reproducibility package with de-identified data, and DIME Analytics verifies that the package produces exactly the same results that appear in the paper (Andrade et al. 2019). The team also assesses whether the package includes sufficient documentation. Once the computational reproducibility check is complete, the team receives a completed reproducibility certificate that also lists any publicly available materials to accompany the package, for use as an appendix to the publication. The DIME Analytics team organizes frequent peer reviews of code for works in progress, and the general recommendation is to ensure that projects are *always* externally reproducible instead of waiting until the final stages to prepare this material. In this way, code is continuously maintained, clearly documented, and easy to read and understand in terms of structure, style, and syntax.

For research to be reproducible, all code files for data cleaning, construction, and analysis should be public, unless they contain confidential information. Nobody should have to guess exactly what a given index comprises, what controls are included in the main regression, or whether standard errors are clustered correctly. That is, as a purely technical matter, nobody should have to "just trust you" or have to work to find out what would happen if any or all of these tasks were done slightly differently (Simonsohn, Simmons, and Nelson 2015). Letting people play around with a project's data and code is a great way to have new questions asked and answered on the basis of valuable work already done (Daniels et al. 2019).

A **master script** (in Stata, a **master do-file**) is a single code script that can be used to execute all of the data work for a project, from importing the original data to exporting the final outputs. Any team member should be able to run this script and all the data work scripts executed by it by changing only the directory file path in one line of code in the master script. For more details, see the DIME Wiki at https:// dimewiki.worldbank.org /Master_Do-files.

A reproducibility package should include the complete materials needed to recreate the final analysis exactly and should be accessible and well documented so that others can identify and adjust potential decision points in which they are interested. They should be able to identify easily what data are used and how the data can be accessed; what code generates each table, figure, and in-text number; how key outcomes are constructed; and how all project results can be reproduced. It is important to plan for reproducibility, because doing so supports the researcher's ability to obtain the proper documentation and permissions for all data, code, and materials used throughout the project. A well-organized reproducibility package usually takes the form of a complete directory, including documentation and a *master script*. When considered in combination with the corresponding publication, this package leads readers through the process and rationale for the code behind each of the outputs. See box 1.4 for an example of a reproducibility package.

The Demand for Safe Spaces team published all final study materials to a repository on the World Bank GitHub account. The repository holds the abstract of the paper, ungated access to the most recent version of the full paper, an online appendix including robustness checks and supplemental material, and the project's reproducibility package.

(Box continues on next page)

The data for this project are published in the Microdata Catalog, under survey ID number BRA_2015-2016_DSS_v01_M. The Microdata Catalog entry includes metadata on the study, documentation such as survey instruments and technical reports, terms of use for the data, and access to downloadable data files. Both the crowdsourced data and the platform survey data are accessible through the Microdata Catalog.

The "Reproducibility Package" folder on GitHub contains instructions for executing the code. Among other things, it provides licensing information for the materials, software and hardware requirements including time needed to run, and instructions for replicators (which are presented below). Finally, it has a detailed list of the code files that will run, the required data inputs, and the outputs of each process.

Instructions to Replicators

To recreate the outputs, follow the steps below:

1. Click on the green `Code` button shown above the list of files in this repository to download a local copy of this repository.

2. Open the downloaded folder and navigate to `rio-safe-space/Reproducibility Package`.

3. The data used for this paper are available in the Microdata Catalogue, under the survey ID number BRA_2015-2016_DSS_v01_M. Copy these data to the `data` folder.

4. In the folder `rio-safe-space/Reproducibility Package`, you will see two scripts called `MASTER`: one in R, one in Stata.

5. To run the Stata `MASTER`, open it and edit line 23 to reflect the path of the repository copy in your computer. This do-file creates all the non-map tables and graphs included in the working paper. You may need to install some of the user-written packages the code uses before it runs. To do so modify line 29 by replacing `0` with `1`. This only needs to be done once on every computer.

6. To run the R `MASTER`, open it and edit line 52. The only package needed to run the code is `pacman`. If you don't have this package installed, uncomment line 29. As before, running this line once on a new computer is enough. This code will recreate the maps included in the paper.

7. The outputs will be recreated in the `rio-safe-space/Reproducibility Package/outputs` folder. The only output that cannot be reproduced is figure A1. Personally identifying information is necessary to recreate this graph, so the package contains only the code for transparency.

For the Demand for Safe Spaces GitHub repository, see https://github.com/worldbank/rio-safe-space. For the Microdata Catalog entry for the study, see https://microdata.worldbank.org/index.php /catalog/3745.

Looking ahead

With the ongoing rise of empirical research and increased public scrutiny of scientific evidence, making analysis code and data available is necessary but not sufficient to guarantee that findings will be credible. Even if the methods used are highly precise, the evidence is only as good as the data—and plenty of mistakes that would compromise the conclusions can be made between establishing a design and generating final results. For this reason, transparency is key for research credibility. It allows other researchers and research consumers to verify the steps to reach a conclusion by themselves and decide whether their standards for accepting a finding as evidence are met. Every investment made up front in documentation and transparency protects the project down the line, particularly as these standards continue to tighten. With these principles in mind, the approach taken to the development, structure, and documentation of data work in this handbook provides a system for implementing these ideas in everyday work. The next chapter discusses the workspace needed to work in an efficient, organized, secure, and reproducible manner.

References

Andrade, Luíza, Guadalupe Bedoya, Benjamin Daniels, Maria Jones, and Florence Kondylis. 2019. "What Development Economists Talk about When They Talk about Reproducibility ..." *Development Impact* (blog), September 16, 2019. https://blogs.worldbank.org/impactevaluations/what-development-economists -talk-about-when-they-talk-about-reproducibility.

Angrist, Joshua D., and Jörn-Steffen Pischke. 2010. "The Credibility Revolution in Empirical Economics: How Better Research Design Is Taking the Con out of Econometrics." *Journal of Economic Perspectives* 24 (2): 3–30.

Banerjee, Abhijit, Esther Duflo, Amy Finkelstein, Lawrence F. Katz, Benjamin A. Olken, and Anja Sautmann. 2020. "In Praise of Moderation: Suggestions for the Scope and Use of Pre-Analysis Plans for RCTs in Economics." NBER Working Paper 26993, National Bureau of Economic Research, Cambridge, MA.

Bedoya, Guadalupe, Aidan Coville, Johannes Haushofer, Mohammad Isaqzadeh, and Jeremy Shapiro. 2019. "No Household Left Behind: Afghanistan Targeting the Ultra Poor Impact Evaluation." Policy Research Working Paper 8877, World Bank, Washington, DC.

Christensen, Garret, and Edward Miguel. 2018. "Transparency, Reproducibility, and the Credibility of Economics Research." *Journal of Economic Literature* 56 (3): 920–80.

Coville, Aidan, Vincenzo Di Maro, Felipe Alexander Dunsch, and Siegfried Zottel. 2019. "The Nollywood Nudge: An Entertaining Approach to Saving." Policy Research Working Paper 8920, World Bank, Washington, DC.

Cusolito, Ana Paula, Ernest Dautovic, and David McKenzie. 2018. "Can Government Intervention Make Firms More Investment-Ready? A Randomized Experiment in the Western Balkans." Policy Research Working Paper 8541, World Bank, Washington, DC.

Daniels, Benjamin, Luíza Andrade, Anton Prokopyev, and Trevor Monroe. 2019. "Making Analytics Reusable." *Data Blog*, March 25, 2019. https://blogs .worldbank.org/opendata/making-analytics-reusable.

Duvendack, Maren, Richard Palmer-Jones, and W. Robert Reed. 2017. "What Is Meant by 'Replication' and Why Does It Encounter Resistance in Economics?" *American Economic Review* 107 (5): 46–51.

Foster, Andy, Dean Karlan, and Ted Miguel. 2018. "Registered Reports: Piloting a Pre-Results Review Process at the *Journal of Development Economics*." *Development Impact* (blog), March 9, 2018. https://blogs .worldbank.org/impactevaluations/registered-reports-piloting-pre-results -review-process-journal-development-economics.

Gelman, Andrew, and Eric Loken. 2013. "The Garden of Forking Paths: Why Multiple Comparisons Can Be a Problem, Even When There Is No 'Fishing Expedition' or 'P-Hacking' and the Research Hypothesis Was Posited Ahead of Time." Department of Statistics, Columbia University, New York.

Huntington-Klein, Nick, Andreu Arenas, Emily Beam, Marco Bertoni, Jeffrey Bloem, Pralhad H. Burli, Naibin Chen, et al. 2021. "The Influence of Hidden Researcher Decisions in Applied Microeconomics." IZA Discussion Paper 13233, Institute of Labor Economics (IZA), Bonn. https://ssrn.com/abstract = 3602409.

Ioannidis, John P. A. 2005. "Why Most Published Research Findings Are False." *PLoS Medicine* 2 (8): e124.

Ioannidis, John P. A., Tom D. Stanley, and Hristos Doucouliagos. 2017. "The Power of Bias in Economics Research." *Economic Journal* 127 (605): F236–65.

Kerr, Norbert L. 1998. "HARKing: Hypothesizing after the Results Are Known." *Personality and Social Psychology Review* 2 (3): 196–217.

McKenzie, David. 2012. "A Pre-analysis Plan Checklist." *Development Impact* (blog), October 28, 2012. https://blogs.worldbank.org /impactevaluations/a-pre-analysis-plan-checklist.

McKenzie, David, and Berk Özler. 2020. "Pre-analysis Plans and Registered Reports: What the New Opinion Piece Does and Doesn't Imply." *Development Impact* (blog), April 24, 2020. https://blogs.worldbank.org /impactevaluations/pre-analysis-plans-and-registered-reports-what-new -opinion-piece-does-and-doesnt.

Nosek, Brian A., G. Alter, G. C. Banks, D. Borsboom, S. D. Bowman, S. J. Breckler, S. Buck, et al. 2015. "Promoting an Open Research Culture." *Science* 348 (6242): 1422–25.

Nosek, Brian A., Charles R. Ebersole, Alexander C. DeHaven, and David T. Mellor. 2018. "The Preregistration Revolution." *Proceedings of the National Academy of Sciences* 115 (11): 2600–06.

Olken, Benjamin A. 2015. "Promises and Perils of Pre-Analysis Plans." *Journal of Economic Perspectives* 29 (3): 61–80.

Pain, Elisabeth. 2019. "How to Keep a Lab Notebook." *Science* (blog), September 3, 2019. https://www.sciencemag.org/careers/2019/09/how-keep-lab-notebook.

Simmons, Joseph P., Leif D. Nelson, and Uri Simonsohn. 2011. "False-Positive Psychology: Undisclosed Flexibility in Data Collection and Analysis Allows Presenting Anything as Significant." *Psychological Science* 22 (11): 1359–66.

Simonsohn, Uri, Leif D. Nelson, and Joseph P. Simmons. 2014. "P-Curve: A Key to the File-Drawer." *Journal of Experimental Psychology: General* 143 (2): 534–47.

Simonsohn, Uri, Joseph P. Simmons, and Leif D. Nelson. 2015. "Specification Curve: Descriptive and Inferential Statistics on All Reasonable Specifications." http://dx.doi.org/10.2139/ssrn.2694998.

Stodden, Victoria, Peixuan Guo, and Zhaokun Ma. 2013. "Toward Reproducible Computational Research: An Empirical Analysis of Data and Code Policy Adoption by Journals." *PLoS One* 8 (6): e67111.

Vilhuber, Lars, James Turrito, and Keesler Welch. 2020. "Report by the AEA Data Editor." *AEA Papers and Proceedings* 110 (May): 764–75.

Vilhuber, Lars, Miklós Kóren, Joan Llull, Marie Connolly, and Peter Morrow. 2020. "A Template README for Social Science Replication Packages." *Zenodo*, December 8, 2020. https://doi.org/10.5281/zenodo.4319999.

Wicherts, Jelte M., Coosje L. S. Veldkamp, Hilde E. M. Augusteijn, Marjan Bakker, Robbie C. M. van Aert, and Marcel A. L. M. van Assen. 2016. "Degrees of Freedom in Planning, Running, Analyzing, and Reporting Psychological Studies: A Checklist to Avoid P-Hacking." *Frontiers in Psychology* 7 (November 25): 1832.

Yishay, Ariel Ben, Maria Jones, Florence Kondylis, and Ahmed Mushfiq. 2016. "Are Gender Differences in Performance Innate or Socially Mediated?" Policy Research Working Paper 7689, World Bank, Washington, DC.

Chapter 2

Setting the stage for effective and efficient collaboration

In order to conduct effective data work in a team environment, researchers need to determine the structure of the workflow in advance. Preparation for collaborative data work begins long before data are acquired. It involves planning both software tools and collaboration platforms for the team and knowing what types of data will be acquired, whether the data will require special handling because of size or privacy considerations, which data sets and outputs will be needed at the end of the process, and how all data files and versions will stay organized throughout. It is important to plan data workflows in advance because changing software or protocols halfway through a project is costly and time-consuming. Seemingly small decisions such as file-sharing services, folder structures, and filenames can be extremely painful to alter down the line.

This chapter provides guidance on setting up an effective environment for collaborative data work, structuring data work to be well organized and clearly documented, and setting up processes to handle confidential data securely. The first section outlines how to set up a working environment to collaborate effectively with others on technical tasks and how to document tasks and decisions. The second section discusses how to organize code and data so that others will be able to understand and interact with them easily. The third section provides guidelines for ensuring privacy and security when working with confidential data. Box 2.1 summarizes the most important points, lists the responsibilities of different members of the research team, and provides a list of key tools and resources for implementing the recommended practices.

The technical environment for data work needs to be established at the start of a research project. Agreeing on software choices, code standards and data structure, and data security protocols will prepare the team to implement technical tasks successfully, safely, and efficiently throughout the project life cycle. Consider the following.

1. *Technical collaboration environment.* All software and workflows need to be standardized and interoperable across the team regardless of the different hardware used:

   - Secure all physical computing hardware through encryption and password protection. If specialized or more powerful hardware is required, initiate requests for access, purchase orders, or other processes now.
   - Agree on tools for collaboration and documentation. Key conversations and decisions need to be archived and organized outside of instant messages and email conversations.
   - Decide which programming languages and environments to use. Setting up a comfortable, modern digital work environment takes time, but it is time well spent.

2. *Organization of code and data.* The team needs to agree on where and how code files and databases will be stored, down to the level of the folder structure:

   - Set up a standardized and scalable folder structure. This structure should give all documents an unambiguous location, and the location and naming of files should describe their purpose and function and be intuitive to all team members.
   - Set up a backup and version-control system appropriate for each type of file. Such a system will ensure that information cannot be lost and that all team members understand how to interoperate and collaborate.
   - Set up master script files. These master files will be used to structure and execute the code.

3. *Information security measures and ethical frameworks.* The team needs to understand why such measures are needed and to adopt practices for ensuring that data are secure and research subjects' information is protected:

   - Formally request and obtain approval from legal entities governing research in all relevant jurisdictions.
   - Understand how to respect the rights and dignity of research subjects, and plan for how to establish informed consent from individuals or groups participating in the research.
   - Adopt standardized digital security practices, including proper encryption of all confidential information, at rest and in transit, both among the team and with external partners.

Key responsibilities for task team leaders and principal investigators

   - Support the acquisition and maintenance of required computing hardware and software, coordinating with procurement, information security, and information technology teams as necessary.
   - Make final decisions regarding code languages and environments.
   - Discuss and agree upon an appropriate project-wide digital organization strategy.
   - Institute and communicate best practices in accordance with legal, ethical, and security obligations.

(Box continues on next page)

Key responsibilities for research assistants

- Communicate technical needs clearly with task team leaders, principal investigators, and relevant service providers.
- Implement a consistent digital organization strategy, and flag issues pertaining to task management, documentation, or materials storage, if they arise.
- Support project compliance with ethical, legal, and security obligations; and flag concerns for task team leaders and principal investigators.

Key resources

- Research ethics in pillar 1 of the DIME Research Standards, at https://github.com /worldbank/dime-standards
- DIME GitHub resources at https://github.com/worldbank/dime-github-trainings
- Data security in pillar 4 of the DIME Research Standards, at https://github.com /worldbank/dime-standards
- Publication guidelines in pillar 5 of the DIME Research Standards, at https://github .com/worldbank/dime-standards

Preparing a collaborative work environment

This section introduces core concepts and tools for organizing data work in an efficient, collaborative, and reproducible manner. Some of these skills may seem elementary, but thinking about simple details from a workflow perspective can make marginal daily improvements that add up to substantial gains over the course of multiple years and projects. Together, these processes form a collaborative workflow that will greatly accelerate the team's ability to complete tasks on all of its projects.

Teams often develop workflows in an ad hoc fashion, solving new challenges as they arise. Adaptation is good, of course, but some tasks exist on every project, and it is more efficient to agree on the corresponding workflow in advance. For example, every project requires research documentation, a file-naming convention, directory organization, coding standards, version control, and code review. These tasks are common to almost every project, and their solutions translate well between projects. Therefore, thinking in advance about the best way to perform these tasks brings greater efficiencies than throwing together a solution when the task arises. Box 2.2 provides an example of these types of decisions made for the Demand for Safe Spaces project. This section outlines the main points to discuss within the team and suggests best-practice solutions for them.

The following are a few highlights demonstrating how the Demand for Safe Spaces team organized the work environment for effective collaboration:

- The data work for the project was done through a private GitHub repository hosted in the World Bank organization account.
- GitHub Issues was used to document research decisions and provide feedback. Even the principal investigators for the study, who did not participate directly in coding, used Github Issues to review code and outputs and to create a record of broader discussions.
- Stata was adopted as the primary software for data analysis, because it was the software that all team members had in common at the start of the project. At a later stage of the project, R code was developed specifically to create maps. The R portion of the code was developed independently because it used different data sets and created separate outputs. The team used two separate master scripts, one for the Stata code and one for the R code.
- Team members shared a synchronized folder (using Dropbox), which included the de-identified data and project documentation such as survey instruments and enumerator training manuals.

Setting up a computer for data work

First things first: almost all data work will be done on a computer, so it needs to be set up for success. The operating system should be fully updated, be in good working order, and use a password-protected login. However, password protection is not sufficient if the computer stores data that are not public. Encryption is essential for sufficient protection and is covered later in this chapter. The computer has to be *backed up* to prevent information loss (https://dimewiki.worldbank.org/Data_Storage). The 3-2-1 rule is highly recommended: maintain three copies of all original or irreplaceable data, with data stored on at least two onsite hardware devices and in one offsite location. Chapter 4 provides a protocol for implementing this rule. It is important to know how to get the *absolute file path* for any given file. On macOS the file path will be something like /users/username/git/project/...; on Windows it will be C:/users/username/git/project/.... Absolute file paths are an obstacle to collaboration unless they are *dynamic absolute file paths*. In a dynamic absolute file path, the relative project path, /git/project/... in the examples above, is added to the user-specific root path for each user, /users/username or C:/users/username, generating an absolute file path unique to each user. Master scripts, which are introduced later in this chapter, implement this process seamlessly. Dynamic absolute file paths, starting from the file system root, are the best way to ensure that files are read and written correctly when multiple users work on the same project across many different platforms, operating systems, and devices. In some contexts—for example, some cloud environments—relative file paths must be used, but in all other contexts dynamic absolute file paths are recommended.

It is recommended to follow standardized *naming conventions* in folder names and filenames. Whenever possible, use only the 26 English letters, numbers, dashes (-), and underscores (_). Give preference to lowercase letters and avoid spaces, which can cause problems when transferred to others. Forward slashes (/) must always be used in file paths to represent folder or directory structures when typed in code, just like in internet addresses. It is good practice to do this even when using a Windows machine, where both forward and backward slashes are allowed; using a backward slash will break the code if anyone tries to run it on a macOS or Linux machine. Making the structure and naming of directories a core part of the workflow is very important, because other-wise it will be impossible to transfer reliable instructions for replicating or carrying out the analytical work.

Most teams use some kind of file-sharing software. The exact services used will depend on the tasks, but in general there are several approaches to file sharing; the three discussed here are the most common. *File syncing* is the most familiar method and is implemented by software like OneDrive, Dropbox, or Box. Syncing software forces everyone to have the same version of every file at the same time, which makes simultaneous editing difficult but other tasks easier. *Distributed version control* is another method, commonly implemented through systems like GitHub, GitLab, and Bitbucket that interact with *Git*. Distributed version control allows everyone to access different versions of a file at the same time. It is optimized only for specific types of files (for example, any type of code file). Finally, *server storage* is the least-common method, because there is only one version of the materials and simultaneous access must be regulated carefully. Server storage ensures that everyone has access to exactly the same files and environment, and it also enables high-powered computing processes for large, complex data.

All three file-sharing methods are used for collaborative workflows, and it is important to review the types of data work that will be done and to plan which types of files will live in which types of sharing services. These services are, in general, not interoperable, meaning that version-controlled files cannot generally be stored inside a syncing service, or vice versa, and files cannot be shifted between services without losing historical information. Therefore, choosing the correct file-sharing service for each of the team's needs at the outset is essential. Teams within DIME typically use file syncing for all project administrative files and data, version control with Git for code, and server storage for backup and large-scale computations when needed.

Establishing effective documentation practices

Once the technical and sharing workspace is set up, the next task is to decide how the team is going to communicate. The first habit that many

Naming conventions are a set of specific rules governing names and structures of files and folders. These conventions ensure that people will know where to place, how to name, and how to find specific pieces of information easily. For details, see the DIME Wiki at https://dimewiki.worldbank.org/Naming_Conventions.

Git is a distributed version-control system for collaborating on and tracking changes to code as it is written.

teams need to break is using instant communication for management and documentation. Email is, simply put, not a system. It is not a system for anything. Neither are instant messaging apps like WhatsApp. Instant messaging tools are developed for communicating "now," and they do it well. They are not structured to manage group membership, to present the same information across a group of people, or to remind individuals when old information becomes relevant. They are not structured to allow people to collaborate over a long period of time or to review old discussions. It is therefore easy to miss or lose communications from the past when they have relevance in the present. Everything with future relevance that is communicated over email or any other instant medium—for example, decisions about research design—should immediately be recorded in a system designed to keep permanent records. These systems are called collaboration tools, and several are very useful.

Good collaboration tools are workflow-oriented systems that allow the team to create and assign tasks, carry out discussions related to single tasks, track progress across time, and quickly see the overall status of the project. They are web-based so that everyone on the team can access them simultaneously and have ongoing discussions about tasks and processes. Such systems link communications to specific tasks so that related decisions are permanently recorded and easy to find in the future when questions about that task arise. Choosing the right tool for the team's needs is essential to designing an effective workflow. What is important is to choose a system and commit to using it, so that decisions, discussions, and tasks are easily reviewable long after they are completed.

GitHub and Dropbox Paper are popular, free collaboration tools that meet these criteria, and DIME Analytics has used both of them. However, any specific list of software will quickly become outdated. Different collaboration tools can be used for different types of tasks. DIME Analytics, for example, uses GitHub for code-related tasks and Dropbox Paper for managerial tasks. GitHub creates incentives for writing down why changes to the code were made in response to specific discussions as they are completed, creating naturally documented code. Tasks in GitHub Issues can be tied clearly to file versions. Dropbox Paper provides a clean interface, with task notifications, assignments, and deadlines, and is very intuitive for people with nontechnical backgrounds. Therefore, it is a useful tool for managing tasks not related to code.

Setting up a code environment

Taking time early in a project to choose a programming language and setting up a productive code environment for that language will make the work significantly easier. Setting up a productive code environment means ensuring that the programming language and all other software that the code requires will run smoothly on all of the hardware used. It also gives the team a productive way to interact with code and gives the code a seamless method for accessing the data.

It is difficult and costly to switch programming languages halfway through a project, so it is important to consider early on the various types of software that the team will use, taking into account the technical abilities of team members, what type of internet access the software will need, the type of data that will be needed, and the level of security required. Big data sets require additional infrastructure and may overburden tools commonly used for small data sets. The cost of licenses, the time to learn new tools, and the stability of the tools also are considerations. Few software choices are strictly right or wrong; what is important is to plan in advance and to understand how the chosen tools will interact with the workflow.

One option is to hold the code environment constant over the life cycle of a single project. However, this means that different projects will inevitably have different code environments and researchers working on multiple projects are likely to have to work in several slightly different code environments. Each successive project's code environment will be better than the last, but it is rarely justified to undertake the costly process of migrating an ongoing project into a new code environment. Code environments should be documented as precisely as possible. The specific version number of the programming languages and the individual packages used should be referenced or maintained so that they can be reproduced going forward, even if different releases contain changes that would break the code or change the results. DIME Analytics developed the command `ieboilstart` in the `ietoolkit` package to support version and settings stability in Stata. If a project requires more than one programming language—for example, if data are analyzed in one language but the results are visualized in another—then the division between the two should be as clear as possible. All tasks done in one language need to be completed before the tasks in the other language are completed. Frequently swapping back and forth between languages is a reproducibility nightmare.

Next, it is important to think about how and where code is written and executed. This book is intended to be agnostic to the size or origin of the data, but it assumes broadly that researchers are using one of the two most popular statistical software packages: R or Stata. (If using another language, like Python, many of the same principles apply, but the specifics will be different.) Most of the code work will be done in a code editor. For working in R, RStudio (https://www.rstudio.com) is the typical choice. For Stata, the built-in do-file editor is the most widely adopted code editor. However, it might be useful to consider using an external editor for R or Stata code. These editors offer great accessibility and quality features. For example, they can access an entire directory—rather than a single file— which provides directory-level views and file management actions, such as folder management, Git integration, and simultaneous work with other types of files, without leaving the editor. Using an external editor can also be preferable because an external editor will not crash if execution of the code causes the statistical software to crash. Finally, it is often possible to use the same external editor for all programming languages used, so any customization done in the code editor of choice will improve productivity across all of the coding work.

ieboilstart is a Stata command to standardize version, memory, and other Stata settings across all users for a project. It is part of the `ietoolkit` package. For more details, see the DIME Wiki at https://dimewiki .worldbank.org/ieboilstart.

Organizing code and data for replicable research

This handbook assumes that the analytical work is done through code with the ambition that all processes will be documented and replicable. Although it is possible to interact with some statistical software through the user interface without writing any code, doing so is strongly discouraged. Writing code creates a record of every task performed. It also prevents direct interaction with the data files, which could lead to nonreproducible steps. It is possible to do some exploratory tasks by point-and-click or typing directly into the console, but anything that is included in a research output must be coded in an organized fashion so that it is possible to release the exact code that produces the final results—up to and including individual statistics in text. Still, organizing code and data into files and folders is not a trivial task. What is intuitive to one person rarely comes naturally to another, and searching for files and folders is the least favorite task of most researchers. This section provides basic tips on managing the folders that store a project's data work.

Maintaining an organized file structure for data work is the best way to ensure that the entire team and others are able to edit and replicate the work easily in the future. It also ensures that automated processes from code and scripting tools are able to interact well, regardless of who created them. File organization makes data work easier as well as more transparent and facilitates integration with tools like version-control systems that aim to cut down on the number of repeated tasks that have to be performed. It is worth thinking in advance about how to store, name, and organize the different types of files with which the team will be working so that there is no confusion down the line and everyone has the same expectations.

Organizing files and folders

Once a research project begins, the number of scripts, data sets, and outputs that need to be managed will grow very quickly. This situation can get out of hand just as quickly, so it is important to organize the data work and follow best practices from the beginning. It is necessary for the team to agree on a specific directory structure and to set it up at the beginning of the project. It also is necessary to agree on a file-naming convention, which will facilitate finding project files and ensure that all team members can easily run the same code.

To support consistent folder organization, DIME Analytics created `iefolder` as a part of the `ietoolkit` package. Box 2.3 describes the folder structure of the Demand for Safe Spaces data work. This Stata command sets up a prestandardized folder structure for what is called the *DataWork folder*. The DataWork folder includes folders for all of the steps in a typical project. Because each project will always have unique needs, the structure is easy to adapt. Having a universally standardized folder structure across the entire portfolio of projects means that everyone can move easily between projects without having to spend time understanding a new organization of files and folders.

`iefolder` is a Stata command to set up a standardized folder structure for all research team members. It is part of the `ietoolkit` package. For more details, see the DIME Wiki at https://dimewiki .worldbank.org/iefolder.

The **DataWork folder** is the root of DIME's recommended folder structure. For more details, see the DIME Wiki at https://dimewiki.worldbank .org/DataWork_Folder.

Figure B2.3.1 illustrates the folder structure of the Demand for Safe Spaces data work. This project started before the `iefolder` structure was created and so differs from the current guidelines. Changing folder organization midway through a project is never recommended. Folder organization requires planning ahead and agreeing with the whole team on the best structure to follow.

FIGURE B2.3.1 **Folder structure of the Demand for Safe Spaces data work**

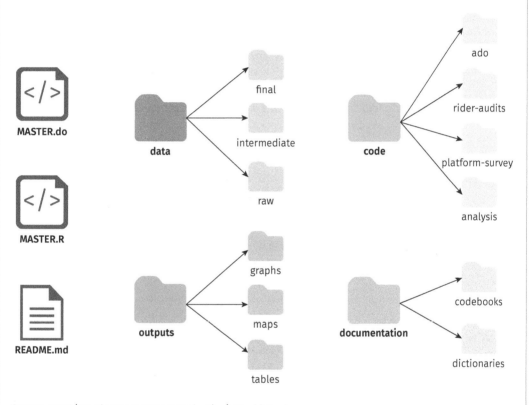

Source: DIME (Development Impact Evaluation), World Bank.

The root folder for the study's data work included two master scripts (one for Stata and one R, which can be run independently), a `README.md` file, and four subfolders: data, code, documentation, and outputs. The folder structure was identical in GitHub and Dropbox, but the files present in each of them differed. All of the code, raw outputs (such as `.tex` table fragments and `.png` images), and plain-text documentation were stored in GitHub. All of the data sets, `.pdf` outputs, and documentation in Word and Excel were stored in Dropbox. When data processing was completed, binary files in the "Documentation" folder that were accessed by the code, such as `iecodebook` and `ieduplicates` spreadsheets, were moved to GitHub to ensure that the repository was complete from a reproducibility perspective.

In the absence of a standard file structure across projects, `iefolder` is an easy template from which to start. The command creates a "DataWork" folder at the project level and, within that folder, creates a standardized directory structure for each data source or survey round. Within each subdirectory, `iefolder` creates folders for raw encrypted data, raw de-identified data, cleaned data, final data, outputs, and documentation. It creates a parallel folder structure for the code files that move data through this progression and for the final analytical outputs. The `ietoolkit` package also includes the `iegitaddmd` command, which places `README.md` placeholder files in folders. Because these placeholder files are written in a plain-text language called Markdown, they also provide an easy way to document the contents of every folder in the structure.

> `iegitaddmd` is a Stata command that automatically generates placeholder files to allow sharing folder structures with empty folders, because Git does not track or share empty folders. It is part of the `ietoolkit` package. For more details, see the DIME Wiki at https://dimewiki .worldbank.org/iegitaddmd.

The DataWork folder may be created either inside an existing project folder or as a separate root folder. It is advisable to keep project management materials (such as contracts, terms of reference, briefs, and other administrative or management work) separate from the DataWork folder structure. Project management materials should be maintained in a sync system like Dropbox, whereas the code folder should be maintained in a version-control system like Git. However, a version-control folder should *never* be stored in a sync folder that is shared with other people. Combining these two types of collaboration tools almost always creates undesirable functionalities.

Establishing common file formats

Each task in the research workflow has specific inputs and outputs that feed into one another. It is common to create incompatibilities, particularly when different people in a team perform different tasks. For example, if the principal investigators are writing a paper using LaTeX, exporting tables from statistical software into a `.csv` format will break the workflow. Therefore, it is important for the team to agree on what tools will be used for what tasks and where inputs and outputs will be stored, before creating them. Taking into account ease of use for different team members and keeping in mind that learning how to use a new tool may require some up-front investment of time will pay off as the project advances.

Knowing how code outputs will be used will help to determine the best format for exporting them. It is typically possible to use the same software to save figures into various formats, such as `.eps`, `.png`, `.pdf`, and `.jpg`. However, the decision to use Office suite software such as Word and PowerPoint (or free alternatives) instead of LaTeX or another plain-text format will influence how the code should be written, because this choice often implies the use of a particular format. This decision will also affect which version-control systems the team can use.

Using version control

Using a *version-control system* is recommended to maintain control of the file history and functionality. A good version-control system tracks who edited each file and when, allows users to revert to previous versions, and provides a protocol for avoiding conflicting versions. Version control is important, for example, if the team needs to find the exact version of a presentation that was delivered to a donor or to understand why the significance level of estimates has changed. Everyone who has ever encountered a file named something like `final_report_v5_LJK_KLE_jun15.docx` can appreciate how useful such a system can be.

Most syncing services offer some kind of rudimentary version control; these services are usually able to manage changes to *binary files* without needing to rely on dreaded filename-based versioning conventions. For code files, however, a more detailed version-control system is usually desirable. Git is the recommended version-control system for all data work. Git documents the changes made to all files, but works best with *plain-text files*. Plain-text files include all code files, most raw outputs, and written outputs that use code languages, such as LaTeX files and many dynamic documents. Git tracks all of the changes made to each plain-text file and makes it possible to return to previous versions without losing information on the changes made. It also makes it possible to work on multiple parallel versions of a file, eliminating the risk that someone who is trying something new will break code for other team members.

Writing code that others can read

Good code is easily understood and run by others. This section discusses a few crucial steps to code organization. They all come from the principle that code is an output in and of itself, not just a means to an end, and should be easy to read. Box 2.4 provides a template for a *master script* do-file in Stata, illustrating the code elements, organization, and structure required.

Binary files are types of computer data that store information and metadata, such as Office suite documents, media files, `.pdf` files, and others. **Plain text files** are types of computer data that store only simple text, such as Stata or R code as well as `.txt`, `.html`, and `.md` files.

A **master script** (in Stata, a master do-file) is a single code script that can be used to execute all of the data work for a project. Any team member should be able to run this script and all the data work scripts executed by it by changing only the directory file path in one line of code in the master script. For more details, see the DIME Wiki at https://dimewiki.worldbank .org/Master_Do-files.

BOX 2.4 DIME MASTER DO-FILE TEMPLATE

```
 1 /************************************************************************
 2 *                    TEMPLATE MASTER DO-FILE                           *
 3 ************************************************************************
 4 *                                                                      *
 5 *    PURPOSE:      Reproduce all data work, map inputs and outputs,    *
 6 *                  facilitate collaboration                            *
 7 *                                                                      *
 8 *    OUTLINE:      PART 1:  Set standard settings and install packages *
 9 *                  PART 2:  Prepare folder paths and define programs   *
10 *                  PART 3:  Run do-files                               *
11 *                                                                      *
```

(Box continues on next page)

BOX 2.4 DIME MASTER DO-FILE TEMPLATE (continued)

```
12 ********************************************************************************
13     PART 1: Install user-written packages and harmonize settings
14 ********************************************************************************/
15
16     local user_commands ietoolkit iefieldkit //Add required user-written commands
17     foreach command of local user_commands {
18       cap which `command'
19       if _rc == 111 ssc install `command'
20     }
21
22     * Harmonize settings across users as much as possible
23     ieboilstart, v(13.1)
24     `r(version)'
25
26 /******************************************************************************
27     PART 2: Prepare folder paths and define programs
28 ********************************************************************************/
29
30     * Research Assistant folder paths
31     if "`c(username)'" == "ResearchAssistant" {
32         global github    "C:/Users/RA/Documents/GitHub/d4di/DataWork"
33         global dropbox   "C:/Users/RA/Dropbox/d4di/DataWork"
34         global encrypted "M:/DataWork/EncryptedData"
35     }
36
37     * Baseline folder globals
38     global bl_encrypt   "${encrypted}/Round Baseline Encrypted"
39     global bl_dt        "${dropbox}/Baseline/DataSets"
40     global bl_doc       "${dropbox}/Baseline/Documentation"
41     global bl_do        "${github}/Baseline/Dofiles"
42     global bl_out       "${github}/Baseline/Output"
43
44 /******************************************************************************
45     PART 3: Run do-files
46 ********************************************************************************/
47
48 /*------------------------------------------------------------------------------
49     PART 3.1: De-identify baseline data
50     REQUIRES:  ${bl_encrypt}/Raw Identified Data/D4DI_baseline_raw_identified.dta
51     CREATES:   ${bl_dt}/Raw Deidentified/D4DI_baseline_raw_deidentified.dta
52     IDS VAR:   hhid
53 ------------------------------------------------------------------------------*/
54     * Change the 0 to 1 to run the baseline de-identification do-file
55     if (0) do "${bl_do}/Cleaning/deidentify.do"
56
```

(Box continues on next page)

```
57 /*------------------------------------------------------------------
58     PART 3.2: Clean baseline data
59     REQUIRES:  ${bl_dt}/Raw Deidentified/D4DI_baseline_raw_deidentified.dta
60     CREATES:   ${bl_dt}/Final/D4DI_baseline_clean.dta
61                ${bl_doc}/Codebook baseline.xlsx
62     IDS VAR:   hhid
63 ------------------------------------------------------------------*/
64     * Change the 0 to 1 to run the baseline cleaning do-file
65     if (0) do "${bl_do}/Cleaning/cleaning.do"
66
67 /*------------------------------------------------------------------
68     PART 3.3: Construct income indicators
69     REQUIRES:  ${bl_dt}/Final/D4DI_baseline_clean.dta
70     CREATES:   ${bl_out}/Raw/D4DI_baseline_income_distribution.png
71                ${bl_dt}/Intermediate/D4DI_baseline_constructed_income.dta
72     IDS VAR:   hhid
73 ------------------------------------------------------------------*/
74     * Change the 0 to 1 to run the baseline variable construction do-file
75     if (0) do "${bl_do}/Construct/construct_income.do"
```

To access this code in do-file format, visit the GitHub repository at https://github.com/worldbank
/dime-data-handbook/tree/main/code.

Comments are components of code that have no function for the computer. They describe in plain language what the code is intended to do and how it is attempting to do it.

To be readable, code must be well documented. This process begins by adding a code header to every file. A code header is a long *comment* that details the functionality of the entire script; refer to lines 5–10 in the template master do-file in box 2.4. The header should include simple information such as the purpose of the script and the name of the person who wrote it. If using version-control software, the software will record the last time a modification was made and the person who most recently edited it. Otherwise, this information should be included in the header. It is essential to track the inputs and outputs of the script as well as the uniquely identifying variable; refer to lines 49–52 in the template master do-file in box 2.4. When trying to determine which code creates which data set, this tracking will be very helpful. Although there are other ways to document decisions related to creating code, the information relevant to understanding the code should always be written in the code file.

Two types of comments should be included in the script itself. The first type of comment describes *what* is being done. Someone familiar with the language might find this information easy to understand from the code itself, if the code is clear, but reverse-engineering the code's intent often requires a great deal of work. Describing the task in plain English (or whatever language the team uses to communicate) will make it easier for everyone to read and understand the code's purpose. It can also help researchers to organize their own work and ensure that they are following logical steps. The second type of comment explains *why* the code is performing a task in a particular way. Writing code requires making a series of decisions that (it is hoped) make perfect sense at the time. These decisions are often highly specialized and may exploit a functionality that is not obvious or that others have not seen before. Well-commented code is, in and of itself, a great way to document the data work that someone can follow to understand everything from data-cleaning decisions that make the published data different from the original data to decisions on how indicators are constructed. In a couple of weeks, even the code writer probably will not remember the exact choices that were made. Documenting the precise processes in code is essential. See box 2.5 for examples of how comments can be used.

BOX 2.5 WRITING CODE THAT OTHERS CAN READ: A CASE STUDY FROM THE DEMAND FOR SAFE SPACES PROJECT

To ensure that all team members were able to read and understand data work easily, Demand for Safe Spaces code files had extensive comments. Comments typically took the form of "what–why": what is this section of code doing, and why is it necessary? The following snippet from a data-cleaning do-file for one of the original data sets illustrates the use of comments:

```
1  ***********************************************************************************
2  *    PART 1: Clean-up                                                            *
3  ***********************************************************************************
4
5      * Drop lines that only work after 8 PM
6      * no rides data are collected outside of rush hour
7      drop if inlist(substr(linha,1,4),"SCZP","JRIP")
8
9      * Drop circular honorio - not present in rides data
10     drop if substr(linha,1,3) == "HON"
11
12     * Adjust var formats - some missing observations are marked as "-",
13     * which causes Stata to read the variable as a string, not a number
14     foreach varAux of varlist boardings exits seatprob {
15         replace `varAux' = subinstr(`varAux',"-","",.) // remove dash character
16         replace `varAux' = strtrim(`varAux')            // remove spaces
17         destring (`varAux'), replace                    // now convertible into a number
18     }
19
20     * Drop null station/line combinations
21     drop if exits == . & boardings == .
```

For the complete do-file, visit the GitHub repository at https://git.io/Jtgev.

Code files should be stored in an easy-to-find location and named in a meaningful way. Breaking code into independently readable "chunks" is good practice for code organization. Each functional element should be written as a chunk that can run completely on its own. This step ensures that each component of code is independent and does not rely on a complex program state created by other chunks of code that are not obvious from the immediate context. One way to achieve this independence is by creating sections in the script to identify where a specific task is completed. RStudio makes it very easy to create sections and compiles them into an interactive script index.

In Stata, comments can be used to create section headers, but they are only intended to make the reading easier and do not have any functionality. For example, to find the line in the code where the directory is set, it is easier to go straight to PART 2: Prepare folder paths and define programs than to read line by line through the entire code (see line 27 in the template master do-file in box 2.4). Since an index is not automated like in RStudio, it must be created manually in the code header by copying and pasting section titles (see lines 8–10 in the template master do-file in box 2.4). It is then possible to add and navigate through the code using the search function in the code editor. Stata code is harder to navigate because it is necessary to scroll through the document; therefore, it is particularly important to avoid writing very long scripts. In Stata at least, breaking code tasks into separate do-files is recommended because there is no limit on the number of do-files, how detailed their names can be, and no advantage to writing longer files. One reasonable rule of thumb is not to write do-files that have more than 200 lines. This is an arbitrary limit, just like the common practice of limiting code lines to 80 characters: it seems to be "enough but not too much" for most purposes.

Writing code that others can run

Bringing all of these smaller code files together is another purpose of the master script. A master script is the map of all of the project's data work, which serves as a table of contents for the instructions that are coded. Anyone should be able to follow and reproduce all of the work from the original data to all outputs simply by running this single script. Someone external to the project who has the master script and all of the input data can (1) run all of the code and recreate all of the outputs, (2) understand generally what is being done at every step, and (3) see how code and outputs are related. All settings required to reproduce all outcomes should be established in the master script, including versions, folder paths, functions, and constants used throughout the project. Box 2.4 shows the DIME Analytics template for a Stata master do-file, but master scripts should be used for reproducibility no matter the programming language used.

A good habit is always to run code from the master script. Creating "section switches" using macros or objects to run only the codes related to a certain task is always preferable to opening different scripts manually and running them in a certain order (see the `if (0)` switches on lines 55, 65, and 75 in the template master do-file in box 2.4 for one way to do this). Furthermore, running all scripts related to a particular task through the master script whenever one of them is edited helps to identify unintended consequences of the changes made. For example, if the name of a variable created in one script changes, this change may break another script that refers to this variable. But, unless both scripts are run when the change is made, it may take time for the break to happen; when it does, it may take time to understand what is causing an error. The same applies to changes in data sets and results.

To link code, data, and outputs, the master script reflects the structure of the DataWork folder in code through globals (in Stata) or string scalars (in R); refer to lines 37–42 of the template master do-file in box 2.4. These coding shortcuts can refer to subfolders, and those folders can be referenced without repeatedly writing out their absolute file paths. Because the DataWork folder is shared by the whole team, its structure is the same in each team member's computer. The only difference between machines is the path to the project root folders—that is, the highest-level shared folder. Depending on the software environment, there may be multiple root folders. In a typical DIME project, there is one Git root folder for the code, one sync software root folder for the de-identified data, and a third encryption software folder for the encrypted data.

This organization is reflected in the master script in such a way that the only change necessary to run the entire code for a new team member is to change the path to the project root folders to reflect the file system and username; refer to lines 30–35 of the template master do-file. The code in the template master file shows how folder structure is reflected in a master do-file. Because writing and maintaining a master script can be challenging as a project grows, an important feature of `iefolder` is to write submaster do-files and add to them whenever new subfolders are created in the DataWork folder. See box 2.6 for an example of the master do-file for the Demand for Safe Spaces project, which was based on the DIME Analytics template and applied the best practices discussed in this section.

All code for the Demand for Safe Spaces study was organized to run from two master scripts, one Stata master script and one R master script. The master scripts were written such that any team member could run all project codes simply by changing the top-level directory. The following is a snippet of the Stata master do-file:

```
1 /**********************************************************************************
2 *   Demand for "Safe Spaces": Avoiding Harassment and Stigma                    *
3 *   MASTER DO-FILE                                                              *
4 **********************************************************************************
5    PART 0: User inputs
6    PART 1: Prepare folder paths
7    PART 2: Load necessary packages
8    PART 3: Run selected code
9 **********************************************************************************
10 *  PART 0: USER INPUTS                                                          *
11 **********************************************************************************/
12
13    ieboilstart, v(14.0) matsize(10000)
14    `r(version)'
15
16 // Set folder paths ------------------------------------------------------------
17
18    if inlist(c(username), "Luiza") {
19        global github   "C:\Users\Documents\GitHub\rio-safe-space\Replication Package"
20        global onedrive "C:\Users\OneDrive - WBG\RJ - Vagao Rosa"
21    }
22
23 // Select sections to run ------------------------------------------------------
24
25    local  packages       0 // Install user-written commands used in the project
26    local  cleaning       0 // Run data cleaning
27    global encrypted      0 // Start from identified data
28    local  construction   0 // Re-create analysis indicators
29    local  mainresults    0 // Re-create analysis outputs
30
31 * Section omitted - see full code on https://github.com/worldbank/rio-safe-space
32
33 **********************************************************************************
34 *   PART 1: Prepare folder paths                                                *
35 **********************************************************************************
36
37    * Confidential folders
38    global encrypt    "${onedrive}/data/raw-identified"
39    global encode     "${onedrive}/dofiles/ado"
40
```

(Box continues on next page)

```
41    * Do-files
42    global do           "${github}/dofiles"
43    global do_analysis  "${do}/analysis"
44    global do_tables    "${do_analysis}/paper/tables"
45    global do_graphs    "${do_analysis}/paper/graphs"
46
47    * Data sets
48    global data         "${github}/data"
49    global dt_final     "${data}/final"
50    global dt_raw       "${data}/raw"
51    global dt_int       "${data}/intermediate"
52
53    * Documentation
54    global doc          "${github}/documentation"
55    global doc_rider    "${doc}/rider-audits"
56    global doc_platform "${doc}/platform-survey"
57
58    * Outputs
59    global out_git      "${github}/outputs"
60    global out_tables   "${out_git}/tables"
61    global out_graphs   "${out_git}/graphs"
62
63 * Section omitted - see full code on https://github.com/worldbank/rio-safe-space
64
65 ********************************************************************************
66 *    PART 3: Run selected code                                                *
67 ********************************************************************************
68
69    if `cleaning'     do "${do}/rider-audits/MASTER_rider_audits_data_prep.do"
70    if `construction' {
71        do "${do}/rider-audits/pooled/7_construct.do"
72        do "${do}/rider-audits/pooled/8_reconstruct_p3_assignment.do"
73    }
74    if `mainresults'  do "${do_analysis}/paper/MASTER_paper_results.do"
```

For the complete Stata master script, visit the GitHub repository at https://git.io/JtgeT. For the R master script, visit the GitHub repository at https://git.io/JtgeY.

In order to maintain well-documented and well-organized code, everyone on the team has to agree on a plan to review code as it is written. Researchers benefit from improving their own skills as they read other people's code and from allowing others to read their code to catch errors and ambiguities. It is normal (and common) to make mistakes while writing code. Reading code again to organize and provide comments while preparing it to be reviewed will help to identify those mistakes. It is best to schedule a code review at regular intervals or when a single task is completed. Waiting a long time to review the code means that the code becomes too complex, and preparation and code review require more time and work, which is a common reason why this step is often skipped. Another important advantage of code review is that making sure that the code is running properly on other machines and that other people can read and understand the code are the easiest ways to prepare in advance for a smooth project handover or for release of the code to the general public.

Preparing to handle confidential data ethically

Personally identifying information (PII) is any piece or set of information that can be linked to the identity of a specific individual. For more details, see the DIME Wiki at https://dimewiki.worldbank .org/Personally_Identifiable _Information_(PII).

Research ethics are the guiding principles of decision-making and the norms of behavior with which research must be conducted to be considered acceptable in the pursuit of the common good. For more details, see the DIME Wiki at https:// dimewiki.worldbank.org /Research_Ethics. See also pillar 1 of the DIME Research Standards at https:// github.com/worldbank /dime-standards.

Most original data in a development research project include *personally identifying information* (PII). PII variables can include names, addresses, geolocations, email addresses, phone numbers, and bank accounts or other financial details. When working in a context or population that is small and specific or has extensive linkable data sources available to others, information like age and gender may be sufficient to disclose a person's identify, even though those variables are not considered PII in general. The remainder of this section addresses the standards for *research ethics* that teams must follow when working with PII.

PII should be separated from the rest of the data at the earliest opportunity and stored in a separate, protected location. This step protects respondent privacy and simplifies workflows, because de-identified data sets do not need to be encrypted. If the PII is required for analysis, research teams must work with encrypted files through-out. There is no one-size-fits-all solution to determine what is PII, and research teams have to use careful judgment in each case to avoid *statistical disclosure risk*. Data privacy principles apply not only to the respondents providing the information but also to their household members or other individuals who are referenced in the data. In all cases involving PII, adhering to several core principles is essential. These principles include ethical approval, participant consent, data security, and participant privacy (for an example, see Baldwin, Muyengwa, and Mvukiyehe 2017). Researchers based in the United States must become familiar with a set of governance standards known as "the Common Rule" (Bierer, Barnes, and Lynch 2017). Researchers interacting with European institutions or persons must also become familiar with the General Data Protection Regulation (GDPR; at https://gdpr-info.eu), a set of regulations governing data ownership and privacy standards. No matter where the researcher is located or what the exact legal require-ments are, similar core principles and practices will apply.

Seeking ethical approval

Most of the field research done in development involves *human subjects*. Researchers ask people to trust them with personal information about themselves: where they live, how rich they are, whether they have committed or been victims of crimes, their names, their national identity numbers, and all sorts of other information. Personal data carry strict expectations about data storage and handling, and the research team is responsible for satisfying these expectations. Donors or employers most likely require researchers to hold a certification from a respected source.

Almost all such data collection and research activities will require the completion of some form of *institutional review board* (IRB) process. Most commonly this process consists of a formal application for approval of a specific protocol for consent, data collection, and data handling. Which IRB has authority over a project is not always apparent, particularly if participating institutions do not have their own IRB. It is customary to obtain approval from a university IRB where at least one principal investigator is affiliated; if work is being done in an international setting, approval from an appropriate local institution subject to the laws of the country where data originate is often required as well.

IRB approval should be obtained well before any data are acquired (see the example of an IRB process in box 2.7). IRBs may have infrequent meeting schedules or require several rounds of review for an application to be approved. If there are any deviations from an approved plan or expected adjustments, these deviations should be reported as early as possible so that the protocol can be updated or revised. IRBs have the authority to deny retroactively the right to use data not acquired in accordance with an approved plan. This situation is extremely rare but shows the seriousness of these considerations because the institution itself may face legal penalties if its IRB is unable to enforce its protocols. As always, researchers who work in good faith should not have any problem complying with these regulations.

Obtaining informed consent

IRBs are principally concerned with protecting the people about whom information is being collected as well as people whose well-being may be affected by the research design. Some jurisdictions (such as those governed by European Union law) view personal data as intrinsically owned by the persons described: those persons have the right to refuse to participate in data collection before it happens, as it is happening, or after it has already happened. In addition, they must explicitly and affirmatively consent to the collection, storage, and use of their information for any purpose, except in cases where IRB regulations allow a waiver of informed consent to be obtained.

BOX 2.7 SEEKING ETHICAL APPROVAL: AN EXAMPLE FROM THE DEMAND FOR SAFE SPACES PROJECT

The Duke University institutional review board (IRB) reviewed and approved the protocol for all components of fieldwork for the Demand for Safe Spaces study (IRB identification number D0190). One of the principal investigators was at Duke University and the World Bank does not have an IRB, so Duke University was the relevant institution in this case. The study was registered with the Duke Campus IRB on September 2015. The protocol was amended four times to reflect additions to the study design, including an implicit association test and a new survey. The IRB approval was renewed twice, in 2016 and 2017. The following are highlights from the study IRB protocols:

- *Voluntary study participation.* The study intervention was conducted through a smartphone application. Through the app, users were offered payment to complete a set of tasks while using the metro. The tasks involved answering questions at different moments of the trip (before boarding the train, during the ride, and after leaving the train). At the start of each task, participants were asked to review the task and the exact value of payment and then decide whether to accept the task or not. There was no obligation to complete any task.
- *Survey instruments.* Translated drafts of all survey instruments were shared with the IRB.
- *Privacy protection.* The intervention was done using a specialized mobile application developed by a partner technology company, which recruited users through social media. User data from the app were encrypted and stored in the cloud using Amazon Web Services. As per the user agreement, access to the raw data was restricted to employees of the tech company, using a virtual private network and encrypted laptops. The tech company processed the raw data and released nonidentifying data to the researchers plus household coordinates (study participants provided informed consent to share this information).
- *Risk.* Participants were tasked with riding the public transport system in Rio de Janeiro. Some general risk is inherent in traveling around Rio de Janeiro. However, the public transport system is widely used, and participants were expected to be persons who regularly take the train, although the assigned task might have caused them to travel on a different route or at a different time than usual. Tasks were assigned around rush hour, so stations and trains were crowded, which was expected to reduce risks. Half of the riders on the system were women, and only a small fraction of the cars were reserved for women, so the task of riding the regular carriage did not require users to enter an all-male environment.
- *Ethical obligation.* When completing an assigned task, participants were asked whether they had experienced any harassment. If harassment was reported, the app directed the participant to the platform guards to whom she could report the harassment (guards are trained to respond to harassment reports) as well as to other resources available in the Rio area.

Appendix C in Kondylis et al. (2020) discusses the ethical aspects of the study, including participant recruitment, informed consent, and how reports of harassment were addressed.

Informed consent is the right of potential research participants to decide whether to participate in research programs or data collection activities, free of any obligation or coercion, and while fully informed of any potential risks or benefits of participation. For more details, see the DIME Wiki at https://dimewiki.worldbank .org/Informed_Consent.

The development of appropriate consent processes is of primary importance. All survey instruments must include a module in which the sampled respondent grants *informed consent* to participate. Research participants must be informed of the purpose of the research, what their participation will entail in terms of duration and procedures, any foreseeable benefits or risks, and how their identity will be protected (see the example in box 2.8). Additional protections are in place for vulnerable populations, such as minors, prisoners, pregnant women, and people with disabilities, and these protections should be confirmed with relevant authorities if the research includes these groups.

BOX 2.8 OBTAINING INFORMED CONSENT: A CASE STUDY FROM THE DEMAND FOR SAFE SPACES PROJECT

Participation in both the study intervention (assignments to take a specific Supervia ride) and the platform survey was fully voluntary and included informed consent. Per the informed consent protocols for the study intervention, participation in each assigned task was voluntary, and participants were paid shortly after each ride was completed, regardless of the total number of rides completed. Thus, participants could choose to stop participating at any time if they felt uncomfortable or for any other reason. Participants were shown the following consent statement:

> If you choose to do this task, you will have to go to a Supervia station, ride the train, and answer questions about your experience on the train. You will have to ride the train for ____ minutes, and answering the questions will take about 10 minutes. You will be paid at least ____ reais for the task, and possibly more. You will be able to review the payment for each task and option before deciding whether to do that task. *You can choose during the task whether to ride either the women-only or the mixed carriage on the Supervia.* Your responses to the task will not be identified in any way with you personally. The anonymous data will be shared with researchers at Duke University in the United States. You can choose to stop the task at any time. To get paid for this task, however, you have to finish the task.

The sentence in italics was removed for the portion of the data collection in which participants were assigned to ride in a particular type of car; the rest of the consent statement applied to all tasks.

Ensuring research subject privacy

In order to safeguard PII data and protect the privacy of respondents, a data protection protocol must be set up from the outset of a project. Secure data storage and transfer are ultimately the researcher's responsibility. Later chapters discuss the proper way to protect data depending on the method used to acquire, store, or share data. This section covers only the computer setup needed for any project. This setup has several components.

First, a system is needed for managing strong and unique passwords for all accounts, including personal accounts like computer logins and email. All passwords should be long, not use common words, and not be reused for multiple accounts. The only way to make that approach practically feasible is to use a password manager (for the DIME step-by-step guide for how to get started with password managers, see pillar 4 of the DIME Research Standards at https://github.com /worldbank/dime-standards). Most password managers offer the ability to securely share passwords for accounts shared with colleagues. Multifactor authentication (sometimes called two-step verification, or 2FA) is a secure alternative to passwords when available.

Second, machines that store confidential data should not be connected to insecure physical or wireless networks; when it is necessary to do so, a *virtual private network* should be used to connect to the internet. Furthermore, USB drives and other devices connecting over USB cables should not be connected to machines storing confidential data unless it is known where the devices came from and who last used them. Machines with confidential data should also be stored in a secure location when not in use.

Third, all confidential data must be *encrypted* at all times. When files are properly encrypted, the information they contain is completely unreadable and unusable even if they are intercepted by a malicious "intruder" (an information-security term for any unauthorized access to information) or accidentally made public. Chapter 4 discusses the implementation of encryption in more detail specific to different stages of data work. Here, suffice it to say that, when setting up a software environment for the project, it is imperative to ensure that the computers of all team members have an encryption solution for all parts of the workflow. Data can be encrypted at the disk (hard drive) level, called *full disk encryption* (FDE), or at the individual file or folder level, called *file system encryption* (FSE). When possible, both types of encryption should be applied, but it is recommended to use file system encryption as the main type of protection and to require all members handling confidential data to use it.

Although most implementations of FDE use a computer's login password to prevent files from being read by anyone but the owner, password protection alone is not sufficient. Password protection makes it more difficult for someone else to gain access to files stored on a computer, but only encryption properly protects files if someone manages to access the computer anyway. Whenever FDE is available in an operating system, it should be enabled. FDE protects data when encrypted just as well as FSE, but FSE is recommended because FDE has several disadvantages. First, FDE is implemented differently in different operating systems, making it difficult to create useful instructions for all computer setups that may be used. Second, when FDE decrypts a disk, it decrypts all of the data on that disk, even files not in use at the time. Because most FDE systems automatically decrypt the full disk each time someone logs in, a malicious intruder would have access to all of the files on the computer. Third and perhaps most important, FDE cannot be used when sharing confidential data over

A **virtual private network** (VPN) is a networking configuration that allows users to connect securely to a trusted network over an insecure network. A VPN makes it possible to communicate securely with other devices on the trusted network and makes traffic to the internet inaccessible to the host of the insecure network.

Encryption is any process that systematically scrambles the information contained in digital files. This process ensures that file contents are unreadable even if laptops are stolen, databases are hacked, or any other type of access is obtained that gives unauthorized people access to the encrypted files. For more details, see the DIME Wiki at https://dimewiki .worldbank.org/Encryption.

insecure channels like file-syncing services or email. So FDE has to be complemented with some other type of protection during collaboration.

With FSE, instead of encrypting a full disk or drive, encrypted folders are created in which to store confidential data securely. These encrypted folders protect data stored on a computer but can also be used to transfer data securely over insecure channels like file-syncing services and email. Encrypted folders in FSE are decrypted only when that specific folder is decrypted. Therefore, a malicious intruder gains access only to the folders that were decrypted while the computer was compromised. Folders that are rarely or never decrypted remain protected even if someone gains access to the computer. DIME uses VeraCrypt for FSE, and DIME protocols are available as part of the DIME Research Standards (for DIME's step-by-step guide for how to get started with VeraCrypt, see pillar 4 of the DIME Research Standards at https://github.com/worldbank/dime-standards). VeraCrypt is free of charge and available for Windows, macOS, and Linux. Although some details are different across platforms, the encryption should be implemented in the same way for all team members.

Regardless of whether full disk encryption or file system encryption is used, it is important to remember that encryption provides no protection when data are decrypted. Therefore, it is important to log out of the computer when not using it and to decrypt folders with confidential data only when those exact files are needed. The latter is possible only when using FSE.

Handling confidential data properly will always add to the workload, even more so when the data contain PII. The easiest way to reduce that workload is to handle PII as infrequently as possible. Acquiring personal data that are not strictly needed to carry out the research should be avoided. Even when PII is necessary for parts of the research, most tasks can be completed with subsets of the data that have had the PII removed. Therefore, all projects should plan to create a version of the data from which PII has been removed and use this version whenever possible.

In practice it is rarely, if ever, possible to *anonymize* data. There is always some statistical chance that an individual's identity will be relinked to the data collected about that person—even if all directly identifying information has been removed—by using some other data that become identifying when analyzed together. For this reason, a two-stage process of *de-identification* is recommended. The *initial de-identification* strips the data of direct identifiers as early in the process as possible, to create a working de-identified data set that can be shared *within the research team* without the need for encryption. This data set should always be used when possible. The *final de-identification* involves making a decision about the trade-off between risk of disclosure and utility of the data before publicly releasing a data set. See box 2.9 for an example of the data privacy protocol used in the Demand for Safe Spaces project.

De-identification is the process of removing or masking PII to reduce the risk that subjects' identities can be connected with the data. For more details, see the DIME Wiki at https://dimewiki.worldbank.org/De-identification.

The Demand for Safe Spaces team adopted the following data security protocols:

- All confidential data were stored in a World Bank OneDrive folder. The World Bank OneDrive was set up to be more secure than regular OneDrive and is the recommended institutional solution for storing confidential data.
- Access to the confidential data was limited to the research analyst and the research assistant working on the data cleaning.
- All de-identified data used for the analysis were stored in the synchronized folder shared by the full research team (in this case, using Dropbox).
- Indirect identifiers such as demographic variables and labels for train lines and stations were removed before the data were published to the Microdata Catalog.

Finally, it is essential to have an end-of-life plan even before data are acquired. This plan includes plans for how to transfer access and control to a new person joining the team and how to revoke that access when someone is leaving the team. It should also include a plan for how the PII will be deleted. Every project should have a clear data retention and destruction plan. After a project is completed and its de-identified data have been made available, research teams should not retain confidential data indefinitely.

Looking ahead

With the computing environment established, it will be clear how the data and code that are received and created will be handled throughout the research process. This structure should prepare the team to work collaboratively, to share code and data across machines and among team members, and to document the work as a group. With an organizational plan and protocols for version control and backup of files, the team will be ready to handle materials ethically and securely. At this point, the approvals needed for any planned work will have been secured, and it is time to translate the project's research design into a measurement framework to answer the project's research questions. The next chapter outlines how to prepare the essential elements of research data. It shows how to map a project's data needs according to both the research design and the planned creation and use of data across the project timeline.

References

Baldwin, Kate, Shylock Muyengwa, and Eric Mvukiyehe. 2017. "Reforming Village-Level Governance via Horizontal Pressure: Evidence from an Experiment in Zimbabwe." Policy Research Working Paper 7941, World Bank, Washington, DC.

Bierer, Barbara E., Mark Barnes, and Holly Fernandez Lynch. 2017. "Revised 'Common Rule' Shapes Protections for Research Participants." *Health Affairs* 36 (5). https://doi.org/10.1377/hlthaff.2017.0307.

Kondylis, Florence, Arianna Legovini, Kate Vyborny, Astrid Zwager, and Luíza Andrade. 2020. "Demand for Safe Spaces: Avoiding Harassment and Stigma." Policy Research Working Paper 9269, World Bank, Washington, DC. https://openknowledge.worldbank.org/handle/10986/33853.

Chapter 3

Establishing a measurement framework

The first step in the data workflow is to establish a measurement framework, which requires understanding a project's data requirements and how to structure the required data to answer the research questions. Setting up the measurement framework involves more than simply listing the key outcome variables. It is also necessary to understand how to structure original data, to determine how different data sources connect together, and to create tools to document these decisions and communicate them to the full research team. This chapter shows how to develop this framework and demonstrates that planning in advance saves time and improves the quality of research.

The first section of this chapter introduces the DIME data map template. The template includes a data linkage table, master data sets, and data flowcharts. These tools are used to communicate the project's data requirements across the team and over time. The second section describes how to translate a project's research design into data needs. It provides examples of the specific data required by common types of impact evaluation research designs and how to document the link between research design and data sources in the data map template. The final section links the measurement framework to the reproducibility and credibility pillars introduced in chapter 1. It covers how to generate research design variables that are reproducible and how to use power calculations and randomization inference to assess credibility. Box 3.1 summarizes the most important points, lists the responsibilities of different members of the research team, and provides a list of key tools and resources for implementing the recommended practices.

BOX 3.1 SUMMARY: ESTABLISHING A MEASUREMENT FRAMEWORK

To be useful for research, original data must be mapped to a research design through a measurement framework. The measurement framework links each of the project's data sets to the research design and establishes their connections and relationships. Elaborating the measurement framework at the start of a research project ensures that all team members have the same understanding and creates documentation that will prove useful over the full research cycle. The measurement framework includes three key outputs.

1. *Data map*. The data map documents all of the data for the project. The materials in the data map provide documentation for

   - All data sets, units of observation, and high-level relationships between data sets, which are provided in a data linkage table;
   - The master data sets for each unit of observation, which define the statistical populations of interest; and
   - The expected ways in which data sets will be combined in data processing and analysis, with data flowcharts as a visual guide.

2. *Research design variables*. The research design variables, which translate the research design into data, describe characteristics like the following:

   - Treatment and sampling variables, such as comparison groups, clusters and strata, and other variables, which describe how units of observation relate to the proposed analytical methodology
   - Time variables, which may be regular or irregular and serve to structure the data temporally
   - Monitoring indicators, which characterize the implementation of interventions or surveys

3. *Outputs of random processes*. Random processes, implemented through statistical software, are often needed to translate research designs into data work. These random processes share common characteristics and can include the following:

   - Random sampling, to choose a subset of the population of interest to observe
   - Random treatment assignment, to determine which units will be placed into which experimental condition in a randomized trial
   - More complex designs, such as clustering or stratification, which require special considerations

Key responsibilities for task team leaders and principal investigators

   - Oversee and provide inputs to the development of data linkage tables, master data set(s), and data flowchart(s); and review and approve the complete data map.
   - Supervise the generation of all research design variables required to execute the study design, and establish guidelines for any research design variables that require data collection.
   - Provide detailed guidance on the expected function and structure of random processes.

(Box continues on next page)

Documenting data needs

Most projects require more than one data source to answer a research question. Data could be sourced from multiple survey rounds, acquired from various partners (such as administrative data or implementation data), acquired from technological tools like satellite imagery or web scraping, or sourced from complex combinations of these and other sources (for an example, see Kondylis and Stein 2018). Regardless of how the study data are structured, it is essential to know how to link data from all sources and analyze the relationships between units to answer the research questions. It is not possible to keep all of the relevant details straight without a structured process because the whole research team is unlikely to have the same understanding, over the whole life cycle of the project, of the relationship between all of the required data sets. To ensure that the full team shares the same understanding, best practice is to create a *data map*. The data map is intended to ensure that all of the data are in hand to answer the intended research questions, well before starting the analysis described in chapter 6. The data map provides documentation for the project. The process of drafting the data map provides a useful opportunity for principal investigators to communicate their vision of the data structure and requirements and for research assistants to communicate their understanding of that vision. The recommended best practice is to complete the data map before acquiring any data and to make it part of the preregistration of the study. However, in practice many research projects evolve as new data sources, observations, and research questions

A **data map** is a set of tools to document and communicate the data requirements in a project and how different data can be linked together. For more details, see the DIME Wiki at https://dimewiki.worldbank.org/Data_Map.

arise, which means that each component of the data map has to be maintained and updated continuously.

The DIME data map template has three components: one data linkage table, one or several master data sets, and one or several data flowcharts. The *data linkage table* lists all of the original data sets that will be used in the project, what data sources they are created from, and how they relate to each other. For each unit of observation in the data linkage table as well as for each unit of analysis to be used, a *master data set* is created and maintained, listing all observations of the unit that are relevant to the project. Finally, using these two resources, *data flowcharts* are created, describing how the original data sets and master data sets are to be combined and transformed to create analysis data sets. Each component is discussed in more detail in the following subsections.

In order to map measurement frameworks into data needs, it is helpful to distinguish between two types of variables: variables that tie the research design to observations in the data, which are called research design variables, and variables that correspond to observations of the real world, which are called measurement variables. Research design variables map information about the research subjects onto the research design. Often, these variables have no meaning outside of the research project— for example, identification variables and treatment status. Others are observations from the real world, but only those that determine how each specific research unit should be handled during the analysis—for example, treatment uptake and eligibility status. Measurement variables, in contrast, are real-world measures that are not determined by the research team. Examples include characteristics of the research subject, outcomes of interest, and control variables, among many others.

Developing a data linkage table

To create a data map according to the DIME template, the first step is to create a data linkage table by listing in a spreadsheet all of the data sources that will be used and the original data sets that will be created from them. If one source of data will result in two different data sets, then each data set is listed on its own row. For each data set, the unit of observation and the name of the *project identifier* (ID) variable for that unit of observation are listed. It is important to include both plain-language terminology as well as technical file and variable names here. For example, the `hh_baseline2020_listmap.csv` data set may be titled the "Baseline Household Listing" data; it may be identified by the `hh_id` variable and listed as being identified at the household level. Establishing such plain-language terminology early in the project allows the team to use these labels unambiguously in communication.

The data linkage table is useful for planning how each unit of observation will be identified in the data. When a data set is listed in the data linkage table, which should be done before the data set is acquired, it is important to ensure that the data will be fully and uniquely identified by the project ID or to plan how the new data set will be linked to the project ID. Working with a data set that does not have an unambiguous link to the project ID is very labor-intensive and a major source of error (for an example of credible matching across data sets in the absence of a unique ID, see Fernandes, Hillberry, and Mendoza Alcántara 2017).

When combining data sets, the data linkage table should indicate whether data sets can be merged one-to-one or appended (for example, with baseline and endline data sets that use the same unit of observation) or whether two data sets need to be merged many-to-one (for example, merging school administrative data with student data). The data map must indicate which ID variables can be used—and how—when combining data sets. The data linkage table is also a great place to list other metadata, such as the source of the data, its backup locations, the nature of the data license, and so on (see the example in box 3.2).

BOX 3.2 DEVELOPING A DATA LINKAGE TABLE: AN EXAMPLE FROM THE DEMAND FOR SAFE SPACES PROJECT

The main unit of observation in the platform survey data sets was the respondent, uniquely identified by the variable ID. However, implicit association tests (IATs) were collected through a specialized software that produced output from two data sets for each IAT instrument: one at the respondent level, containing the final scores, and one with detailed information on each stimulus used in the test (images or expressions to be associated with concepts). Three IAT instruments were used: one testing the association between gender and career choice, one testing the association between car choice and safety concerns, and one testing the association between car choice and openness to sexual advances.

As a result, the original data for the platform survey component of the project consisted of seven data sets: one for the platform survey and six for the IAT—three with IAT scores (one for each instrument) and three with detailed stimuli data (one for each instrument). All seven data sets were stored in the same raw data folder. The data linkage table listed their filenames and indicated how their ID variables are connected. In the table below, the raw stimulus data do not have a unique identifier, because the same stimulus can be shown repeatedly, so the "ID var" field is blank for these data sets.

A sample data linkage table (ID = identifying)

Data source	Raw data set name	Unit of observation (ID var)	Parent unit (ID var)
Platform survey	`platform_survey_raw_ deidentified.dta`	Respondent (id)	

(Box continues on next page)

Gender-career implicit association test	`career_stimuli.dta`	Stimulus	Respondent (`id`) Question block (`block`)
Car choice–safety concerns implicit association test	`security_stimuli.dta`	Stimulus	Respondent (`id`) Question block (`block`)
Car choice–openness to advances implicit association test	`reputation_stimuli .dta`	Stimulus	Respondent (`id`) Question block (`block`)
Gender-career implicit association test	`career_score.dta`	Respondent (`id`)	
Car choice–safety concerns implicit association test	`security_score.dta`	Respondent (`id`)	
Car choice–openness to advances implicit association test	`reputation_score.dta`	Respondent (`id`)	

For the complete project data map, visit the GitHub repository at https://git.io/Jtg3J.

Constructing master data sets

The second step in creating a data map is to create one master data set for each unit of observation that will be used in any research activity. Examples of such activities are data collection, data analysis, sampling, and treatment assignment. The master data set is the authoritative source of the project ID and all research design variables for the corresponding unit of observation, such as sample status and treatment assignment. Therefore, the master data set serves as an unambiguous method of mapping the observations in the data to the research design. A master data set should not include any measurement variables. Research design variables and measurement variables may come from the same source, but should not be stored in the same way. For example, if the project acquires administrative data that include both information on eligibility for the study (research design variables) and data on the topic of study (measurement variables), the research design variables should be stored in the master data set, and the measurement variables should be stored separately and prepared for analysis as described in chapter 5.

Each master data set is to be the authoritative source for how all observations at that unit of analysis are identified. Therefore, the master data sets should include identifying information such as names, contact information, and project ID. The project ID is the ID variable used in the data linkage table and is therefore used to link observations across data sets. The master data set may list alternative IDs—for example, IDs used by a partner organization—but an alternative ID should never be used as the project ID, because doing so would allow individuals outside the research team to identify the research subjects. The project team must create the project ID, and the linkage to direct identifiers should be accessible only to people listed on the protocol approved by the institutional review board. The master data set serves as the link between all other identifying information and the project ID. Because the master data set is full of directly identifying information, it must always be encrypted. If a data set is received with an alternative ID, it should be replaced with the project ID as a part of the de-identification process (see chapters 5 and 7 for more on de-identification). The alternative ID should be stored in the master data set so that it may be linked back to the data using the project ID if needed. Any data set that needs to retain an alternative ID for any reason should be treated as confidential data; it should always be encrypted and never published.

The starting point for the master data set is typically a sampling frame (more on sampling frames later in this chapter). However, it is essential to update the master data set continuously with all observations encountered in the project, even if those observations are not eligible for the study. Examples include new observations that are listed during monitoring activities or observations that are connected to respondents in the study—for example, in a social network module. This updating is useful because errors become less likely in record linkages such as fuzzy matching using string variables as more information is added to the master data set. If it is ever necessary to perform a fuzzy match to a data source that does not have a unique ID, this task should be done using the master data set (for an example, see Benhassine et al. 2018). Data from sources that are not fully and uniquely identified with the project ID should not be cleaned or analyzed until the project IDs have been merged successfully from the master data set. If this process results in the project adding new observations to the master data set, it is necessary to confirm beyond a reasonable doubt that the new observation is indeed a new observation and not simply a failed match to an observation already contained in the master data set. For example, it should be checked whether identifiers such as proper names have inconsistent spellings or romanizations or whether identifiers such as addresses or phone numbers have become outdated.

Creating data flowcharts

The third and final step in creating the data map is to create data flowcharts. Each analysis data set (see chapter 6 for a discussion on why multiple analysis data sets may be needed) should have a data flowchart showing how it was created. The flowchart is a diagram in which each starting point is either a master data set or a data set listed in the data linkage table. The data flowchart should include instructions on how the original data sets can be combined to create the analysis data set. The operations used to combine the data could include appending, one-to-one merging, many-to-one or one-to-many merging, collapsing, reshaping, or a broad variety of other operations. It is important to list which variable or set of variables should be used in each operation and to note whether the operation creates a new variable or a combination of variables to identify the newly linked data. Data sets should be linked by project IDs when possible (exceptions are time variables in longitudinal data and subunits like farm plots, which correspond to a farmer with a project ID but do not themselves have project IDs). Once the data sets listed in the flowchart have been acquired, the number of observations that the starting point data set has and the number of observations that each resulting data set should have after each operation can be added to the data flowcharts. This method is useful for tracking attrition and making sure that the operations used to combine data sets do not create unwanted duplicates or incorrectly drop any observations.

The information that goes into the data flowcharts can be expressed in text, but diagrams generally are the most efficient way to communicate this information across a team (see the example in box 3.3). A data flowchart can be created using a flowchart drawing tool (many free options are available online) or using the shapes or tools in Microsoft Office. It can also be created simply by drawing on a piece of paper and taking a photo, but a digital tool is recommended so that flowcharts can be updated easily over time if needed. As with the data linkage table, the flowchart should include both technical information and plain-language interpretations of the operations that are done and the data that are created. This information is useful for understanding the complex data combinations that often result from merges and appends, such as panel data sets like "person-year" structures and multilevel data like "district-school-teacher-student" structures.

The flowchart summarizes each operation that changes the level of observation of the data and how data sets will be combined. Because these changes are the most error-prone data-processing tasks, having a high-level plan for how they will be executed helps to clarify the process for everyone on the data team, preventing future mistakes.

BOX 3.3 CREATING DATA FLOWCHARTS: AN EXAMPLE FROM THE DEMAND FOR SAFE SPACES PROJECT

The data flowchart indicates how the original data sets were processed and combined to create a final respondent-level data set that was used for analysis. In figure B3.3.1, the analysis data set resulting from this process is shown in green. The original data sets are shown in blue (refer to the sample in box 3.2 for details on the original data sets). The name of the uniquely identifying variable in the data set is indicated in the format (ID: `variable_name`).

(Box continues on next page)

FIGURE B3.3.1 **Flowchart of a project data map**

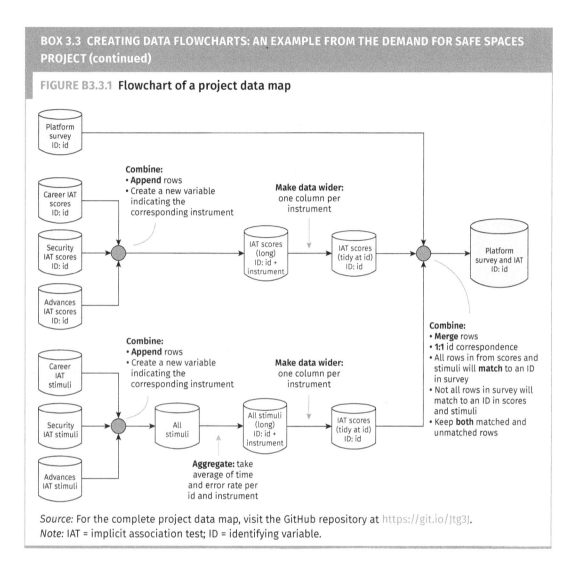

Source: For the complete project data map, visit the GitHub repository at https://git.io/Jtg3J.
Note: IAT = implicit association test; ID = identifying variable.

Translating research design to data needs

A **treatment** is an evaluated intervention or event, which includes things like being offered training or a cash transfer from a program or experiencing a natural disaster, among many others.

A **counterfactual** is a statistical description of what would have happened to specific individuals in an alternative scenario—for example, a different treatment assignment outcome.

An important step in translating the research design into a specific data structure is to determine which research design variables are needed to infer which differences in measurement variables are attributable to the research design. These data needs should be expressed in the data map by listing the data source for each variable in the data linkage table, by adding columns for them in the master data set (the master data set might not have any observations yet; that is not a problem), and by indicating in the data flowcharts how they will be merged with the analysis data. It is important to perform this task before acquiring any data, to make sure that the data acquisition activities described in chapter 4 will generate the data needed to answer the research questions.

Because DIME works primarily on impact evaluations, the discussion here focuses on research designs that compare a group that received some kind of *treatment* against a *counterfactual*. The key assumption is that each person, facility, or village (or whatever the unit of analysis is) has two possible states: the outcome if the unit did receive the treatment and the outcome if it did not receive the treatment. The *average treatment effect* (ATE) is the difference between these two states averaged over all units.

However, it is impossible to observe the same unit in both the treated and untreated state simultaneously, so it is impossible to calculate these differences directly. Instead, the treatment group is compared to a control group that is statistically indistinguishable, which is often referred to as achieving *balance* between two or more groups. DIME Analytics maintains a Stata command to standardize and automate the creation of well-formatted balance tables: `iebaltab` (for instructions and details, see the DIME Wiki at https://dimewiki.worldbank.org/iebaltab). Each research design has a different method for identifying and balancing the counterfactual group. The rest of this section covers how different methods require different research data. What does not differ, however, is that these data requirements are all research design variables that should always be included in the master data set. It is usually necessary to merge the research design variables with other data sets many times during a project, but this task is easy if the project has created a data linkage table.

This chapter assumes that the reader has a working familiarity with the research designs mentioned here. Appendix C provides more details and specific references for common types of impact evaluation designs.

Applying common research designs to data

When using *experimental methods,* such as *randomized control trials* (RCTs), the research team determines which members of the studied population will receive the treatment. This decision is typically made by a randomized process in which a subset of the eligible population is randomly assigned to receive the treatment (implementation is discussed later in this chapter). The intuition is that, if everyone in the eligible population is assigned at random to either the treatment or the control group, the two groups will, on average, be statistically indistinguishable. Randomization makes it generally possible to obtain unbiased estimates of the effects that can be attributed to a specific program or intervention: in a randomized trial, the expected spurious correlation between treatment and outcomes will approach zero as the sample size increases (Duflo, Glennerster, and Kremer 2007; Gibson and Sautmann 2020). The randomized assignment should be done using data from the master data set, and the result should be saved back to the master data set before being merged with other data sets.

Quasi-experimental methods, by contrast, are based on events not controlled by the research team. Instead, they rely on "experiments of nature," in which natural variation in exposure to treatment can be argued to approximate deliberate randomization. This natural variation has to be measured, and the master data set has to document how the variation is categorized as outcomes of a naturally randomized assignment. Unlike carefully planned experimental designs, quasi-experimental designs typically require the luck of having access to data collected at the right times and places to exploit events that occurred in the past. Therefore, these methods often use either secondary data, including administrative data, or other classes of routinely collected information; and it is important for the data linkage table to document how these data can be linked to the rest of the data in the project.

Regardless of the type of design, it is necessary to be very clear about which of the data points observed or collected are research design variables. For example, *regression discontinuity* (RD) designs exploit sharp breaks or limits in policy designs (for an example, see Alix-Garcia et al. 2019). The cutoff determinant—or running variable—should be saved in the master data set. In *instrumental variables* (IV) designs, the instruments influence the probability of treatment (for an example, see Calderon, Iacovone, and Juarez 2017). These research design variables should be collected and stored in the master data set. Both the running variable in RD designs and the instruments in IV designs are among the rare examples of research design variables that may vary over time. In such cases, the research design should clearly indicate ex ante the point in time when they will be recorded, and this information should be clearly documented in the master data set.

In *matching* designs, statistically similar observations are identified using strata, indexes, or propensity scores unrelated to the topic of the study. Matching can be used to pair units that already have or will receive the treatment to identify statistically similarly control units. It can also be used to identify pairs or groups of statistically similar units within which the research team randomizes who will be treated. Like all research design variables, the matching results should be stored in the master data set. This recording is best done by assigning a matching ID to each group and creating a variable in the master data set with the matching ID to which each unit belongs (for an example, see Prennushi and Gupta 2014).

Including multiple time periods

The data map should also consider whether the project uses data from one time period or several. A study that observes data in only one time period is called a *cross-sectional study*. Observations over multiple time periods, referred to as *longitudinal data*, can consist of either *repeated cross sections* or *panel data*. In repeated cross sections, each successive round of data collection uses a new sample of units from the treatment and control groups (which may or may not overlap), whereas in a panel data study the same units are tracked and observed in each round (for an example, see Kondylis et al. 2016). If each round of data collection is a separate activity, then each round should be treated as a separate source of data and given its own row in the data linkage table.

Data that are generated continuously or are acquired at frequent intervals can be treated as a single data source. When data are acquired in discrete batches, the data linkage table must document how the different rounds will be combined. It is important to keep track of the *attrition rate*

Regression discontinuity (RD) designs are causal inference approaches that use cut-offs by which units on both sides are assumed to be statistically similar but only units on one side receive the treatment. For more details, see the DIME Wiki at https://dimewiki.worldbank.org/Regression_Discontinuity.

Instrumental variables (IV) designs are causal inference approaches that overcome endogeneity through the use of a valid predictor of treatment variation, known as an instrument. For more details, see the DIME Wiki at https://dimewiki.worldbank.org/Instrumental_Variables.

Matching designs are causal inference approaches that use characteristics in the data to identify units that are statistically similar. For more details, see the DIME Wiki at https://dimewiki.worldbank.org/Matching.

in panel data, which is the share of intended observations not observed in each round of data collection. The characteristics of units that are not possible to track are often correlated with the outcome being studied (for an example, see Bertrand et al. 2017). For example, poorer households may live in more informal dwellings, patients with worse health conditions might not survive to follow-up, and so on. If this is the case, then estimated treatment effects might in reality only be an artifact of the remaining sample being a subset of the original sample that were better or worse off from the beginning. A research design variable in the master data set is needed to indicate attrition. A balance check using that attrition variable can provide insights about whether the lost observations are systematically different from the rest of the sample.

Incorporating monitoring data

Monitoring data are the data collected to understand take-up and implementation fidelity. They allow the research team to know if the field activities are consistent with the intended research design. For more details, see the DIME Wiki at https://dimewiki.worldbank .org/Administrative_and _Monitoring_Data.

For any study with an ex ante design, *monitoring data* are very important for understanding whether the research design corresponds to reality. The most typical example is to make sure that, in an experimental design, the treatment is implemented according to the treatment assignment. Treatment is often implemented by partners, and field realities may be more complex than foreseen during research design. Furthermore, field staff of the partner organization might not be aware that they are implementing a research design.

In all impact evaluation research designs, fidelity to the design is important to record as well (for an example, see Pradhan et al. 2013). For example, a program intended for students who scored under 50 percent on a test might have some cases in which the program was offered to someone who scored 51 percent on the test and participated in the program or someone who scored 49 percent on the test but declined to participate in the program. Differences between assignments and realizations should also be recorded in the master data sets. Therefore, for nearly all research designs, it is essential to acquire monitoring data to indicate how well the realized treatment implementation in the field corresponds to the intended treatment assignment.

Although monitoring data have traditionally been collected by someone in the field, it is increasingly common for monitoring data to be collected remotely. Some examples of remote monitoring include the use of local collaborators to upload geotagged images for visible interventions (such as physical infrastructure), the installation of sensors to broadcast measurements (such as air pollution or water flow), the distribution of wearable devices to track location or physical activity, or the application of image recognition to satellite data. In-person monitoring activities are often preferred, but cost and travel dangers, such as conflicts or disease outbreaks, make remote monitoring innovations increasingly appealing. If cost alone is the constraint, it is worthwhile to consider monitoring a subset of the implementation area in person. The information collected may not be detailed enough to be used as a control in the analysis, but it will provide a means to estimate the validity of the research design assumptions.

Linking monitoring data to the rest of data in the project is often complex and a major source of errors. Monitoring data are rarely received in the same format or structure as research data (for an example, see Goldstein et al. 2015). For example, the project may receive a list of the names of all people who attended a training or administrative data from a partner organization without any unique ID. In both of these cases, it can be difficult to ensure a one-to-one match between units in the monitoring data and the master data sets. Planning ahead and collaborating closely with the implementing organization from the outset of the project are the best ways to avoid these difficulties. Often, it is ideal for the research team to prepare forms (paper or electronic) for monitoring, preloading them with the names of sampled individuals or ensuring that a consistent ID is directly linkable to the project ID. If monitoring data are not handled carefully and actively used in fieldwork, treatment implementation may end up being poorly correlated with treatment assignment, without a way to tell if the lack of correlation is a result of bad matching of monitoring data or a meaningful problem of implementation.

Creating research design variables by randomization

Randomization is the process of generating a sequence of unrelated numbers, typically for the purpose of implementing a research design that requires a key element to exhibit zero correlation with all other variables. For more details, see the DIME Wiki at https://dimewiki.worldbank.org/Randomization.

Random sampling and *random treatment assignment* are two core research activities that generate important research design variables. These processes directly determine the set of units that will be observed and what their status will be for the purpose of estimating treatment effects. *Randomization* is used to ensure that samples are representative and that treatment groups are statistically indistinguishable. Randomization is often used to produce random samples and random treatment assignments. In this book, the term "randomization" is used only to describe the process of generating a sequence of unrelated numbers, even though it is often used in practice to refer to random treatment assignment.

Randomization in statistical software is nontrivial, and its mechanics are not intuitive for the human mind. The principles of randomization apply not just to random sampling and random assignment but also to all statistical computing processes that have random components, such as simulations and bootstrapping. Furthermore, all random processes introduce statistical noise or uncertainty into the estimates of effect sizes. Choosing one random sample from all of the possibilities produces some probability of choosing a group of units that are not, in fact, representative. Similarly, choosing one random assignment produces some probability of creating groups that are not good counterfactuals for each other. *Power calculation* and *randomization inference* are the main methods by which these probabilities of error are assessed. These analyses are particularly important in the initial phases of development research—typically conducted before any data acquisition or field work occur—and have implications for feasibility, planning, and budgeting.

Randomizing sampling and treatment assignment

Random sampling is the process of randomly selecting observations from a list of units to create a subsample that is representative or that has specific statistical properties (such as selecting only from eligible units, oversampling populations of interest, or other techniques such as weighted probabilities). This process can be used, for example, to select a subset from all eligible units to be included in data collection when the cost of collecting data on everyone is prohibitive. For more details on sampling, see the DIME Wiki at https://dimewiki.worldbank.org/Sampling. It can also be used to select a subsample of observations to test a computationally heavy process before running it on the full data.

Randomized treatment assignment is the process of assigning observations to different treatment arms. This process is central to experimental research design. Most of the code processes used for randomized assignment are the same as those used for sampling, which also entails randomly splitting a list of observations into groups. Whereas sampling determines whether a particular unit will be observed at all in the course of data collection, randomized assignment determines whether each unit will be observed in a treatment state or in a counterfactual state.

The list of units to sample or assign from may be called a *sampling universe*, a *listing frame*, or something similar. In almost all cases, the starting point for randomized sampling or assignment should be a master data set, and the result of the randomized process should always be saved in the master data set before it is merged with any other data. The only exceptions are when the sampling universe cannot be known in advance. For example, randomized assignment cannot start from a master data set when sampling is done in real time, such as randomly sampling patients as they arrive at a health facility or when treatment is assigned through an in-person lottery. In those cases, it is important to collect enough data during real-time sampling or to prepare the inputs for the lottery such that all units can be added to the master data set afterward.

The simplest form of sampling is *uniform-probability random sampling*, which means that every eligible observation in the master data set has an equal probability of being selected. The most explicit method of implementing this process is to assign random numbers to all of the potential observations, order them by the number they are assigned, and mark as "sampled" those with the lowest numbers, up to the desired proportion. It is important to become familiar with exactly how the process works. The do-file in box 3.4 provides an example of how to implement uniform-probability sampling in practice. The code there uses a Stata built-in data set and is fully reproducible (more on reproducible randomization in next section), so anyone who runs this code in any version of Stata later than 13.1 (the version set in this code) will get the exact same, but still random, results.

```
1 * Set up reproducible randomization - VERSIONING, SORTING and SEEDING
2     ieboilstart, v(13.1)      // Version
3     `r(version)'              // Version
4     sysuse bpwide.dta, clear  // Load data
5     isid patient, sort        // Sort
6     set seed 215597           // Seed - drawn using https://bit.ly/stata-random
7
8 * Generate a random number and use it to sort the observations.
9 * Then the order the observations are sorted in is random.
10    gen   sample_rand = rnormal() // Generate a random number
11    sort sample_rand              // Sort based on the random number
12
13 * Use the sort order to sample 20% (0.20) of the observations.
14 * _N in Stata is the number of observations in the active dataset,
15 * and _n is the row number for each observation. The bpwide.dta has 120
16 * observations and 120*0.20 = 24, so (_n <= _N * 0.20) is 1 for observations
17 * with a row number equal to or less than 24, and 0 for all other
18 * observations. Since the sort order is randomized, this means that we
19 * have randomly sampled 20% of the observations.
20    gen sample = (_n <= _N * 0.20)
21
22 * Restore the original sort order
23    isid patient, sort
24
25 * Check your result
26    tab sample
```

To access this code in do-file format, visit the GitHub repository at https://github.com/worldbank/dime-data-handbook/tree/main/code.

Sampling typically has only two possible outcomes: observed and unobserved. Similarly, a simple randomized assignment has two outcomes: treatment and control; the logic in the code is identical to the sampling code example. However, randomized assignment often involves multiple treatment arms, each representing different varieties of treatment to be delivered (for an example, see De Andrade, Bruhn, and McKenzie 2013); in some cases, multiple treatment arms are intended to overlap in the same sample. Randomized assignment can quickly grow in complexity, and it is doubly important to understand fully the conceptual process described in the experimental design and to fill in any gaps before implementing it in code. The do-file in box 3.5 provides an example of how to implement randomized assignment with multiple treatment arms.

```
1 * Set up reproducible randomization - VERSIONING, SORTING and SEEDING
2    ieboilstart, v(13.1)      // Version
3    `r(version)'              // Version
4    sysuse bpwide.dta, clear  // Load data
5    isid patient, sort        // Sort
6    set seed 654697           // Seed - drawn using https://bit.ly/stata-random
7
8 * Generate a random number and use it to sort the observation.
9 * Then the order the observations are sorted in is random.
10    gen   treatment_rand = rnormal() // Generate a random number
11    sort treatment_rand             // Sort based on the random number
12
13 * See simple-sample.do example for an explanation of "(_n <= _N * X)".
14 * The code below randomly selects one third of the observations into group 0,
15 * one third into group 1 and one third into group 2.
16 * Typically 0 represents the control group
17 * and 1 and 2 represents the two treatment arms
18    generate treatment = 0                       // Set all observations to 0 (control)
19    replace  treatment = 1 if (_n <= _N * (2/3)) // Set only the first two thirds to 1
20    replace  treatment = 2 if (_n <= _N * (1/3)) // Set only the first third to 2
21
22 * Restore the original sort order
23    isid patient, sort
24
25 * Check your result
26    tab treatment
```

To access this code in do-file format, visit the GitHub repository at https://github.com /worldbank/dime-data-handbook/tree/main/code.

A **pseudo-random number generator** is an algorithm that creates a long, fixed sequence of numbers in which no statistical relationship exists between the position or value of any set of those numbers.

Reproducible randomization is a random process that will produce the same results each time it is executed. For more details on reproducible randomization in Stata, see the DIME Wiki at https:// dimewiki.worldbank.org /Randomization_in_Stata.

Programming reproducible random processes

For statistical programming to be reproducible, it is necessary to be able to reobtain its exact outputs in the future (Orozco et al. 2018). This section focuses on what is needed to produce truly random results and to ensure that those results can be obtained again. This effort takes a combination of strict rules, solid understanding, and careful programming. The rules are not negotiable (but thankfully are simple). Stata, like most statistical software, uses a *pseudo-random number generator*, which, in ordinary research use, produces sequences of numbers that are as good as random. However, for *reproducible randomization*, two additional properties are needed: the ability to fix the sequence of numbers generated and the ability to ensure that the first number is independently randomized. In Stata, reproducible randomization is accomplished through three concepts: versioning, sorting, and seeding. Stata is used in the examples, but the same principles translate to all other programming languages.

- *Rule 1: Versioning* requires using the same version of the software each time the random process is run. If anything is different, the underlying list of pseudo-random numbers may have changed, and it may be impossible to recover the original result. In Stata, the version command ensures that the list of numbers is fixed. Most important is to use the same version across a project, but, at the time of writing, using Stata version 13.1 is recommended for backward compatibility. The algorithm used to create this list of random numbers was changed after Stata 14, but the improvements are unlikely to matter in practice. The ieboilstart command in ietoolkit provides functionality to support this requirement. Using ieboilstart at the beginning of the *master do-file* is recommended. Testing the do-files without running them via the master do-file may produce different results, because Stata's version setting expires after code execution completes.

- *Rule 2: Sorting* requires using a fixed order of the actual data on which the random process is run. Because random numbers are assigned to each observation row by row starting from the top row, changing their order will change the result of the process. In Stata, using isid [id_variable], sort is recommended to guarantee a unique sorting order. This command does two things. First, it tests that all observations have unique values in the sorting variable, because duplicates would cause an ambiguous sort order. If all values are unique, then the command sorts on this variable, guaranteeing a unique sort order. It is a common misconception that the sort, stable command may also be used; however, by itself, this command cannot guarantee an unambiguous sort order and therefore is not appropriate for this purpose. Because the exact order must remain unchanged, the underlying data must remain unchanged between runs. If the number of observations is expected to change (for example, to increase during ongoing data collection), randomization will not be reproducible unless the data are split into smaller fixed data sets in which the number of observations does not change. Those smaller data sets can be combined after randomization.

- *Rule 3: Seeding* requires manually setting the start point in the list of pseudo-random numbers. A seed is a single number that specifies one of the possible start points. It should be at least six digits long and contain exactly one unique, different, and randomly created seed for each randomization process. To create a seed that satisfies these conditions, see https://bit.ly/stata-random. (This link is a shortcut to a page of the website https://www.random.org where the best practice criteria for a seed are predefined.) In Stata, set seed [seed] will set

ieboilstart is a Stata command to standardize version, memory, and other Stata settings across all users for a project. It is part of the ietoolkit package. For more details, see the DIME Wiki at https://dimewiki .worldbank.org/ieboilstart.

A **master script** (in Stata, a **master do-file**) is a single code script that can be used to execute all of the data work for a project, from importing the original data to exporting the final outputs. Any team member should be able to run this script and all the data work scripts executed by it by changing only the directory file path in one line of code in the master script. For more details, see the DIME Wiki at https:// dimewiki.worldbank.org /Master_Do-files.

the generator to the start point identified by the seed. In R, the `set.seed` function does the same. To be clear: setting a single seed once in the master do-file is not recommended; instead, a new seed should be set in code right before each random process. The most important task is to ensure that each of these seeds is truly random; shortcuts such as the current date or a previously used seed should not be used. Comments in the code should describe how the seed was selected.

How the code was run needs to be confirmed carefully before finalizing it, because other commands may induce randomness in the data, change the sorting order, or alter the place of the pseudo-random number generator. The process for confirming that randomization has worked correctly before finalizing its results is to save the outputs of the process in a temporary location, rerun the code, and use the Stata commands `cf` or `datasignature` to ensure that nothing has changed. It is also advisable to let someone else reproduce the randomization results on another machine to remove any doubt that the results are reproducible. Once the result of a randomization is used in the field, there is no way to correct mistakes. The code in box 3.6 provides an example of a fully reproducible randomization.

BOX 3.6 AN EXAMPLE OF REPRODUCIBLE RANDOMIZATION

```
 1 * VERSIONING - Set the version
 2     ieboilstart, v(13.1)
 3     `r(version)'
 4
 5 * Load the auto dataset (auto.dta is a test dataset included in all Stata installations)
 6     sysuse auto.dta, clear
 7
 8 * SORTING - sort on the uniquely identifying variable "make"
 9     isid make, sort
10
11 * SEEDING - Seed picked using https://bit.ly/stata-random
12     set seed 287608
13
14 * Demonstrate stability after VERSIONING, SORTING and SEEDING
15     gen check1 = rnormal()  // Create random number
16     gen check2 = rnormal()  // Create a second random number without resetting seed
17
18     set seed 287608          // Reset the seed
19     gen check3 = rnormal()  // Create a third random number after resetting seed
20
```

(Box continues on next page)

As discussed previously, at times it may not be possible to use a master data set for randomized sampling or treatment assignment (for example, when sampling patients on arrival or through live lotteries). Methods like a real-time lottery typically do not leave a record of the randomization and, as such, are never reproducible. However, a reproducible randomization can be run in advance even without an advance list of eligible units. For example, to select a subsample of patients randomly as they arrive at various health facilities, it is possible to compile a pregenerated list with a random order of "in sample" and "not in sample." Field staff would then go through this list in order and cross off one randomized result as it is used for a patient.

This method is especially beneficial when implementing a more complex randomization. For example, a hypothetical research design may call for enumerators to undertake the following:

1. Sample 10 percent of people observed in a particular location.

2. Show a video to 50 percent of the sample.

3. Administer a short questionnaire to 80 percent of all persons sampled.

4. Administer a longer questionnaire to the remaining 20 percent, with the mix of questionnaires equal between those who were shown the video and those who were not.

In real time, such a complex randomization is much more likely to be implemented correctly if field staff can simply follow a list of the randomized categories for which the project team is in control of the predetermined proportions and the random order. This approach makes it possible to control precisely how these categories are distributed across all of the locations where the research is to be conducted.

Finally, if this real-time implementation of randomization is done using survey software, then the pregenerated list of randomized categories can be preloaded into the questionnaire. Then the field team can follow a list of respondent IDs that are randomized into the appropriate categories, and the survey software can show a video and control which version of the questionnaire is asked. This approach can help to reduce the risk of errors in field randomization.

Implementing clustered or stratified designs

Clustering is a research design in which the unit of randomization or unit of sampling differs from the unit of analysis. For more details, see the DIME Wiki at https://dimewiki.worldbank .org/Clustered_Sampling_and _Treatment_Assignment.

Stratification is a statistical technique that ensures that subgroups of the population are represented in the sample and treatment groups. For more details, see the DIME Wiki at https:// dimewiki.worldbank.org /Stratified_Random_Sample.

For a variety of reasons, random sampling and random treatment assignment are rarely as straightforward as a uniform-probability draw. The most common variants are clustering and stratification (Athey and Imbens 2017). *Clustering* occurs when the unit of analysis is different from the unit of randomization in a research design. For example, a policy may be implemented at the village level or the project may only be able to send enumerators to a limited number of villages, but the outcomes of interest for the study are measured at the household level. In such cases, the higher-level groupings by which lower-level units are randomized are called *clusters* (for an example, see Keating et al. 2011).

Stratification splits the full set of observations into subgroups, or strata, before performing randomized assignment within each subgroup, or stratum. Stratification ensures that members of each stratum are included in all groups of the randomized assignment process or that members of all groups are observed in the sample. Without stratification, randomization may put all members of a given subgroup into just one of the treatment arms or fail to select any of them into a sample. For both clustering and stratification, implementation is nearly identical in both random sampling and random assignment.

Clustered randomization is procedurally straightforward in Stata, although it typically needs to be performed manually. The process for clustering a sampling or randomized assignment is to randomize on the master data set for the unit of observation of the cluster and then merge the results with the master data set for the unit of analysis. This is a many-to-one merge, and the data map should document how those data sets can be merged correctly. If the project does not yet have a master data set for the unit of observation of the cluster, then it is necessary to create one and update the data map accordingly. When sampling or randomized assignment is conducted using clusters, the cluster ID variable should be clearly identified in the master data set for the unit of analysis because it will need to be used in subsequent statistical analysis. Typically, standard errors for clustered designs must be clustered at the level at which the design is clustered (McKenzie 2017). This clustering accounts for the design covariance within the clusters—the information that, if one unit is observed or treated from that cluster, the other members of the cluster are as well.

Although procedurally straightforward, implementing stratified designs in statistical software is prone to error. Even for a relatively simple multiple-arm design, the basic method of randomly ordering the observations will often create very skewed assignments in the presence of strata (McKenzie 2011). The user-written `randtreat` Stata command properly implements stratification (Carril 2017). The options and outputs (including messages) from the command should be reviewed carefully so that it is clear exactly what has been implemented—`randtreat` performs a two-step process in which it takes the straightforward approach as far as possible and then, according to the user's instructions, handles the remaining observations in a consistent fashion. Notably, it is extremely hard to target exact numbers of observations in stratified designs because exact allocations are rarely round fractions.

Performing power calculations

Random sampling and treatment assignment are noisy processes: it is impossible to predict the result in advance. By design, the exact choice of sample or treatment will not be correlated with the key outcomes, but this lack of correlation is only true "in expectation"—that is, the correlation between randomization and other variables will only be zero on average across a large number of randomizations. In any particular randomization, the correlation between the sampling or randomized assignments and the outcome variable is guaranteed to be nonzero: this is called *in-sample* or *finite-sample correlation*.

Because the true correlation (over the "population" of potential samples or assignments) is zero, the observed correlation is considered an error. In sampling, this error is called the *sampling error*, and it is defined as the difference between a true population parameter and the observed mean due to the chance selection of units. In randomized assignment, this error is called *randomization noise* and is defined as the difference between a true treatment effect and the estimated effect due to the placement of units in treatment groups. The intuition for both measures is that, from any group, it is possible to find some subsets that have higher-than-average values of some measure and some that have lower-than-average values. The random sample or treatment assignment will fall into one of these categories, and it is necessary to assess the likelihood and magnitude of this occurrence. Power calculation and randomization inference are the two key tools for doing so.

Power calculations report the likelihood that the experimental design will be able to detect the treatment effects of interest given these sources of noise. This measure of power can be described in various ways, each of which has different practical uses. The purpose of power calculations is to identify where the strengths and weaknesses are located and to understand the relative trade-offs that the project will face if the randomization scheme is changed for the final design. It is important to consider take-up rates and attrition when doing power calculations. Incomplete take-up will significantly reduce power, and understanding what minimum level of take-up is required can help to guide field operations (for this reason, monitoring take-up in real time is often critical).

The *minimum detectable effect* (MDE) is the smallest true effect that a given research design can reliably detect. It is useful as a check on whether a study is worthwhile. If, in a field of study, a "large" effect is just a few percentage points or a small fraction of a standard deviation, then it is nonsensical to run a study whose MDE is much larger than that. Given the sample size and variation in the population, the effect needs to be much larger to be statistically detected, so such a study would never be able to

The **minimum detectable effect** (MDE) is the effect size that an impact evaluation is able to estimate for a given level of significance. For more details, see the DIME Wiki at https://dimewiki.worldbank.org/Minimum_Detectable_Effect.

say anything about the size of effect that is practically relevant. Conversely, the *minimum sample size* prespecifies expected effect sizes and indicates how large a study's sample would need to be to detect that effect, which can determine what resources are needed to implement a useful study.

Randomization inference
is a method of calculating regression p-values that takes into account variability in data that arises from randomization itself. For more details, see the DIME Wiki at https:// dimewiki.worldbank.org /Randomization_Inference.

Randomization inference is used to analyze the likelihood that the randomized assignment process, by chance, would have created a false treatment effect as large as the one estimated. Randomization inference is a generalization of placebo tests, because it considers what the estimated results would have been from a randomized assignment that did not happen in reality. Randomization inference is particularly important in quasi-experimental designs and in small samples, in which the number of possible randomizations is itself small. Randomization inference can therefore be used proactively during experimental design to examine the potential spurious treatment effects the exact design is able to produce. If results heap significantly at particular levels or if results seem to depend dramatically on the outcome of randomization for a small number of units, randomization inference will flag those issues before the study is fielded and allow adjustments to the design.

Looking ahead

This chapter introduced the DIME data map template, a toolkit to document a data acquisition plan and to describe how each data source relates to the design of a study. The data map contains research design variables and the instructions for using them in combination with measurement variables, which together form the data set(s) for the analytical work. It then discussed ways to use this planning data to inform and execute research design tasks, such as randomized sampling and assignment, and to produce concrete measures of whether the project design is sufficient to answer the research questions posed. The next chapter turns to data acquisition—the first step toward answering those questions. It details the processes of obtaining original data, whether those data are collected by the project or received from another entity.

References

Alix-Garcia, Jennifer M., Katharine R. E. Sims, Victor Hugo Orozco-Olvera, Laura Costica, Jorge David Fernandez Medina, Sofia Romo-Monroy, and Stefano Pagiola. 2019. "Can Environmental Cash Transfers Reduce Deforestation and Improve Social Outcomes? A Regression Discontinuity Analysis of Mexico's National Program (2011–2014)." Policy Research Working Paper 8707, World Bank, Washington, DC.

Athey, Susan, and Guido W. Imbens. 2017. "The Econometrics of Randomized Experiments." In *Handbook of Economic Field Experiments,* vol. 1, edited by Abjihit Banerjee and Esther Duflo, 73–140. Amsterdam: North Holland.

Benhassine, Najy, David McKenzie, Victor Pouliquen, and Massimiliano Santini. 2018. "Does Inducing Informal Firms to Formalize Make Sense? Experimental Evidence from Benin." *Journal of Public Economics* 157 (January): 1–14.

Bertrand, Marianne, Bruno Crépon, Alicia Marguerie, and Patrick Premand. 2017. "Contemporaneous and Post-Program Impacts of a Public Works Program: Evidence from Côte d'Ivoire." Working Paper, World Bank, Washington, DC.

Calderon, Gabriela, Leonardo Iacovone, and Laura Juarez. 2017. "Opportunity versus Necessity: Understanding the Heterogeneity of Female Micro-Entrepreneurs." *World Bank Economic Review* 30 (Suppl. 1): S86–S96.

Carril, Alvaro. 2017. "Dealing with Misfits in Random Treatment Assignment." *Stata Journal* 17 (3): 652–67.

De Andrade, Gustavo Henrique, Miriam Bruhn, and David McKenzie. 2013. "A Helping Hand or the Long Arm of the Law? Experimental Evidence on What Governments Can Do to Formalize Firms." Policy Research Working Paper 6435, World Bank, Washington, DC.

Duflo, Esther, Rachel Glennerster, and Michael Kremer. 2007. "Using Randomization in Development Economics Research: A Toolkit." In *Handbook of Development Economics*, vol. 4, edited by T. Paul Schultz and John Strauss, 3895–962. Amsterdam: North Holland.

Fernandes, Ana M., Russell Hillberry, and Alejandra Mendoza Alcántara. 2017. "An Evaluation of Border Management Reforms in a Technical Agency." Policy Research Working Paper 8208, World Bank, Washington, DC.

Gibson, Mike, and Anja Sautmann. 2020. "Introduction to Randomized Evaluations." Abdul Latif Jameel Poverty Action Lab, Cambridge, MA. https://www.povertyactionlab.org/resource/introduction-randomized-evaluations.

Goldstein, Markus, Kenneth Houngbedji, Florence Kondylis, Michael O'Sullivan, and Harris Selod. 2015. "Formalizing Rural Land Rights in West Africa: Early Evidence from a Randomized Impact Evaluation in Benin." Policy Research Working Paper 7435, World Bank, Washington, DC.

Keating, Joseph, Andrea Locatelli, Andemariam Gebremichael, Tewolde Ghebremeskel, Jacob Mufunda, Selam Mihreteab, Daniel Berhane, and Pedro Carneiro. 2011. "Evaluating Indoor Residual Spray for Reducing Malaria Infection Prevalence in Eritrea: Results from a Community Randomized Control Trial." *Acta Tropica* 119 (2-3): 107–13.

Kondylis, Florence, Valerie Mueller, Glenn Sheriff, and Siyao Zhu. 2016. "Do Female Instructors Reduce Gender Bias in Diffusion of Sustainable Land Management Techniques? Experimental Evidence from Mozambique." *World Development* 78 (February): 436–49.

Kondylis, Florence, and Mattea Stein. 2018. "The Speed of Justice." Policy Research Working Paper 8372, World Bank, Washington, DC.

McKenzie, David. 2011. "Tools of the Trade: Doing Stratified Randomization with Uneven Numbers in Some Strata." *Development Impact* (blog), November 6, 2011. https://blogs.worldbank.org/impactevaluations/tools-of-the-trade-doing-stratified-randomization-with-uneven-numbers-in-some-strata.

McKenzie, David. 2017. "When Should You Cluster Standard Errors? New Wisdom from the Econometrics Oracle." *Development Impact* (blog), October 16, 2017. https://blogs.worldbank.org/impactevaluations/when-should-you-cluster-standard-errors-new-wisdom-econometrics-oracle.

Orozco, Valerie, Christophe Bontemps, Elise Maigne, Virginie Piguet, Annie Hofstetter, Anne Marie Lacroix, Fabrice Levert, and Jean-Marc Rousselle. 2018. "How to Make a Pie? Reproducible Research for Empirical Economics and Econometrics." TSE Working Paper 933, Toulouse School of Economics, Toulouse.

Pradhan, Menno, Sally A. Brinkman, Amanda Beatty, Amelia Maika, Elan Satriawan, Joppe de Ree, and Amer Hasan. 2013. "Evaluating a Community-Based Early Childhood Education and Development Program in Indonesia: Study Protocol for a Pragmatic Cluster Randomized Controlled Trial with Supplementary Matched Control Group." *Trials* 14 (259).

Prennushi, Giovanna, and Abhishek Gupta. 2014. "Women's Empowerment and Socio-Economic Outcomes: Impacts of the Andhra Pradesh Rural Poverty Reduction Program." Policy Research Working Paper 6841, World Bank, Washington, DC.

Chapter 4

Acquiring development data

Many research questions require original data because no source of publicly available data addresses the inputs or outcomes of interest for the relevant population. Data acquisition can take many forms, including primary data generated through surveys; private sector partnerships granting access to new data sources, such as administrative and sensor data; digitization of paper records, including administrative data; web scraping; data captured by unmanned aerial vehicles or other types of remote sensing; and novel integration of various types of data sets, such as combining survey and sensor data. Much of the recent push toward credibility in the social sciences has focused on analytical practices. However, credible development research depends, first and foremost, on the quality of the data acquired. Clear and careful documentation of the data acquisition process is essential for research to be reproducible.

This chapter covers reproducible data acquisition, special considerations for generating high-quality survey data, and protocols for handling confidential data safely and securely. The first section discusses acquiring data reproducibly, by establishing and documenting the right to use the data. This discussion applies to all original data, whether collected for the first time through surveys or sensors or acquired through a unique partnership. The second section examines the process of acquiring data through surveys, which is typically more involved than acquiring secondary data and has more in-built opportunities for quality control. It provides detailed guidance on the electronic survey workflow, from designing electronic survey instruments to monitoring data quality once fieldwork is ongoing. The final section discusses handling data safely, providing guidance on how to receive, transfer, store, and share confidential data. Secure file management is a basic requirement for complying with the legal and ethical agreements that allow access to personal information for research purposes. Box 4.1 summarizes the main points, lists the responsibilities of different members of the research team, and supplies a list of key tools and resources for implementing the recommended practices.

BOX 4.1 SUMMARY: ACQUIRING DEVELOPMENT DATA

The process of obtaining research data is unique to every project. However, some basic structures and processes are common to both data acquired from others and data generated by surveys:

1. *When receiving data from others, ownership and licensing are critical.* Before any data are transferred, knowing all of the formal rights associated with those data is essential:

   - Ensure that the partner has the right to share the data, especially data containing personally identifying information.
   - Identify the data owner and any restrictions on the use, storage, or handling of data.
   - Secure a data use agreement or license from the partner, outlining the rights and responsibilities regarding analysis, publication of results and derived data, redistribution of data, and data destruction.

2. *Collecting high-quality data requires careful planning and attention to detail throughout the workflow.* The following best practices apply to all surveys, with further details for electronic surveys:

   - Produce and pilot draft instruments on paper and focus on survey content.
   - Structure questionnaires for electronic programming and pilot them for function, considering features like pagination, ordering, looping, conditional execution, and instructions for enumerators.
   - Test data outputs for analytical compatibility, such as code-friendly variable and value labels.
   - Train enumerators carefully, using a paper survey before an electronic template, assess their performance objectively throughout training, and transparently select the top performers.
   - Assess data quality in real time, through scripted high-frequency checks and diligent field validation.

3. *No matter how data are acquired, handling data securely is essential:*

   - Encrypt data on all devices, in transit and at rest, beginning from the point of collection and including all intermediate locations such as servers and local devices.
   - Store encryption keys using appropriate password management software with strong, unique passwords for all applications and devices with access.
   - Back up data in case of total loss or failure of hardware and software at any site.

Key responsibilities for task team leaders and principal investigators

   - Obtain appropriate legal documentation and permission agreements for all data.
   - For surveys, guide and supervise development of all instruments.
   - For surveys, review and provide inputs to the project's data quality assurance plan.
   - For surveys, guide decisions on how to correct issues identified during data quality checks.

(Box continues on next page)

BOX 4.1 SUMMARY: ACQUIRING DEVELOPMENT DATA (continued)

- Oversee implementation of security measures and manage access codes, encryption keys, and hardware.
- Determine and communicate institutionally appropriate data storage and backup plans.

Key responsibilities for research assistants

- Coordinate with data providers, develop required technical documentation, and archive all final documentation.
- For surveys, draft, refine, and program all survey instruments, following best practices for electronic survey programming and maintaining up-to-date and version-controlled paper and electronic versions.
- For surveys, coordinate closely with field staff on survey pilots and contribute to enumerator manuals.
- For surveys, draft a data quality assurance plan and manage the quality assurance process.
- Implement storage and security measures for all data.

Key resources

- Manage Successful Impact Evaluation Surveys, a course covering best practices for the survey workflow, from planning to piloting instruments and monitoring data quality, at https://osf.io/resya
- DIME Analytics Continuing Education for field coordinators, technical trainings and courses for staff implementing field surveys that are updated regularly, at https://osf.io/gmn38
- SurveyCTO coding practices, a suite of DIME Wiki articles covering common approaches to sophisticated design and programming in SurveyCTO, at https://dimewiki.worldbank .org/SurveyCTO_Coding_Practices
- Monitoring data quality, a DIME Wiki article covering communication, field monitoring, minimizing attrition, back-checks, and data quality checks, at https://dimewiki.worldbank .org/Monitoring_Data_Quality

Acquiring data ethically and reproducibly

Clearly establishing and documenting access to data are critical for reproducible research. This section provides guidelines for establishing data ownership, receiving data from development partners, and documenting the research team's right to use data. Researchers are responsible not only for respecting the rights of both people who own and people who are described by the data but also for making that information as available and as accessible as possible. These twin responsibilities can and do come into tension, so it is important for everyone on the team to be informed about what everyone else is doing. Writing down and agreeing to specific details is a good way to do that.

Determining data ownership

Data ownership is the assignment of rights and privileges over data sets, including control over who may access, possess, copy, use, distribute, or publish data or products created from the data. For more details, see the DIME Wiki at https://dimewiki.worldbank.org/Data_Ownership.

Before acquiring any data, it is critical to establish *data ownership*. Data ownership can sometimes be challenging to establish, because different jurisdictions have different laws regarding data and information, and the research team may have its own regulations. In some jurisdictions, data are implicitly owned by the people to whom the information pertains. In others, data are owned by the people who collect the information. In still others, ownership is highly unclear, and there are varying norms. The best approach is always to consult with a local partner and to enter into specific legal agreements establishing ownership, access, and publication rights. These agreements are particularly critical when confidential data are involved—that is, when people are disclosing information that could not be obtained simply by observation or through public records.

If the research team is requesting access to existing data, it must enter into data license agreements to access the data and publish research outputs based on the information. These agreements should make clear from the outset whether and how the research team can make the original data public or whether it can publish any portion or *derivatives* of the data. If the data are publicly accessible, these agreements may be as simple as agreeing to terms of use on the website from which the data can be downloaded. If the data are original and not yet publicly accessible, the process is typically more complex and requires a documented legal agreement or memorandum of understanding.

Derivatives of data are new data points, new data sets, or outputs such as indicators, aggregates, visualizations, and other research products created from the original data.

If the research team is generating data directly, such as survey data, it is important to clarify up front who owns the data and who will have access to the information (see box 4.2 for an example of how data ownership considerations may vary within a project). These details need to be shared with respondents when they are offered the opportunity to consent to participate in the study. If the research team is not collecting the data directly—for example, if a government, private company, or research partner is collecting the data—an explicit agreement is needed establishing who owns the resulting data.

BOX 4.2 DETERMINING DATA OWNERSHIP: A CASE STUDY FROM THE DEMAND FOR SAFE SPACES PROJECT

The Demand for Safe Spaces study used three data sources, all of which had different data ownership considerations.

1. *Crowdsourced ride data from the mobile app.* The research team acquired crowdsourced data through a contract with the technology firm responsible for developing and deploying the application. The terms of the contract specified that all intellectual property in derivative works developed using the data set are the property of the World Bank.

(Box continues on next page)

2. *Platform survey and implicit association test data.* A small team of consultants collected original data using a survey instrument developed by the research team. The contract specified that the data collected by the consultants and all derivative works are the sole intellectual property of the World Bank.

3. *Crime data.* The team also used one variable (indicating crime rate at the Supervia stations) from publicly accessible data produced by Rio's Public Security Institute. The data are published under Brazil's Access to Information Law and are available for download from the institute's website.

The contract for data collection should include specific terms as to the rights and responsibilities of each stakeholder. It must clearly stipulate which party owns the data produced and that the research team maintains full intellectual property rights. The contract should also explicitly indicate that the contracted firm is responsible for protecting the privacy of respondents, that the data collection will not be delegated to any third parties, and that the data will not be used by the firm or subcontractors for any purpose not expressly stated in the contract, before, during, or after the assignment. The contract should also stipulate that the vendor is required to comply with ethical standards for social science research and to adhere to the specific terms of agreement with the relevant *institutional review board* (IRB) or applicable local authority. Finally, it should include policies on the reuse, storage, and retention or destruction of data.

Research teams that acquire original data must also consider data ownership downstream, through the terms they use to release those data to other researchers or to the general public. The team should consider whether it can publish the data in full after removing personal identifiers. For example, the team must consider whether it would be acceptable for the data to be copied and stored on servers anywhere in the world, whether it would be preferable to manage permissions on a case-by-case basis, and whether data users would be expected to cite or credit them. Similarly, the team can require users to release the derivative data sets or publications under similar licenses or offer use without restriction. Simple license templates are available for offering many of these permissions, but, at the planning stage, all licensing agreements, data collection contracts, and informed consent processes used to acquire the data need to detail those future uses specifically.

An **institutional review board** (IRB) is an institutional body formally responsible for ensuring that research under its oversight meets minimum ethical standards. For more details, see the DIME Wiki at https://dimewiki.worldbank.org/IRB_Approval.

Obtaining data licenses

Data licensing is the process of formally granting rights and privileges over data sets to people who are not the owner of the data. For more details, see the DIME Wiki at https://dimewiki.worldbank.org/Data_License_Agreement.

Data licensing is the formal act of the owner giving some rights to a specific user, while retaining ownership of the data set. If the team does not own the data set to be analyzed, it must enter into a licensing agreement to access the data for research purposes. Similarly, if the team does own a data set, it must consider whether the data set will be made accessible to other researchers and what terms of use will be required.

If the research team requires access to existing data for novel research, it is necessary to agree on the terms of use with the data owner, typically through a data license agreement. These terms should specify what data elements will be received, the purposes for which the data will be used, and who will have access to the data. The data owner is unlikely to be highly familiar with the research process and may be surprised at some of the uses to which the data could be put. It is essential to be forthcoming about the uses up front. Researchers typically want to hold intellectual property rights to all research outputs developed with the data and a license for all uses of derivative works, including public distribution (unless ethical considerations contraindicate this right). Holding these rights allows the research team to store, catalog, and publish, in whole or in part, either the original licensed data set or data sets derived from the original. It is important to ensure that the license obtained from the data owner allows these uses and that the owner is consulted if exceptions for specific portions of the data are foreseen.

The Development Impact Evaluation (DIME) department follows the World Bank's template data license agreement. The template specifies the specific objectives of the data sharing and whether the data can be used for the established purpose only or for other objectives as well. It classifies data into one of four access categories, depending on who can access the data by default and whether case-by-case authorization for access is needed. The data provider may impose similar restrictions on sharing derivative data and any or all of the associated metadata. The template also specifies the required citation for the data. Although it is not necessary to use the World Bank's template or its access categories if the team is not working on a World Bank project, the information in the template is useful in two ways. First, it is necessary to base the data license agreement on a template. Ad hoc agreements can leave many legal ambiguities or gaps where the permissions given to the research team are unclear or incomplete. Second, it is strongly recommended that the data be categorized using some variation of this system. Doing so will create different standard procedures for each category, so that the intended processes for handling the data are clear.

Documenting data received from partners

Research teams granted access to existing data may receive those data in several ways: access to an existing server, physical access to extract certain information, or a one-time data transfer. In all cases, action is required to ensure that data are transferred through secure channels so that confidentiality is not compromised. The section on handling data securely explains how to do that. Compliance with ethical research standards may in some cases require a stricter level of security than initially proposed by the partner agency. It is also critical to request any and all available documentation for the data; this documentation could take the form of a data dictionary or codebook, a manual for the administrative data collection system, detailed reports or operating procedures, or another format. If no written documentation is available, the person(s) responsible for managing the data should be interviewed to learn as much as possible about the data; the interview notes should be archived with data documentation.

At this stage, it is very important to assess the documentation and cataloging of data and associated metadata. It is not always clear what pieces of information will jointly constitute a research data set, and many data sets are not organized for research. The original data should be retained exactly as received, alongside a copy of the corresponding ownership agreement or license. A simple README document is needed, noting the date of receipt, the source and recipient of the data, and a brief description of each file received. All too often data are provided in vaguely named spreadsheets or digital files with nonspecific titles. Documentation is critical for future access and reproducibility.

Eventually, a set of documents will be created that can be submitted to a data catalog and given a reference and citation. *Metadata*— documentation about the data—are critical for future use of the data. Metadata should include documentation of how the data were created, what they measure, and how they are to be used. For survey data, this documentation should include the survey instrument and associated manuals; the sampling protocols and field adherence to those protocols and any sampling weights; what variable(s) uniquely identifies the data set(s) and how different data sets can be linked; and a description of field procedures and quality controls. DIME uses the Data Documentation Initiative (DDI), which is supported by the World Bank's Microdata Catalog (https://microdata.worldbank.org).

As soon as the desired pieces of information are stored together, it is time to think about which ones are the components of what will be called a data set. Often, when receiving data from a partner, even highly structured materials such as registers or records are not, as received, equivalent to a research data set; they require initial cleaning, restructuring, or recombination to be considered an original research data set. This process is as much an art as a science: it is important to keep information together that is best contextualized together, but information also needs to be as granular as possible, particularly when there are varying units of observation. There is often no single correct way to structure a data set, and the research team will need to decide how to organize the materials received. Soon, research data sets will be built from this set of information and become the original clean data, which will be the material published, released, and cited as the starting point of the data. (If funders or publishers request that "raw" data be published or cataloged, for example, they should receive this data set, unless they specifically require data in the original format received.) These first data sets created from the received materials need to be cataloged, licensed, and prepared for release. This is a good time to begin assessing the *disclosure risk* and to seek publication licenses in collaboration with data providers, while still in close contact with them.

Statistical **disclosure risk** is the likelihood of revealing information that can be used to associate data points with individual research participants, especially through indirect identifiers. For more details, see the DIME Wiki at https://dimewiki.worldbank.org/De-identification.

Collecting high-quality data using electronic surveys

This section details specific considerations for acquiring high-quality data through electronic surveys of study subjects. If the project will not use any survey data, skip this section. Many excellent resources address how to design questionnaires and field supervision, but few cover the particular challenges and opportunities presented by electronic surveys. Many survey software options are available to researchers, and the market is evolving rapidly. Therefore, this section focuses on specific workflow considerations for digitally collected data and on basic concepts rather than on software-specific tools.

Electronic data collection technologies have greatly accelerated the ability to collect high-quality data using purpose-built survey instruments and therefore have improved the precision of research. At the same time, electronic surveys create new pitfalls to avoid. Programming electronic surveys efficiently requires a very different mind-set than writing paper-based surveys; careful preparation can improve the efficiency and data quality of surveys. This section outlines the major steps and technical considerations to follow when fielding a custom survey instrument, no matter the scale.

Designing survey instruments

Questionnaire design is the process of creating a survey instrument, typically for data collection with human subjects. For details and best practices, see the DIME Wiki at https:// dimewiki.worldbank.org /Questionnaire_Design.

A well-designed questionnaire results from careful planning, consideration of analysis and indicators, close review of existing questionnaires, survey pilots, and research team and stakeholder review. Many excellent resources discuss *questionnaire design*, such as that of the World Bank's Living Standards Measurement Survey (Glewwe and Grosh 2000). This section focuses on the design of electronic field surveys, often referred to as *computer-assisted personal interviews* (CAPIs). Although most surveys are now collected electronically, by tablet, mobile phone, or web browser, questionnaire design (content development) and questionnaire programming (functionality development) should be seen as two strictly separate tasks. Therefore, the research team should agree on the content of all questionnaires and design a version of the survey on paper before beginning to program the electronic version. Doing so facilitates a focus on content during the design process and ensures that teams have a readable, printable version of the questionnaire. Most important, it means that the research, not the technology, drives the questionnaire's design.

Computer-assisted personal interviews (CAPIs) are interviews that use a survey instrument programmed on a tablet, computer, or mobile phone using specialized survey software. For more details, see the DIME Wiki at https://dimewiki.worldbank .org/Computer-Assisted _Personal_Interviews_(CAPI). For CAPI questionnaire programming resources, see the DIME Wiki at https:// dimewiki.worldbank.org /Questionnaire_Programming.

This approach is recommended for three reasons. First, an easy-to-read paper questionnaire is very useful for training data collection staff, which is discussed further in the section on training enumerators. Second, finalizing the paper version of the questionnaire before beginning any programming avoids version-control concerns that arise from concurrent work on paper and electronic survey instruments. Third, a readable paper questionnaire is a necessary component of data

A **theory of change** is a theoretical structure for conceptualizing how interventions or changes in environment might affect behavior or outcomes, including intermediate concepts, impacts, and processes. For more details, see the DIME Wiki at https://dimewiki.worldbank.org/Theory_of_Change.

Research design is the process of planning a scientific study so that data can be generated, collected, and used to estimate specific parameters accurately in the population of interest. For more details, see the DIME Wiki at https://dimewiki.worldbank.org/Experimental_Methods and https://dimewiki.worldbank.org/Quasi-Experimental_Methods.

A **preanalysis plan** is a document containing extensive details about a study's analytical approach, which is archived or published using a third-party repository in advance of data acquisition. For more details, see the DIME Wiki at https://dimewiki.worldbank.org/Preanalysis_Plan.

A **survey pilot** is intended to test the theoretical and practical performance of an intended data collection instrument. For more details on how to plan, prepare for, and implement a survey pilot, see the DIME Wiki at https://dimewiki.worldbank.org/Survey_Pilot.

documentation, because it is difficult to work backward from the survey program to the intended concepts.

The workflow for designing a questionnaire is much like writing an essay: it begins from broad concepts and slowly fleshes out the specifics. It is essential to start with a clear understanding of the *theory of change* and *research design* of the project. The first step of questionnaire design is to list key outcomes of interest, the main covariates to control for, and any variables needed for the specific research design. The ideal starting point for this process is a *preanalysis plan*.

The list of key outcomes is used to create an outline of questionnaire modules. The modules are not numbered; instead, a short prefix is used, because numbers quickly become outdated when modules are reordered. For each module, it is necessary to determine if the module is applicable to the full sample or only to specific respondents and whether or how often the module should be repeated. For example, a module on maternal health applies only to households with a woman who has children, a household income module should be answered by the person responsible for household finances, and a module on agricultural production might be repeated for each crop cultivated by the household. Each module should then be expanded into specific indicators to observe in the field. To the greatest extent possible, using questions from reputable survey instruments that have already been fielded is recommended rather than creating questions from scratch (for links to recommended questionnaire libraries, see the DIME Wiki at https://dimewiki.worldbank.org/Literature_Review_for_Questionnaire). Questionnaires for impact evaluation must also include ways to document the reasons for *attrition* and treatment *contamination*. These data components are essential for completing CONSORT records, a standardized system for reporting enrollment, intervention allocation, follow-up, and data analysis through the phases of a randomized trial (Begg et al. 1996).

Piloting survey instruments

A *survey pilot* is critical to finalize survey design. The pilot must be done out-of-sample, but in a context as similar as possible to the study sample. The survey pilot includes three steps: a prepilot, a content-focused pilot, and a data-focused pilot (see box 4.3 for a description of the pilots for the Demand for Safe Spaces project).

The first step is a *prepilot*. The prepilot is a qualitative exercise, done early in the questionnaire design process. The objective is to answer broad questions about how to measure key outcome variables and gather qualitative information relevant to any of the planned survey modules. A prepilot is particularly important when designing new survey instruments.

The second step is a *content-focused pilot*. The objectives at this stage are to improve the structure and length of the questionnaire, refine the phrasing and translation of specific questions, check for potential sensitivities and enumerator-respondent interactions, and confirm that coded-response options are exhaustive. In addition, it provides an opportunity to test and refine all of the survey protocols, such as how units will be sampled or preselected units identified. The content-focused pilot is best done with pen and paper, before the questionnaire is programmed, because changes resulting from this pilot may be deep and structural, making them hard to adjust in code. At this point, it is important to test both the validity and the reliability of the survey questions, which requires conducting the content-focused pilot with a sufficiently large sample (the exact requirement will depend on the research sample, but a very rough rule of thumb is a minimum of 30 interviews). For a checklist for how to prepare for a survey pilot, see the DIME Wiki at https://dimewiki.worldbank .org/Checklist:_Preparing_for_a_Survey_Pilot. The sample for the pilot should be as similar as possible to the sample for the full survey, but the two should never overlap. For details on selecting appropriate pilot respondents, see the DIME Wiki at https://dimewiki.worldbank .org/Survey_Pilot_Participants. For checklists detailing activities in a content-focused pilot, see the DIME Wiki at https://dimewiki.worldbank .org/Checklist:_Content-focused_Pilot and https://dimewiki.worldbank.org /Checklist:_Piloting_Survey_Protocols.

The final stage is a *data-focused pilot*. After the content is finalized, it is time to begin programming a draft version of the electronic survey instrument. The objective of this pilot is to refine the programming of the questionnaire; this process is discussed in detail in the following section.

BOX 4.3 PILOTING SURVEY INSTRUMENTS: A CASE STUDY FROM THE DEMAND FOR SAFE SPACES PROJECT

The context for the platform survey and implicit association test presented some unique design challenges. The respondents to the survey were commuters on the platform waiting to board the train. Given the survey setting, respondents might need to leave at any time, so only a random subset of questions was asked to each participant. The survey included a total of 25 questions on commuting patterns, preferences about use of the reserved car, perceptions about safety, and perceptions about gender issues and how they affect riding choices. While waiting for their train, 1,000 metro riders answered the survey. The team tested the questions extensively through pilots before commencing data collection. On the basis of pilot data and feedback, questions that were causing confusion were reworded, and the questionnaire was shortened to reduce attrition. The research team designed a custom instrument to test for implicit association between using or not using the women-reserved space and openness to sexual advances. To determine the best words to capture social stigma, two versions of the implicit association test instrument were tested, one with "strong" and one with "weak" language (for example, "vulgar" vs. "seductive"), and the response times were compared to other well-established instruments. For the development of all protocols and sensitive survey questions, the research team requested input and feedback from gender experts at the World Bank and local researchers working on gender-related issues to ensure that the questions were worded appropriately.

For the survey instrument, visit the GitHub repository at https://git.io/JtgqD. For the survey protocols, visit the GitHub repository at https://git.io/Jtgqy.

Programming electronic survey instruments

Once the team is satisfied with the content and structure of the survey, it is time to move on to implementing it electronically. Electronic data collection has great potential to simplify survey implementation and improve data quality. But it is critical to ensure that electronic survey instruments flow correctly and produce data that can be used in statistical software, before data collection begins. Electronic questionnaires are typically developed in a spreadsheet (usually using Excel or Google Sheets) or a software-specific form builder, all of which are accessible even to novice users.

This book does not address software-specific design; rather, it focuses on coding and design conventions that are important to follow for electronic surveys regardless of the choice of software. (At the time of publication, SurveyCTO is the most commonly used survey software in DIME. For best practices for SurveyCTO code, which almost always apply to other survey software as well, see the DIME Wiki at https://dimewiki .worldbank.org/SurveyCTO_Coding_Practices.) Survey software tools provide a wide range of features designed to make implementing even highly complex surveys easy, scalable, and secure. However, these features are not fully automatic: the survey must be designed and managed actively. This section discusses specific practices that take advantage of electronic survey features and ensure that the exported data are compatible with the statistical software used.

From the perspective of quantitative analysis, questions with *coded-response options* are always preferable to *open-ended questions*. The content-based pilot is an excellent time to ask open-ended questions and refine fixed responses for the final version of the questionnaire—it is rarely practical to code lots of free text after the full survey has been conducted. Two examples help to illustrate this point. First, instead of asking, "How do you feel about the proposed policy change?" use techniques like *Likert scales*. Second, if collecting data on things like medication use or food supplies, collect, for example, the brand name of the product, the generic name of the product, a coded identifier for the item, and the broad category to which each product belongs (for example, "antibiotics" or "staple foods") (for an example, see Wafula et al. 2017).

All four identifiers may be useful for different reasons, but the latter two are likely to be the most useful for rapid data analysis. The coded identifiers require providing field staff with a translation dictionary, but also enable automated rapid recoding for analysis with no loss of information. The broad category requires agreement on the groups of interest, but allows for much more comprehensible top-line statistics and data quality checks. Rigorous field testing is required to ensure that the answer categories are comprehensive; additionally, it is best practice always to include an "other, specify" option. Keeping track of such responses in the first few weeks of fieldwork is recommended because adding an answer category for a response frequently showing up as "other" can save time by avoiding extensive coding later in the project.

Coded-response options are responses to questions that require respondents to select from a list of choices, corresponding to underlying numerical response codes.

Open-ended questions are responses to questions that do not impose any structure on the response, typically recorded as free-flowing text.

A **Likert scale** is an ordered selection of choices indicating the respondent's level of agreement or disagreement with a proposed statement.

It is essential to provide variable names and value labels for the fields in the questionnaire in a way that will work well in the data analysis software. Most survey programs do not require such names by default, because naming restrictions vary across statistical software. Instead, most survey software implicitly encourages the use of complete sentences as question labels and detailed descriptions as choice options. This practice is desirable for the enumerator-respondent interaction, but analysis-compatible labels should now be programmed in the background so that the resulting data can be imported rapidly into the analytical software.

There is some debate over how exactly individual questions should be identified: formats like dem_1 are hard to remember and unpleasant to reorder, but formats like dem_sex_of_respondent quickly become cumbersome. Using short descriptive names with clear prefixes is recommended so that variables within a module stay together when sorted alphabetically—for example, formats like dem_woman. Variable names should never include spaces or mixed cases (DIME prefers using all lowercase; for more details on naming conventions, see the DIME Wiki at https://dimewiki.worldbank.org/Naming_Conventions), and they should not be so long that the software cuts them off, which could result in a loss of uniqueness and requires a lot of manual work to restore compatibility. Numbering questions is discouraged, at least at first, because it makes reordering questions difficult, which is a common change recommended after the pilot. In the case of follow-up surveys, numbering can quickly become convoluted, too often resulting in uninformative variables names like ag_15a, ag_15_new, ag_15_fup2, and so on.

Using electronic survey features to enhance data quality

Electronic surveys are more than simply a paper questionnaire displayed on a mobile device or web browser. All common survey software products make it possible to automate survey logic and include hard or soft constraints on survey responses. These features make enumerators' work easier and create an opportunity to identify and resolve data issues in real time, which simplifies data cleaning and improves the quality of responses. Well-programmed questionnaires should include most or all of the following features:

- *Localization.* The survey instrument should display full-text questions and responses in all potential survey languages and should also have English (or the primary language of the research team) and code-compatible versions of all text and labels.

- *Survey logic.* Built-in tests should be included for all logic connections between questions, so that only relevant questions appear. Enumerators should not have to implement complex survey logic themselves. The research team should program the instruments to embed simple skip patterns as well as more complex interdependencies (for example, a child health module is asked only of households that report the presence of a child under five).

- *Range checks.* Range checks should be added for all numeric variables to catch data entry mistakes (for example, age must be less than 120).

- *Confirmation of key variables.* Double entry of essential information (such as a contact phone number in a survey with planned phone follow-up) is required, with automatic validation that the two entries match and with rejection and reentry otherwise.

- *Multimedia.* Electronic questionnaires facilitate the collection of images, video, and geolocation data directly during the survey, using the camera and global positioning system (GPS) built into the tablet or phone.

- *Preloaded data.* Data from previous rounds or related surveys can be used to prepopulate certain sections of the questionnaire and be validated during the survey.

- *Filtered-response options.* Filters dynamically reduce the number of response options (for example, filtering a "cities" choice list based on the state selected).

- *Location checks.* Enumerators submit their actual location using built-in GPS, to confirm that they are in the right place for the interview.

- *Consistency checks.* It is essential to check that answers to related questions align and that a warning is triggered if they do not so that enumerators can probe further (for example, if a household reports producing 800 kilograms of maize, but selling 900 kilograms of maize from its own production).

- *Calculations.* The electronic survey instrument should do all of the math; enumerators should not be asked to do their own calculations.

---

ietestform is a Stata command to test for common errors and Stata best practices in electronic survey forms based on Open Data Kit (ODK), thereby ensuring that data are easily managed. It is part of the iefieldkit package. For more details, see the DIME Wiki at https://dimewiki.worldbank.org/ietestform.

All established survey software packages include debugging and test options to correct syntax errors and ensure that the survey instruments will compile successfully. Such options are not sufficient, however, to ensure that the resulting data set will load without errors in the data analysis software of choice. To address this issue, DIME Analytics developed the ietestform command (https://dimewiki.worldbank.org/ietestform), part of the Stata package iefieldkit (Bjärkefur, Andrade, and Daniels 2020). Intended for use during questionnaire programming and before fieldwork, ietestform tests for best practices in coding, naming, labeling, and compiling choice lists. Although ietestform is software specific, many of the tests it runs are general and important to consider regardless of the software chosen. For example, ietestform tests that no variable name exceeds 32 characters, the limit in Stata (variable names exceeding that limit will be truncated and, as a result, may no longer be unique). It checks whether ranges are included for numeric variables. It also removes all leading and trailing blanks from response lists, which could be handled inconsistently across software.

The final stage of survey piloting, the data-focused pilot, should be done at this stage (after the questionnaire is programmed). The data-focused pilot is intended to validate the programming and to export a sample data set. Significant desk-testing of the instrument is required to debug the programming as fully as possible before going into the field. It is important to plan for multiple days of piloting, so that the electronic survey instrument can be debugged or otherwise revised at the end of each day and tested the following day, until no further field errors arise. The data-focused pilot should be done in advance of enumerator training. (For a checklist with best practices important to remember during a data-focused pilot, see the DIME Wiki at https://dimewiki.worldbank.org /Checklist:_Data-focused_Pilot.)

Training enumerators

Once a survey instrument is designed, piloted on paper to refine content, programmed, piloted electronically to refine the data, and fully translated to any local languages, it is time to train the field staff who will conduct the interviews. The following guidelines for enumerator training apply regardless of whether data will ultimately be collected in person or remotely, with the only significant differences being in the survey protocols and the nature of the field practice (which could be in-person or by phone).

The first step is to develop a detailed *enumerator manual.* The manual should explain each question in the survey instrument, address any issues that arose during piloting, and cover frequently asked questions. The manual should also describe survey protocols and conventions, such as how to select or confirm the identity of respondents and standardized means for recording responses such as "don't know." The enumerator manual serves as the basis for the *enumerator training.* Dividing the training into two sessions is recommended: first, the training-of-trainers and, then, the enumerator training. The training-of-trainers should include the field supervisors and any other relevant management staff from the organization responsible for data collection and should be led by the research team. The objective is to ensure that the survey leaders are deeply familiar with the survey instrument and protocols, so that they can support and supervise enumerators going forward. The training-of-trainers typically lasts a few days, although the exact length will depend on the complexity of the survey instrument and experience level of the staff. (For more details on how to design an enumerator manual and a template for enumerator manuals, among other materials for survey protocol design, see the DIME Wiki at https://dimewiki.worldbank.org/Enumerator_Training and https://dimewiki.worldbank.org/Survey_Protocols.)

Enumerator training includes all field staff and should be led jointly by the research team and the survey managers. This training typically lasts one to two weeks, although the exact length will depend, again, on the complexity of the survey and experience level of the enumerators; training for particularly challenging surveys may take a full month. Enumerator training has three components: review of the paper questionnaire, review of the electronic survey instrument, and field practice. The training schedule should allow for significant discussion and feedback after each component. Training with a paper survey instrument is critical, even for surveys that will be deployed electronically. Starting with paper ensures that enumerators will focus on the content and structure of the survey before diving into the technical components of the survey software. It is much easier for enumerators to understand the overall flow of a survey instrument and the range of possible participant responses using a paper survey than using a tablet, and it is easier to translate that understanding to digital functionality later. The classroom training should be very interactive, using methods such as role playing and mock interviews to test enumerators' understanding of survey protocols and modules. The field practice should be supervised carefully to provide individualized feedback to each enumerator.

When first using the digital form of the survey, enumerators should submit data from practice interviews to the server, and the research team should run the standard *data quality checks* to familiarize enumerators with those standards for data quality and how quality issues will be communicated and resolved. It is essential to train more enumerators than required for the survey and to include objective assessments throughout the training. These assessments can take the form of pop quizzes (which should be done daily, using the same software as the survey), points for participation, and a score for the field practice. At the end of the training, the aggregate score should be used to select the final team of enumerators.

Data quality assurance checks or simply **data quality checks** are the set of processes put in place to detect incorrect data points due to survey programming errors, data entry mistakes, misrepresentation, and other issues. For more details, see the DIME Wiki at https://dimewiki.worldbank.org/Monitoring_Data_Quality.

Checking data quality in real time

Once all field staff have been trained, it is time to start collecting data. Following the guidance in this handbook will set the stage for collecting quality data. To ensure high-quality data in practice, the research team should develop a *data quality assurance plan*. A key advantage of electronic data collection methods, as compared to traditional paper surveys and one-time data dumps, is the ability to access and analyze the data while they are being collected, allowing issues to be identified and resolved in real time. The process of designing systematic data checks and running them routinely throughout data collection simplifies field monitoring and improves data quality. Two types of checks are important for monitoring data quality: high-frequency quality checks and field validation.

A **data quality assurance plan** is the outline of tasks and responsibilities for ensuring that data collected in the field are accurate. For more details, see the DIME Wiki at https://dimewiki.worldbank.org/Data_Quality_Assurance_Plan.

High-frequency data quality checks (HFCs) are data quality checks run in real time during data collection so that any issues can be addressed while the data collection is still ongoing. For more details, see the DIME Wiki at https://dimewiki.worldbank .org/High_Frequency_Checks.

High-frequency data quality checks (HFCs) should be scripted before data collection begins, so that data checks can start as soon as data start to arrive. A research assistant should run the HFCs on a daily basis for the duration of the survey. HFCs should include monitoring the consistency and range of responses to each question, validating survey programming, testing for enumerator-specific effects, and checking for duplicate entries and completeness of online submissions vis-à-vis the field log.

HFCs will improve data quality only if the issues they catch are communicated to the team collecting the data and if corrections are documented and applied to the data. This effort requires close communication with the field team, so that enumerators are promptly made aware of data quality issues and have a transparent system for documenting issues and corrections. There are many ways to communicate the results of HFCs to the field team, with the most important being to create actionable information. `ipacheck`, for example, generates a spreadsheet with flagged errors; these spreadsheets can be sent directly to the data collection teams. Many teams display results in other formats, such as online dashboards created by custom scripts. It is also possible to automate the communication of errors to the field team by adding scripts to link the HFCs with a messaging platform. Any of these solutions is possible: what works best for the team will depend on factors such as cellular networks in fieldwork areas, whether field supervisors have access to laptops, internet speed, and coding skills of the team preparing the HFC workflow (see box 4.4. for how data quality assurance was applied in the Demand for Safe Spaces project).

BOX 4.4 CHECKING DATA QUALITY IN REAL TIME: A CASE STUDY FROM THE DEMAND FOR SAFE SPACES PROJECT

The Demand for Safe Spaces project created protocols for checking the quality of the platform survey data. In this case, the survey instrument was programmed for electronic data collection using the SurveyCTO platform.

- Enumerators submitted surveys to the server upon completing interviews.
- The team's field coordinator made daily notes of any unusual field occurrences in the documentation folder in the project folder shared by the research team.
- The research team downloaded data daily; after each download the research assistant ran coded data quality checks. The code was prepared in advance of data collection, based on the pilot data.
- The data quality checks flagged any duplicated identifications, outliers, and inconsistencies in the day's data. Issues were reported to the field team the next day. In practice, the only issues flagged were higher-than-expected rates of refusal to answer and wrongly entered identification numbers. The field team responded on the same day to each case, and the research assistant documented any resulting changes to the data set through code.

(Box continues on next page)

BOX 4.4 CHECKING DATA QUALITY IN REAL TIME: A CASE STUDY FROM THE DEMAND FOR SAFE SPACES PROJECT (continued)

The team developed a customized data quality monitoring dashboard to keep all team members up to date on the survey's progress and quality. The dashboard included indicators of progress such as refusal rates, number of surveys completed, and number of respondents on the previous day or week by gender. Figure B4.4.1 presents an example of the progress indicators on the dashboard. The dashboard also illustrated participation in the implicit association test, by gender and by various demographic characteristics of interest. Visual descriptive statistics for the main variables of interest were also displayed to monitor and flag concerns easily.

FIGURE B4.4.1 **A sample dashboard of indicators of progress**

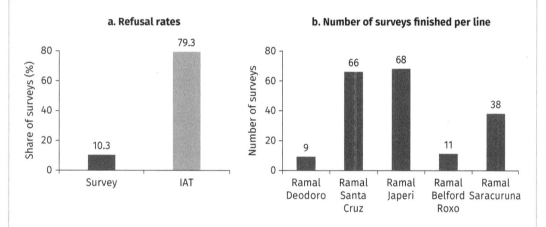

Source: DIME (Development Impact Evaluation), World Bank.
Note: IAT = implicit association test.

Careful *field validation* is essential for high-quality survey data. Although it is impossible to control natural measurement errors (for an example, see Kondylis, Mueller, and Zhu 2015), which are the result of variation in the realization of key outcomes, there is often an opportunity to reduce errors arising from inaccuracies in the data generation process. *Back-checks*, spot checks, and other validation audits help to ensure that data are not falsified, incomplete, or otherwise suspect. Field validation also provides an opportunity to ensure that all field protocols are followed. For back-checks, a random subset of observations is selected, and a subset of information from the full survey is verified through a brief targeted survey with the original respondent. For spot checks, field supervisors (and, if contextually appropriate, research team staff) should make unannounced field visits to each enumerator, to confirm first-hand that the enumerator is following survey protocols and understands the survey questions well. The design of the back-checks or validations follows the same survey design principles discussed above: the analysis plan or a list of key outcomes is used to establish which subset of variables to prioritize and to focus on errors that would be major flags of poor-quality data.

Back-checks are revisits to already interviewed respondents, in which the interviewer asks a subset of the survey questions a second time to audit survey accuracy. For more details, see the DIME Wiki at https://dimewiki.worldbank.org/Back_Checks.

Real-time access to the data massively increases the potential utility of back-checks and both simplifies and improves the rigor of the associated workflows. Raw data can be used to draw the back-check or validation sample, which ensures that the validation is apportioned correctly across observations. As soon as HFCs are complete, the back-check data can be tested against the original data to identify areas of concern in real time. The `bcstats` command is a useful tool for analyzing back-check data in Stata (White 2016). Some electronic survey software also provides a unique opportunity to do audits through audio recordings of the interview, typically short recordings triggered at random throughout the questionnaire. Such audio audits can be a useful means to assess whether enumerators are conducting interviews as expected. However, they must be included in the informed consent for the respondents, and the recordings will have to be assessed by specially trained staff.

Handling data securely

All confidential data must be handled so that only people specifically approved by an IRB or specified in the data license agreement can access the data. Data can be confidential for multiple reasons; two very common reasons are that the data contain *personally identifying information* (PII) or that the data owner has specified restricted access.

Encrypting data

Data *encryption* is a group of tools and methods to prevent unauthorized access to confidential files. Encryption is a system that is only as secure as its weakest link. Therefore, proper encryption can rarely be condensed into a single tool or method, because the data must be handled securely as they travel through many servers, devices, and computers from the source of the data to the final analysis. This section recommends a streamlined encryption workflow, so that it is as straightforward as possible to ensure that the entire chain is easy to manage and sufficiently secure. For more about data security and encryption practices, see the DIME Wiki at https://dimewiki.worldbank.org/Data_Security or pillar 4 of the DIME Research Standards at https://github.com /worldbank/dime-standards.

All encryption relies on a password or encryption key for both encrypting and decrypting information. Encryption makes data files completely unusable to anyone who does not have the decryption key. This is a higher level of security than most password protection, because password-protected information is often readable if the password is bypassed or the storage hard drive is compromised. Encryption keys have to be shared and stored carefully; if they are lost or cannot be matched to encrypted information, the information is permanently lost. Therefore, access to encryption keys should be treated the same as access to

Personally identifying information (PII) is any piece or set of information that can be linked to the identity of a specific individual. For more details, see the DIME Wiki at https://dimewiki.worldbank .org/Personally_Identifiable _Information_(PII) and pillar 4 of the DIME Research Standards at https:// github.com/worldbank /dime-standards.

Encryption is a process of systematically masking the underlying information contained in digital files. This process ensures that file contents are unreadable even if laptops are stolen, databases are hacked, or any other type of access is obtained which gives unauthorized people access to the encrypted files. For more about encryption methods, see the DIME Wiki at https://dimewiki .worldbank.org/Encryption.

confidential information. These passwords or keys should never be shared by email, WhatsApp, or other common modes of communication; instead, using a secure password manager built for this purpose is recommended. (For DIME's step-by-step guide for how to get started with password managers, see pillar 4 of the DIME Research Standards at https://github .com/worldbank/dime-standards.)

There are two main types of encryption algorithms: symmetric encryption and asymmetric encryption. In *symmetric encryption*, the same key is used both to encrypt and to decrypt the data. In *asymmetric encryption*, one key is used to encrypt data, and another key from the same "pair" is used to decrypt data. It is essential to keep track of these keys. While encryption keys for asymmetric encryption are often provided automatically to the devices recording or inputting information, only people listed on the IRB should have access to decryption keys or any key used in symmetric encryption.

There are two important contexts for encryption. *Encryption-in-transit* protects data sent over the internet. It is a standard, passive protection that almost all internet-based services use; it rarely needs to be implemented by the research team unless the project is creating a custom transfer solution. *Encryption-at-rest* protects data stored on a server, computer, or drive.

Typically, unless the project has access to an approved enterprise version of data-sharing software, encryption-at-rest will have to be set up for data in two locations: server or web storage during data acquisition and local storage afterward. It is never wise to assume that encryption-at-rest is implemented automatically unless a cybersecurity expert within the organization has specified that a specific service is appropriate to the particular case. In all other cases, readers should follow the steps laid out in this section to set up their own encryption for which they, and only they, are in full control of who has access to the key.

Collecting and storing data securely

Most data collection software will automatically encrypt all data in transit (that is, uploaded from the field or downloaded from the server). However, it is necessary to ensure that confidential data are protected when stored on a server owned by the data collection software provider or when people not on the research team (including local IT support or system administrators trusted by the research team) can access the location where the information is stored. In most data collection platforms, users need to enable and operate encryption-at-rest explicitly. When collecting data, the tablets or the browsers used for data collection should encrypt all information before submitting it to the server; information should be decrypted only after it has been downloaded to the computer where the data will be used.

This case is perfect for using asymmetric encryption in which two keys form a "public-private key pair." The public key can safely be sent to all tablets or browsers so that it can be used for encrypting the data before the information is submitted to the server. Only the private key in the same key pair can be used to decrypt those data so the information can be accessed after it has been received. The private key should be kept secret and not given to anyone not listed on the IRB. Again, it is essential to store the key pair in a secure location, such as a secure note in a password manager, because there is no way to access the data if the private key is lost. If the data collection service allows users to view data in a web browser, then the encryption is implemented correctly only if the user is asked for the key each time or is allowed to see only fields explicitly marked as publishable by the research team.

The data security standards that apply when receiving confidential data from the field also apply when transferring confidential data to the field, such as sampling or enumeration lists containing PII. In some survey software, the same encryption that is used to receive data securely from the field can also be used to send confidential data, such as an identifying list of respondents, to the field. Otherwise, it is necessary to create an encrypted folder where the file is stored, transfer this folder to the field team using any method, and have them decrypt the information locally using a key that is transferred securely using a password manager. This process is more similar to the process for storing data securely, which is discussed next.

Before planning how to send or receive data securely, it is necessary to plan how to store data securely after the information has been transferred. Typically, data should be stored so that the information can be decrypted and accessed, interacted with, and then encrypted again. (Usually, these data will not be edited, but nonsensitive pieces may be extracted to a less secure location.) This case is perfect for using symmetric encryption to create an encrypted folder for which the same key is used both to encrypt and to decrypt the information. This type of encryption is similar to a physical safe, for which one key is used to both add and access contents.

An encrypted folder can be set up using, for example, VeraCrypt. Users can interact with and modify files in an encrypted folder if and only if they have the key. This is an example of the implementation of encryption-at-rest. There is absolutely no way to restore the data if the key is lost, so it is impossible to overstress the importance of using a password manager, or an equally secure solution, to store these encryption keys.

It is becoming more and more common for development research to use data that are too big to be stored on a regular computer and need to be stored and processed in a cloud environment instead. Many cloud storage solutions are available, and it is necessary to understand how the data are encrypted and how the keys are handled. In this case, the research team will probably have to ask a cybersecurity expert. After a secure cloud storage is set up, it is vital to remember to encrypt the data if samples are downloaded to—for example, to develop code on—a local computer.

Backing up original data

In addition to encrypting data, protection is needed to keep the information from being accidentally overwritten or deleted. This protection is achieved through a backup protocol, which creates additional copies of the original data, exactly as received and finalized, in secure locations that remain permanently available but are not intended for frequent access. The following is an example of such a protocol:

1. Create an encrypted folder on a local computer in the shared project folder using VeraCrypt.

2. Download the original data from the data source to the encrypted folder. If the data source is a survey and the data were encrypted during data collection, *both* keys will be needed: the private key used during data collection will be needed to download the data *and* the key used when creating the encrypted folder will be needed to save the information there. This is the *working copy* of the original data, and it is the copy that will be the starting point for data cleaning.

3. Create a second encrypted folder on an external drive that is kept in a location where it is physically secure. The data downloaded in the previous step will be copied to this second encrypted folder. This is the *master backup copy* of the original data. No one should ever work with these data on a day-to-day basis. The encrypted folder for the master backup copy must not be the same encrypted folder used for the working copy. It should not use the same key, because if the same key is used and lost, access to both encrypted folders will be lost. If it is possible to store the external drive in a locked physical safe, then it is not necessary to encrypt the data, thereby removing the risk associated with losing encryption keys.

4. Finally, create a third encrypted folder. Either create this folder on a computer and upload it to a long-term cloud storage service (not a sync software) or create it on another external hard drive or computer that is then stored in a second location—for example, in another office. This is the *golden master backup copy* of the original data. The golden master copy should never be stored in a synced folder, because it will be deleted in the cloud storage if it is deleted on the computer. These data exist for recovery purposes only; they are not to be worked on or changed.

This handling satisfies the 3-2-1 rule: there are two onsite copies of the data and one offsite copy, so the data can never be lost in the event of hardware failure. If all goes well, it will never be necessary to access the master or golden master copies—but it is important to know that they are there, safe, if they are ever needed.

FIGURE 4.1 **Data acquisition tasks and outputs**

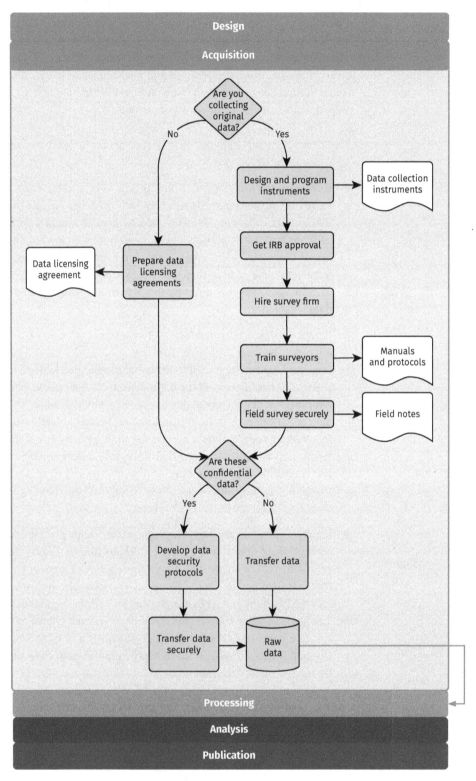

Source: DIME (Development Impact Evaluation), World Bank.
Note: IRB = institutional review board.

Looking ahead

This chapter provided a road map to the acquisition of original data. It outlined guidelines for ensuring that the team has effective ownership or licensing of data that were obtained or collected and for determining how to make those materials available in the future. It also provided an extensive guide for one of the most common—and challenging—methods of data collection: primary electronic surveys. Finally, it emphasized the secure handling of this potentially sensitive information, providing a range of tools and a complete workflow for transferring and storing data securely at all times. Once original data are completely transferred, securely stored, and backed up, the data acquisition stage is complete, as summarized in figure 4.1. This is when the heavy lifting with statistical software starts. Before analyzing the data and answering the project's research questions, it is necessary to check the quality of the data acquired, make sure that the right information is in hand and in the right format, and prepare the information for analysis. This process, called data cleaning and processing, is described in the next chapter.

References

Begg, Colin, Mildred Cho, Susan Eastwood, Richard Horton, David Moher, Ingram Olkin, Roy Pitkin, et al. 1996. "Improving the Quality of Reporting of Randomized Controlled Trials: The CONSORT Statement." *JAMA* 276 (8): 637–39.

Bjärkefur, Kristoffer, Luíza Cardoso de Andrade, and Benjamin Daniels. 2020. "Iefieldkit: Commands for Primary Data Collection and Cleaning." *Stata Journal* 20 (4): 892–915.

Glewwe, Paul, and Margaret E. Grosh. 2000. *Designing Household Survey Questionnaires for Developing Countries: Lessons from 15 Years of the Living Standards Measurement Study.* Vol. 3. Washington, DC: World Bank.

Kondylis, Florence, Valerie Mueller, and Siyao Zhu. 2015. "Measuring Agricultural Knowledge and Adoption." *Agricultural Economics* 46 (3): 449–62.

Wafula, Francis, Amy Dolinger, Benjamin Daniels, Njeri Mwaura, Guadalupe Bedoya, Khama Rogo, Ana Goicoechea, Jishnu Das, and Bernard Olayo. 2017. "Examining the Quality of Medicines at Kenyan Healthcare Facilities: A Validation of an Alternative Post-Market Surveillance Model That Uses Standardized Patients." *Drugs—Real World Outcomes* 4 (1): 53–63.

White, Matthew. 2016. "BCSTATS: Stata Module to Analyze Back Check (Field Audit) Data and Compare It to the Original Survey Data." Statistical Software Components S458173, Department of Economics, Boston College, Boston, MA.

Chapter 5

Cleaning and processing research data

Original data come in a variety of formats, most of which are not immediately suited for analysis. The process of preparing data for analysis has many different names—data cleaning, data munging, data wrangling—but they all mean the same thing: transforming data into an appropriate format for the intended use. This task is the most time-consuming step of a project's data work, particularly when primary data are involved; it is also critical for data quality. A structured workflow for preparing newly acquired data for analysis is essential for efficient, transparent, and reproducible data work. A key point of this chapter is that no changes are made to the contents of data at this point. Therefore, the clean data set, which is the main output from the workflow discussed in this chapter, contains the same information as the original data, but in a format that is ready for use with statistical software. Chapter 6 discusses tasks that involve changes to the data based on research decisions, such as creating new variables, imputing values, and handling outliers.

This chapter describes the various tasks involved in making newly acquired data ready for analysis. The first section teaches how to make data *tidy*, which means adjusting the organization of the data set until the relationship between rows and columns is well defined. The second section describes quality assurance checks, which are necessary to verify data accuracy. The third section covers de-identification, because removing direct identifiers early in the data-handling process helps to ensure privacy. The final section discusses how to examine each variable in the data set and ensure that it is as well documented and as easy to use as possible. Each of these tasks is implemented through code, and the resulting data sets can be reproduced exactly by running this code. The original data files are kept precisely as they were acquired, and no changes are made directly to them. Box 5.1 summarizes the main points, lists the responsibilities of different members of the research team, and supplies a list of key tools and resources for implementing the recommended practices.

BOX 5.1 SUMMARY: CLEANING AND PROCESSING RESEARCH DATA

After being acquired, data must be structured for analysis in accordance with the research design, as laid out in the data linkage tables and the data flowcharts discussed in chapter 3. This process entails the following tasks.

1. *Tidy the data.* Many data sets do not have an unambiguous identifier as received, and the rows in the data set often do not match the units of observation specified by the research plan and data linkage table. To prepare the data for analysis requires two steps:

   - Determine the unique identifier for each unit of observation in the data.
   - Transform the data so that the desired unit of observation uniquely identifies rows in each data set.

2. *Validate data quality.* Data completeness and quality should be validated upon receipt to ensure that the information is an accurate representation of the characteristics and individuals it is supposed to describe. This process entails three steps:

   - Check that the data are complete—that is, that all the observations in the desired sample were received.
   - Make sure that data points are consistent across variables and data sets.
   - Explore the distribution of key variables to identify outliers and other unexpected patterns.

3. *De-identify, correct, and annotate the data.* After the data have been processed and de-identified, the information must be archived, published, or both. Before publication, it is necessary to ensure that the processed version is highly accurate and appropriately protects the privacy of individuals:

   - De-identify the data in accordance with best practices and relevant privacy regulations.
   - Correct data points that are identified as being in error compared to ground reality.
   - Recode, document, and annotate data sets so that all of the content will be fully interpretable by future users, whether or not they were involved in the acquisition process.

Key responsibilities for task team leaders and principal investigators

- Determine the units of observation needed for experimental design and supervise the development of appropriate unique identifiers.
- Indicate priorities for quality checks, including key indicators and reference values.
- Provide guidance on how to resolve all issues identified in data processing, cleaning, and preparation.
- Publish or archive the prepared data set.

Key responsibilities for research assistants

- Develop code, data, and documentation linking data sets with the data map and study design, and tidy all data sets to correspond to the required units of observation.

(Box continues on next page)

BOX 5.1 SUMMARY: CLEANING AND PROCESSING RESEARCH DATA (continued)

- Manage data quality checks, and communicate issues clearly to task team leaders, principal investigators, data producers, and field teams.
- Inspect each variable, recoding and annotating as required. Prepare the data set for publication by de-identifying data, correcting field errors, and documenting the data.

Key resources

- The `iefieldkit` Stata package, a suite of commands to enable reproducible data cleaning and processing:

  - Explanation at https://dimewiki.worldbank.org/iefieldkit
  - Code at https://github.com/worldbank/iefieldkit

- The `ietoolkit` Stata package, a suite of commands to enable reproducible data management and analysis:

  - Explanation at https://dimewiki.worldbank.org/ietoolkit
  - Code at https://github.com/worldbank/ietoolkit

- DIME Analytics Continuing Education Session on tidying data at https://osf.io/p4e8u/
- De-identification article on the DIME Wiki at https://dimewiki.worldbank.org/De-identification

Making data "tidy"

Data tables are data that are structured into rows and columns. They are also called **tabular data sets** or **rectangular data**. By contrast, nonrectangular data types include written text, NoSQL files, social graph databases, and files such as images or documents.

The **unit of observation** is the type of entity that is described by a given data set. In tidy data sets, each row should represent a distinct entity of that type. For more details, see the DIME Wiki at https://dimewiki.worldbank.org/Unit_of_Observation.

The first step in creating an analysis data set is to understand the data acquired and use this understanding to translate the data into an intuitive format. This section discusses what steps may be needed to make sure that each row in a *data table* represents one observation. Getting to such a format may be harder than expected, and the *unit of observation* may be ambiguous in many data sets. This section presents the tidy data format, which is the ideal format for handling tabular data. Tidying data is the first step in data cleaning; quality assurance is best done using tidied data, because the relationship between row and unit of observation is as simple as possible. In practice, tidying and quality monitoring should proceed simultaneously as data are received.

This book uses the term "original data" to refer to the data in the state in which the information was first acquired by the research team. In other sources, the terms "original data" or "raw data" may be used to refer to the corrected and compiled data set created from received information, which this book calls "clean data"—that is, data that have been processed to have errors and duplicates removed, that have been transformed to the correct level of observation, and that include complete metadata such as labels and documentation. This phrasing applies to data provided by partners as well as to original data collected by the research team.

Establishing a unique identifier

A **unique identifier** is a variable or combination of variables that distinguishes each entity described in a data set at that level of observation (for example, person, household) with a distinct value. For more details, see the DIME Wiki at https://dimewiki.worldbank.org/ID_Variable_Properties.

The **data linkage table** is the component of a data map that lists all the data sets in a particular project and explains how they are linked to each other. For more details and an example, see the DIME Wiki at https://dimewiki.worldbank.org/Data_Linkage_Table.

A **master data set** is the component of a data map that lists all individual units for a given level of observation in a project. For more details and an example, see the DIME Wiki at https://dimewiki.worldbank.org/Master_Data_Set.

A **project identifier** (ID) is a research design variable used consistently throughout a project to identify observations. For each level of observation, the corresponding project ID variable must uniquely and fully identify all observations in the project. For more details, see the DIME Wiki at https://dimewiki.worldbank.org/ID_Variable_Properties.

Before starting to tidy a data set, it is necessary to understand the unit of observation that the data represent and to determine which variable or set of variables is the *unique identifier* for each observation. As discussed in chapter 3, the unique identifier will be used to link observations in this data set to data in other data sources according to the *data linkage table*, and it must be listed in the *master data set*.

Ensuring that observations are uniquely and fully identified is arguably the most important step in data cleaning because the ability to tidy the data and link them to any other data sets depends on it. It is possible that the variables expected to identify the data uniquely contain either missing or duplicate values in the original data. It is also possible that a data set does not include a unique identifier or that the original unique identifier is not a suitable *project identifier* (ID). Suitable project IDs should not, for example, involve long strings that are difficult to work with, such as names, or be known outside of the research team.

In such cases, cleaning begins by adding a project ID to the acquired data. If a project ID already exists for this unit of observation, then it should be merged carefully from the master data set to the acquired data using other identifying information. (In R and some other languages, this operation is called a "data set join"; this book uses the term "merge.") If a project ID does not exist, then it is necessary to generate one, add it to the master data set, and then merge it back into the original data. Although digital survey tools create unique identifiers for each data submission, these identifiers are not the same as having a unique ID variable for each observation in the sample, because the same observation can have multiple submissions.

The DIME Analytics team created an automated workflow to identify, correct, and document duplicated entries in the unique identifier using the `ieduplicates` and `iecompdup` Stata commands. One advantage of using `ieduplicates` to correct duplicate entries is that it creates a duplicates report, which records each correction made and documents the reason for it. Whether using this command or not, it is important to keep a record of all cases of duplicate IDs encountered and how they were resolved (see box 5.2 for an explanation of how a unique identifier was established for the Demand for Safe Spaces project).

All data sets have a unit of observation, and the first columns of each data set should uniquely identify which unit is being observed. In the Demand for Safe Spaces project, as should be the case in all projects, the first few lines of code that imported each original data set immediately ensured that this was true and applied any corrections from the field needed to fix errors related to uniqueness.

The code segment below was used to import the crowdsourced ride data; it used the `ieduplicates` command to remove duplicate values of the uniquely identifying variable in the data set. The screen shot of the corresponding `ieduplicates` report shows how the command documents and resolves duplicate identifiers in data collection. After applying the corrections, the code confirms that the data are uniquely identified by riders and ride identifiers and documents the decisions in an optimized format.

```
 1 // Import to Stata format ==============================================================
 2
 3    import delimited using "${encrypt}/Baseline/07112016/Contributions 07112016", ///
 4        delim(",")        ///
 5        bindquotes(strict) ///
 6        varnames(1)       ///
 7        clear
 8
 9 * There are two duplicated values for obs_uid, each with two submissions.
10 * All four entries are demographic surveys from the same user, who seems to
11 * have submitted the data twice, each time creating two entries.
12 * Possibly a connectivity issue
13    ieduplicates obs_uid using "${doc_rider}/baseline-study/raw-duplicates.xlsx", ///
14        uniquevars(v1) ///
15        keepvars(created submitted started)
16
17 * Verify unique identifier, sort, optimize storage,
18 * remove blank entries and save data
19    isid user_uuid obs_uid, sort
20    compress
21    dropmiss, force
22    save "${encrypt}/baseline_raw.dta", replace
```

	A	B	C	D	E	F	G	H	I
1	obs_uid	duplistid	datelisted	datefixed	correct	drop	newid	initials	notes
2	00bf3083-32f2-474c-b3e0-92e23f0d6191	1	31Jan2021	31Jan2021	correct			LA	These are all the same user
3	00bf3083-32f2-474c-b3e0-92e23f0d6191	2	31Jan2021	31Jan2021		drop		LA	These are all the same user
4	5675f57c-f415-48b9-8b4c-1fe6969722e6	3	31Jan2021	31Jan2021		drop		LA	These are all the same user
5	5675f57c-f415-48b9-8b4c-1fe6969722e6	4	31Jan2021	31Jan2021		drop		LA	These are all the same user

To access this code in do-file format, visit the GitHub repository at https://github.com/worldbank /dime-data-handbook/tree/main/code.

Tidying data

ieduplicates is a Stata command to identify duplicate values in ID variables. It is part of the `iefieldkit` package. For more details, see the DIME Wiki at https://dimewiki .worldbank.org/ieduplicates.

iecompdup is a Stata command to compare duplicate entries and understand why they were created. It is part of the `iefieldkit` package. For more details, see the DIME Wiki at https://dimewiki .worldbank.org/iecompdup.

A **variable** is the collection of all data points that measure the same attribute for each observation.

An **observation** is the collection of all data points that measure attributes for the same instance of the unit of observation in the data table.

Wide format refers to a data table in which the data points for a single variable are stored in multiple columns, one for each subunit. In contrast, **long format** refers to a data table in which a subunit is represented in one row and values representing its parent unit are repeated for each subunit.

Although data can be acquired in all shapes and sizes, they are most commonly received as one or multiple data tables. These data tables can organize information in multiple ways, and not all of them result in easy-to-handle data sets. Fortunately, a vast literature of database management has identified the format that makes interacting with the data as easy as possible. While this is called normalization in database management, data in this format are called *tidy* in data science. A data table is tidy when each column represents one *variable*, each row represents one *observation*, and all variables in it have the same unit of observation. Every other format is *untidy*. This distinction may seem trivial, but data, and original survey data in particular, are rarely received in a tidy format.

The most common case of untidy data acquired in development research is a data set with multiple units of observations stored in the same data table. When the rows include multiple nested observational units, then the unique identifier does not identify all observations in that row, because more than one unit of observation is in the same row. Survey data containing nested units of observation are typically imported from survey platforms in *wide format*. Wide format data could have, for instance, one column for a household-level variable (for example, `owns_fridge`) and a few columns for household member–level variables (for example, `sex_1`, `sex_2`). Original data are often saved in this format because it is an efficient way to transfer the data: adding different levels of observation to the same data table allows data to be transferred in a single file. However, doing so leads to the widespread practice of interacting with data in wide format, which is often inefficient and error-prone.

To understand how dealing with wide data can be complicated, imagine that the project needs to calculate the share of women in each household. In a wide data table, it is necessary first to create variables counting the number of women and the total number of household members and then to calculate the share; otherwise, the data have to be transformed to a different format. In a tidy data table, however, in which each row is a household member, it is possible to aggregate the share of women by household, without taking additional steps, and then to merge the result to the household-level data tables. Tidy data tables are also easier to clean, because each attribute corresponds to a single column that needs to be checked only once, and each column corresponds directly to one question in the questionnaire. Finally, summary statistics and distributions are much simpler to generate from tidy data tables.

As mentioned earlier, there are unlimited ways for data to be untidy; wide format is only one of those ways. Another example is a data table containing both information on transactions and information on the firms involved in each transaction. In this case, the firm-level information is repeated for all transactions in which a given firm is involved. Analyzing firm data in this format gives more weight to firms that conducted more transactions, which may not be consistent with the research design.

The basic process behind tidying a data table is simple: first, identify all of the variables that were measured at the same level of observation; second, create separate data tables for each level of observation; and third, *reshape* the data and remove duplicate rows until each data table is uniquely and fully identified by the unique identifier that corresponds to its unit of observation. Reshaping data tables is one of the most intricate tasks in data cleaning. It is necessary to be very familiar with commands such as `reshape` in Stata and `pivot` in R. It is also necessary to ensure that identifying variables are consistent across data tables, so they can always be linked. Reshaping is the type of transformation referred to in the example of how to calculate the share of women in a wide data set. The important difference is that in a tidy workflow, instead of reshaping the data for each operation, each such transformation is done once during cleaning, making all subsequent operations much easier.

In the earlier household survey example, household-level variables are stored in one tidy data table, and household-member variables are reshaped and stored in a separate, member-level, tidy data table, which also contains the household ID for each individual. The household ID is intentionally duplicated in the household-member data table to allow one or several household members to be linked to the same household data. The unique identifier for the household member–level data will be either a single household member ID or a combination of household ID and household member ID. In the transaction data example, the tidying process creates one transaction-level data table, containing variables indicating the ID of all firms involved, and one firm-level data table, with a single entry for each firm. Then, firm-level analysis can be done easily by calculating appropriate statistics in the transactions data table (in Stata, often through `collapse`) and then merging or joining those results with the firm data table.

In a tidy workflow, the clean data set contains one or more tidy data tables (see box 5.3 for an example of how data sets were tidied in the Demand for Safe Spaces project). In both examples in the preceding paragraphs, the clean data set is made up of two tidy data tables. There must be a clear way to connect each tidy data table to a master data set and thereby also to all other data sets. To implement this connection, one data table is designated as the main data table, and that data table's unit of observation is the main unit of observation of the data set. It is important that the main unit of observation correspond directly to a master data set and be listed in the data linkage table. There must be an unambiguous way to merge all other data tables in the data set with the main data table. This process makes it possible to link all data points in all of the project's data sets to each other. Saving each data set as a folder of data tables, rather than as a single file, is recommended: the main data table shares the same name as the folder, and the names of all other data tables start with the same name, but are suffixed with the unit of observation for that data table.

Reshape means to transform a data table in such a way that the unit of observation it represents changes.

The unit of observation in an original data set does not always match the relevant unit of analysis for a study. One of the first steps required is to create data sets at the unit of analysis desired. In the case of the crowdsourced ride data used in the Demand for Safe Spaces project, study participants were asked to complete three tasks in each metro trip: one before boarding the train (check-in task), one during the ride (ride task), and one after leaving the train (check-out task). The raw data sets show one *task* per row. As a result, each unit of analysis, a metro *trip*, was described in three rows in this data set.

To create a data set at the trip level, the research team took two steps, outlined in the data flowchart (for an example of how data flowcharts can be created, see box 3.3 in chapter 3). First, three separate data sets were created, one for each task, containing only the variables and observations created during that task. Then the trip-level data set was created by combining the variables in the data tables for each task at the level of the individual trip (identified by the session variable).

The following code shows an example of the ride task script, which keeps only the ride task rows and columns from the raw data set.

```
1 /********************************************************************************
2     Load data set and keep ride variables
3 ********************************************************************************/
4
5     use "${dt_raw}/baseline_raw_deidentified.dta", clear
6
7 * Keep only entries that refer to ride task
8     keep if inlist(spectranslated, "Regular Car", "Women Only Car")
9
10 * Sort observations
11     isid user_uuid session, sort
12
13 * Keep only questions answered during this task
14 * (all others will be missing for these observations)
15     dropmiss, force
```

The script then encodes categorical variables and saves a tidy ride task data set:

```
1 /********************************************************************************
2     Clean up and save
3 ********************************************************************************/
4
5     iecodebook apply using "${doc_rider}/baseline-study/codebooks/ride.xlsx", drop
6     order   user_uuid session RI_pa - RI_police_present CI_top_car RI_look_pink ///
7             RI_look_mixed RI_crowd_rate RI_men_present
8
9     * Optimize memory and save data
10     compress
11     save "${dt_int}/baseline_ride.dta", replace
```

(Box continues on next page)

In the household data set example, the household-level data table is the main table. This means that there must be a master data set for households. (The project may also have a master data set for household members if it is important for the research, but having one is not strictly required.) The household data set would then be stored in a folder called, for example, `baseline-hh-survey`. That folder would contain both the household-level data table with the same name as the folder, for example, `baseline-hh-survey.csv`, and the household member-level data, named in the same format but with a suffix, for example, `baseline-hh-survey-hhmember.csv`.

The tidying process gets more complex as the number of nested groups increases. The steps for identifying the unit of observation of each variable and reshaping the separated data tables need to be repeated multiple times. However, the larger the number of nested groups in a data set, the more efficient it is to deal with tidy data than with untidy data. Cleaning and analyzing wide data sets, in particular, constitute a repetitive and error-prone process.

The next step of data cleaning—data quality monitoring—may involve comparing different units of observation. Aggregating subunits to compare to a higher unit is much easier with tidy data, which is why tidying data is the first step in the data cleaning workflow. When collecting primary data, it is possible to start preparing or coding the data tidying even before the data are acquired, because the exact format in which the data will be received is known in advance. Preparing the data for analysis, the last task in this chapter, is much simpler when tidying has been done.

Data quality assurance checks or simply **data quality checks** are the set of processes put in place to detect incorrect data points due to survey programming errors, data entry mistakes, misrepresentation, and other issues. For more details, see the DIME Wiki at https://dimewiki .worldbank.org/Monitoring _Data_Quality.

Implementing data quality checks

Whether receiving data from a partner or collecting data directly, it is important to make sure that data faithfully reflect realities on the ground. It is necessary to examine carefully any data collected through surveys or received from partners. Reviewing original data will inevitably reveal errors, ambiguities, and data entry mistakes, such as typos and inconsistent values. The key aspects to keep in mind are the completeness, consistency, and distribution of data (Andrade et al. 2021). *Data quality assurance checks* should be performed as soon as the data are acquired. When data are being collected and transferred to the team in real time, conducting *high-frequency checks* is recommended. Primary data require

High-frequency data quality checks (HFCs) are data quality checks run in real time during data collection so that any issues can be addressed while the data collection is still ongoing. For more details, see the DIME Wiki at https://dimewiki.worldbank .org/High_Frequency_Checks.

paying extra attention to quality checks, because data entry by humans is susceptible to errors, and the research team is the only line of defense between data issues and data analysis. Chapter 4 discusses survey-specific quality monitoring protocols.

Data quality checks should carefully inspect key treatment and outcome variables to ensure that the data quality of core study variables is uniformly high and that additional effort is centered where it is most important. Checks should be run every time data are received to flag irregularities in the acquisition progress, in sample completeness, or in response quality. The faster issues are identified, the more likely they are to be solved. Once the field team has left a survey area or high-frequency data have been deleted from a server, it may be impossible to verify whether data points are correct or not. Even if the research team is not receiving data in real time, the data owners may not be as knowledgeable about the data or as responsive to the research team queries as time goes by. ipacheck is a very useful Stata command that automates some of these tasks, regardless of the data source.

It is important to check continuously that the observations in data match the intended sample. In surveys, electronic survey software often provides case management features through which sampled units are assigned directly to individual enumerators. For data received from partners, such as administrative data, this assignment may be harder to validate. In these cases, cross-referencing with other data sources can help to ensure completeness. It is often the case that the data as origi-nally acquired include *duplicate observations* or missing entries, which may occur because of typos, failed submissions to data servers, or other mistakes. Issues with data transmission often result in missing obser-vations, particularly when large data sets are being transferred or when data are being collected in locations with limited internet connection. Keeping a record of what data were submitted and then comparing it to the data received as soon as transmission is complete reduces the risk of noticing that data are missing when it is no longer possible to recover the information.

Duplicate observations are instances in which two or more rows of data are identified by the same value of the ID variable or in which two or more rows unintentionally represent the same respondent. They can be created by situations such as data entry mistakes in the ID variable or repeated surveys or submissions. For more details, see the DIME Wiki at https://dimewiki.worldbank .org/Duplicates_and_Survey _Logs.

Once data completeness has been confirmed, observed units must be validated against the expected sample: this process is as straightfor-ward as merging the sample list with the data received and checking for mismatches. Reporting errors and duplicate observations in real time allows for efficient corrections. ieduplicates provides a workflow for resolving duplicate entries with the data provider. For surveys, it is also important to track the progress of data collection to monitor attrition, so that it is known early on if a change in protocols or additional tracking is needed (for an example, see Özler et al. 2016). It is also necessary to check survey completion rates and sample compliance by surveyors and survey teams, to compare data missingness across administrative regions, and to identify any clusters that may be providing data of suspect quality.

Quality checks should also include checks of the quality and consistency of responses. For example, it is important to check whether the values for each variable fall within the expected range and whether related variables contradict each other. Electronic data collection systems often incorporate many quality control features, such as range restrictions and logical flows. Data received from systems that do not include such controls should be checked more carefully. Consistency checks are project specific, so it is difficult to provide general guidance. Having detailed knowledge of the variables in the data set and carefully examining the analysis plan are the best ways to prepare. Examples of inconsistencies in survey data include cases in which a household reports having cultivated a plot in one module but does not list any cultivated crops in another. Response consistency should be checked across all data sets, because this task is much harder to automate. For example, if two sets of administrative records are received, one with hospital-level information and one with data on each medical staff member, the number of entries in the second set of entries should match the number of employed personnel in the first set.

Finally, no amount of preprogrammed checks can replace actually looking at the data. Of course, that does not mean checking each data point; it does mean plotting and tabulating distributions for the main variables of interest. Doing so will help to identify outliers and other potentially problematic patterns that were not foreseen. A common source of outlier values in survey data are typos, but outliers can also occur in administrative data if, for example, the unit reported changed over time, but the data were stored with the same variable name. Identifying unforeseen patterns in the distribution will also help the team to gather relevant information—for example, if there were no harvest data because of a particular pest in the community or if the unusual call records in a particular area were caused by temporary downtime of a tower. Analysis of metadata can also be useful in assessing data quality. For example, electronic survey software generates automatically collected timestamps and trace histories, showing when data were submitted, how long enumerators spent on each question, and how many times answers were changed before or after the data were submitted. See box 5.4 for examples of data quality checks implemented in the Demand for Safe Spaces project.

BOX 5.4 ASSURING DATA QUALITY: A CASE STUDY FROM THE DEMAND FOR SAFE SPACES PROJECT

The Demand for Safe Spaces team adopted three categories of data quality assurance checks for the crowdsourced ride data. The first—*completeness*—made sure that each data point made technical sense in that it contained the right elements and that the data as a whole covered all of the expected spaces. The second—*consistency*—made sure that real-world details were right: stations were on

(Box continues on next page)

the right line, payments matched the value of a task, and so on. The third—*distribution*—produced visual descriptions of the key variables of interest to make sure that any unexpected patterns were investigated further. The following are examples of the specific checks implemented:

Completeness

- Include the following tasks in each trip: check-in, ride, and check-out.
- Plot the number of observations per day of the week and per half-hour time-bin to make sure that there are no gaps in data delivery.
- Plot all observations received from each combination of line and station to visualize data coverage.

Consistency

- Check the correspondence between stations and lines. This check identified mismatches that were caused by the submission of lines outside the research sample. These observations were excluded from the corrected data.
- Check the correspondence between task and premium for riding in the women-only car. This check identified a bug in the app that caused some riders to be offered the wrong premium for some tasks. These observations were excluded from the corrected data.
- Check task times to make sure they were applied in the right order. The task to be completed before boarding the train came first, then the one corresponding to the trip, and finally the one corresponding to leaving the station.

Distribution

- Compare platform observations data and rider reports of crowding and male presence to ensure general data agreement.
- Visualize distribution of rides per task per day and week to ensure consistency.
- Visualize patterns of the presence of men in the women-only car throughout the network.

Personally identifying information (PII) is is any piece or set of information that can be linked to the identity of a specific individual. For more details, see the DIME Wiki at https://dimewiki .worldbank.org/Personally _Identifiable_Information_(PII) and pillar 4 of the DIME Research Standards at https:// github.com/worldbank /dime-standards.

Processing confidential data

When implementing the steps discussed up to this point, the team is likely to be handling confidential data. Effective monitoring of data quality frequently requires identifying individual observations in the data set and the people or other entities that the data describe. Using identified data enables rapid follow-up on and resolution of identified issues. Handling confidential data such as *personally identifying information* (PII) requires a secure environment and, typically, encryption. De-identifying the data simplifies the workflow and reduces the risk of harmful leaks. This section describes how to de-identify data in order to share the information with a wider audience.

Protecting research subject privacy

Human subjects are any living individuals about whom a research team collects data through intervention or interaction with them, as well as any living individuals who can be identified readily using research data. For more details, see the DIME Wiki at https://dimewiki.worldbank .org/Protecting_Human _Research_Subjects.

Most development data involve *human subjects*. Researchers often have access to personal information about people: where they live, how much they earn, whether they have committed or been victims of crimes, their names, their national identity numbers, and other sensitive data (for an example, see Banerjee, La Ferrara, and Orozco 2019). There are strict requirements for safely storing and handling personally identifying data, and the research team is responsible for satisfying these requirements. Everyone working with research on human subjects should have completed an ethics certification course, such as Protecting Human Research Participants (https://phrptraining.com) or one of the CITI Program course offerings (https://citiprogram.org). A plan for handling data securely is typically also required for institutional review board (IRB) approval.

The best way to avoid risk is to minimize interaction with PII as much as possible. First, only PII that is strictly necessary for the research should be collected. Second, there should never be more than one copy of any identified data set in the working project folder, and this data set must always be encrypted. Third, data should be de-identified as early as possible in the workflow. Even within the research team, access to identified data should be limited to team members who require it for their specific tasks. Data analysis rarely requires identifying information, and, in most cases, masked identifiers can be linked to research information, such as treatment status and weight, and then unmasked identifiers can be removed.

De-identification is the process of removing or masking PII to reduce the risk that subjects' identities can be connected with the data. For more details, see the DIME Wiki at https://dimewiki.worldbank .org/De-identification.

Once data are acquired and data quality checks have been completed, the next task typically is to *de-identify* the data by removing or masking all personally identifying variables. In practice, it is rarely, if ever, possible to anonymize data. There is always some statistical chance that an individual's identity will be relinked to the project data by using some other data—even if the project data have had all of the directly identifying information removed. For this reason, de-identification should typically be conducted in two stages. The *initial de-identification* process, performed as soon as data are acquired, strips the data of direct identifiers, creating a working de-identified data set that can be shared within the research team without the need for encryption. The *final de-identification* process, performed before data are released publicly, involves careful consideration of the trade-offs between the risk of identifying individuals and the utility of the data; it typically requires removing a further level of indirect identifiers. The rest of this section describes how to approach the de-identification process.

Implementing de-identification

Initial de-identification reduces risk and simplifies workflows. Having created a de-identified version of the data set, it is no longer necessary to interact directly with the identified data. If the data tidying has resulted in multiple data tables, each table needs to be de-identified separately, but the workflow will be the same for all of them.

During the initial round of de-identification, data sets must be stripped of directly identifying information. To do so requires identifying all of the variables that contain such information. For data collection, when the research team designs the survey instrument, flagging all potentially identifying variables at the questionnaire design stage simplifies the initial de-identification process. If that was not done or original data were received by another means, a few tools can help to flag variables with directly identifying data. The Abdul Latif Jameel Poverty Action Lab (J-PAL) PII-scan and Innovations for Poverty Action (IPA) PII_detection scan variable names and labels for common string patterns associated with identifying information. The sdcMicro package lists variables that uniquely identify observations, but its more refined method and need for higher processing capacity make it better suited for final de-identification (Benschop and Welch, n.d.). The iefieldkit command iecodebook lists all variables in a data set and exports an Excel sheet that makes it easy to select which variables to keep or drop.

It is necessary to assess the resulting list of variables that contain PII against the analysis plan, asking for each variable, *Will this variable be needed for the analysis?* If not, the variable should be removed from the de-identified data set. It is preferrable to be conservative and remove all identifying information at this stage. It is always possible to include additional variables from the original data set if deemed necessary later. However, it is not possible to go back in time and drop a PII variable that was leaked (see box 5.5 for an example of how de-identification was implemented for the Demand for Safe Spaces project).

iecodebook is a Stata command to document and execute repetitive data-cleaning tasks such as renaming, recoding, and labeling variables; to create complete codebooks for data sets; and to harmonize and append data sets containing similar variables. It is part of the iefieldkit package. For more details, see the DIME Wiki at https://dimewiki .worldbank.org/iecodebook.

> ## BOX 5.5 IMPLEMENTING DE-IDENTIFICATION: A CASE STUDY FROM THE DEMAND FOR SAFE SPACES PROJECT
>
> The Demand for Safe Spaces team used the iecodebook command to drop identifying information from the data sets as they were imported. Additionally, before data sets were published, the labels indicating line and station names were removed from them, leaving only the masked number for the underlying category. This was done so that it would not be possible to reconstruct individuals' commuting habits directly from the public data.
>
> The code fragment below shows an example of the initial de-identification when the data were imported. The full data set was saved in the folder for confidential data (using World Bank OneDrive accounts), and a short codebook listing variable names, but not their contents, was saved elsewhere. iecodebook was then used with the drop option to remove confidential information from the data set before it was saved in a shared Dropbox folder. The specific variables removed in this operation contained information about the data collection team that was not needed after quality checks were implemented (deviceid, subscriberid, simid, devicephonenum, username, enumerator, enumeratorname) and the phone numbers of survey respondents (phone_number).

(Box continues on next page)

For each identifying variable that is needed in the analysis, it is necessary to ask, *Is it possible to encode or otherwise construct a variable that masks the confidential component and then drop this variable?* For example, it is easy to encode identifiers for small localities like villages and provide only a masked numerical indicator showing which observations are in the same village without revealing which villages are included in the data. This process can be done for most identifying information. If the answer to either of the two questions posed is yes, all that needs to be done is to write a script to drop the variables that are not required for analysis, encode or otherwise mask those that are required, and save a working version of the data. For example, after constructing measures of distance or area, drop the specific geolocations in the data; after constructing and verifying numeric identifiers in a social network module, drop all names. If identifying information is strictly required for the analysis and cannot be masked or encoded, then at least the identifying part of the data must remain encrypted and be decrypted only when used during the data analysis process. Using identifying data in the analysis process does *not* justify storing or sharing the information in an insecure way.

After initial de-identification is complete, the data set will consist of one or multiple tidy, de-identified data tables. This is the data set with which the team will interact during the remaining tasks described in this chapter. Initial de-identification should not affect the usability of the data. Access to the initially de-identified data should still be restricted to the research team only, because indirect identifiers may still present a high risk of disclosure. It is common, and even desirable, for teams to make data publicly available once the tasks discussed in this chapter have been concluded. Making data publicly available will allow other researchers to conduct additional analysis and to reproduce the findings. Before that can be done, however, it is necessary to consider whether the data can be reidentified, in a process called final de-identification, which is discussed in more detail in chapter 7.

Preparing data for analysis

The last step in the process of data cleaning involves making the data set easy to use and understand and carefully examining each variable to document distributions and identify patterns that may bias the analysis. The resulting data set will contain only the variables collected in the field, and data points will not be modified, except to correct mistaken entries. There may be more data tables in the data set now than originally received, and they may be in a different format, but the information contained is still the same. In addition to the cleaned data sets, cleaning will also yield extensive documentation describing the process.

Such detailed examination of each variable yields in-depth under-standing of the content and structure of the data. This knowledge is key to correctly constructing and analyzing final indicators, which are covered in the next chapter. Careful inspection of the data is often the most time-consuming task in a project. It is important not to rush through it! This section introduces some concepts and tools to make it more efficient and productive. The discussion is separated into four subtopics: exploring the data, making corrections, recoding and annotating, and documenting data cleaning. They are separated here because they are different in nature and should be kept separate in the code. In practice, however, they all may be done at the same time.

Exploring the data

The first time a project team interacts with the data contents is during quality checks. However, these checks are usually time-sensitive, and there may not be time to explore the data at length. As part of data processing, each variable should be inspected closely. Tabulations, summary statistics, histograms, and density plots are helpful for under-standing the structure of data and finding patterns or irregularities. Critical thinking is essential: the numerical values need to be consistent with the information the variable represents. Statistical distributions need to be realistic and not be unreasonably clumped or skewed. Related variables need to be consistent with each other, and outliers and missing values need to be found. If unusual or unexpected distributional patterns are found for any of these characteristics, data entry errors could be the cause.

At this point, it is more important to document the findings than to address any irregularities. A very limited set of changes should be made to the original data set during cleaning. They are described in the next two sections and are usually applied to each variable as it is examined. Most of the transformations that result in new variables occur during *data construction*, a process discussed in the next chapter. For now, the task is to focus on creating a record of what is observed and to document extensively the data being explored. This documentation is useful during the construction phase when discussing how to address irregularities and also valuable during exploratory data analysis.

Data construction is the process of developing analysis data sets from information or data obtained as part of research, including variable creation, changes in unit of analysis, data integration, and data subsetting.

Correcting data points

As mentioned earlier, corrections to issues identified during data quality monitoring are the only changes made to individual data points during the data-cleaning stage. However, there is a lot of discussion about whether such data points should be modified at all. On the one hand, some argue that following up on the issues identified is costly and adds limited value. Because it is not possible to check each and every possible data entry error, identifying issues on just a few main variables can create a false sense of security. Additionally, manually inspected data may suffer from considerable inspector variability. In many cases, the main purpose of data quality checks is to detect fraud and identify problems with data collection protocols. On the other hand, others argue against keeping clear errors or not correcting missing values. DIME Analytics recommends correcting any entries that are clearly identified as errors. However, there is some subjectivity involved in deciding which cases fall into this category. A common rule of thumb is to include the set of corrections based on information that the team has privileged access to and other research teams would not be able to make, and no more. Making this decision involves deep knowledge of the data and the particular circumstances of each research project.

Whether the decision is made to modify data or not, it is essential to keep a careful record of all the issues identified. If no data points are modified, it may still be helpful to add flags to observations containing potentially problematic values so that it is possible to verify how they affect results during analysis. If the team decides to follow up on and correct these issues, the follow-up process must be documented thoroughly. Confidential information should never be included in documentation that is not stored securely or that will be released as part of a replication package or data publication. Finally, no changes should be made directly to the original data set. Instead, any corrections must be made as part of data cleaning, applied through code, and saved to a new data set (see box 5.6 for a discussion of how data corrections were made for the Demand for Safe Spaces project).

BOX 5.6 CORRECTING DATA POINTS: A CASE STUDY FROM THE DEMAND FOR SAFE SPACES PROJECT

Most of the issues that the Demand for Safe Spaces team identified in the raw crowdsourced data during data quality assurance were related to incorrect station and line identifiers. Two steps were taken to address this issue. The first was to correct data points. The second was to document the corrections made.

The correct values for the line and station identifiers, as well as notes on how they were identified, were saved in a data set called `station_correction.dta`. The team used the command `merge` to replace the values in the raw data in memory (called the "master data" in `merge`) with the `station_correction.dta` data (called the "using data" in `merge`).

The following options were used for the following reasons:

- `update replace` was used to update values in the "master data" with values from the same variable in the "using data."
- `keepusing(user_station)` was used to keep only the `user_station` variable from the "using data."
- `assert(master match_update)` was used to confirm that all observations were either only in the "master data" or were in both the "master data" and the "using data" and that the values were updated with the values in the "using data." This quality assurance check was important to ensure that data were merged as expected.

To document the final contents of the original data, the team published supplemental materials on GitHub as well as on the World Bank Microdata Catalog.

```
1 * There was a problem with the line option for one of the stations.
2 * This fixes it:
3 * ----------------------------------------------------------------------
4
5     merge 1:1 obs_uuid                                              ///
6         using "${doc_rider}/compliance-pilot/station_corrections.dta", ///
7         update replace                                             ///
8         keepusing(user_station)                                    ///
9         assert(master match_update)                                ///
10        nogen
```

For the complete script, visit the GitHub repository at https://git.io/Jt2ZC.

Recoding and annotating data

The clean data set is the starting point of data analysis. It is manipulated extensively to construct analysis indicators, so it must be easy to process using statistical software. To make the analysis process smoother, the data set should have all of the information needed to interact with it. Having this information will save people opening the data set from having to go back and forth between the data set and its accompanying documentation, even if they are opening the data set for the first time.

Often, data sets are not imported into statistical software in the most efficient format. The most common example is string (text) variables: *categorical variables* and open-ended responses are often read as strings. However, variables in this format cannot be used for quantitative analysis. Therefore, categorical variables must be transformed into other formats, such as *factors* in R and *labeled integers* in Stata. Additionally, open-ended responses stored as strings usually have a high risk of including identifying information, so cleaning them requires extra attention. The choice names in categorical variables (called *value labels* in Stata and *levels* in R) should be accurate, concise, and linked directly to the data collection instrument. Adding choice names to categorical variables makes it easier to understand the data and reduces the risk that small errors will make their way into the analysis stage.

In survey data, it is common for nonresponse categories such as "don't know" and "declined to answer" to be represented by arbitrary *survey codes*. The presence of these values would bias the analysis, because they do not represent actual observations of an attribute. They need to be turned into *missing values*. However, the fact that a respondent did not know how to answer a question is also useful information that would be lost by simply omitting all information. In Stata, this information can be elegantly conserved using extended missing values.

The clean data set should be kept as similar to the original data set as possible, particularly with regard to variable names: keeping them consistent with the original data set makes data processing and construction more transparent. Unfortunately, not all variable names are informative. In such cases, one important piece of documentation makes the data easier to handle: the variable dictionary. When a data collection instrument (for example, a questionnaire) is available, it is often the best dictionary to use. But, even in these cases, going back and forth between files can be inefficient, so annotating variables in a data set is extremely useful. *Variable labels* must always be present in a clean data set. Labels should include a short and clear description of the variable. A lengthier description, which may include, for example, the exact wording of a question, may be added through *variable notes* in Stata or using *data frame attributes* in R.

Finally, any information that is not relevant for analysis may be removed from the data set. In primary data, it is common to collect information for quality monitoring purposes, such as notes, duration fields, and surveyor IDs. Once the quality monitoring phase is

In statistical software, **categorical variables** are stored as numeric integers, each representing one category. **Value labels** or **levels** are the names assigned to each category in a categorical variable in Stata and R, respectively. For more details, see the DIME Wiki at https:// dimewiki.worldbank.org /Data_Cleaning.

Survey codes are values that are used as placeholders in survey questions to indicate types of outcomes other than responses to the question, such as refusal to answer. For more details, see the DIME Wiki at https://dimewiki.worldbank .org/Data_Cleaning.

Variable labels are short descriptors of the information contained in a variable in statistical software. For more details, see the DIME Wiki at https://dimewiki.worldbank .org/Data_Cleaning.

completed, these variables may be removed from the data set. In fact, starting from a minimal set of variables and adding new ones as they are cleaned can make the data easier to handle. Using commands such as `compress` in Stata so that the data are always stored in the most efficient format helps to ensure that the cleaned data set file does not get too big to handle.

Although all of these tasks are key to making the data easy to use, implementing them can be quite repetitive and create convoluted scripts. The `iecodebook` command suite, part of the `iefieldkit` Stata package, is designed to make some of the most tedious components of this process more efficient. It also creates a self-documenting workflow, so the data-cleaning documentation is created alongside the code, with no extra steps (see box 5.7 for a description of how `iecodebook` was used in the Demand for Safe Spaces project). In R, the Tidyverse (https://www.tidyverse.org) packages provide a consistent and useful grammar for performing the same tasks and can be used in a similar workflow.

BOX 5.7 RECODING AND ANNOTATING DATA: A CASE STUDY FROM THE DEMAND FOR SAFE SPACES PROJECT

The Demand for Safe Spaces team relied mostly on the `iecodebook` command for this part of the data-cleaning process. The screenshot below shows the `iecodebook` form used to clean the crowd-sourced ride data. This process was carried out for each task.

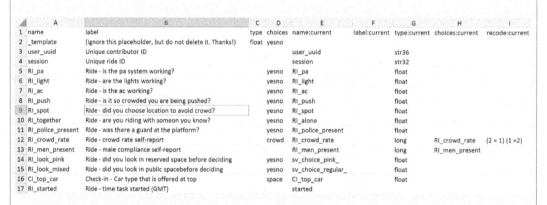

	A	B	C	D	E	F	G	H	I
1	name	label	type	choices	name:current	label:current	type:current	choices:current	recode:current
2	_template	(Ignore this placeholder, but do not delete it. Thanks!)	float	yesno					
3	user_uuid	Unique contributor ID			user_uuid		str36		
4	session	Unique ride ID			session		str32		
5	RI_pa	Ride - is the pa system working?		yesno	RI_pa		float		
6	RI_light	Ride - are the lights working?		yesno	RI_light		float		
7	RI_ac	Ride - is the ac working?		yesno	RI_ac		float		
8	RI_push	Ride - is it so crowded you are being pushed?		yesno	RI_push		float		
9	RI_spot	Ride - did you choose location to avoid crowd?		yesno	RI_spot		float		
10	RI_together	Ride - are you riding with someon you know?		yesno	RI_alone		float		
11	RI_police_present	Ride - was there a guard at the platform?		yesno	RI_police_present		float		
12	RI_crowd_rate	Ride - crowd rate self-report		crowd	RI_crowd_rate		long	RI_crowd_rate	(2 = 1) (1 =2)
13	RI_men_present	Ride - male compliance self-report			RI_men_present		long	RI_men_present	
14	RI_look_pink	Ride - did you look in reserved space before deciding		yesno	sv_choice_pink_		float		
15	RI_look_mixed	Ride - did you look in public spacebefore deciding		yesno	sv_choice_regular_		float		
16	CI_top_car	Check-in - Car type that is offered at top		space	CI_top_car		float		
17	RI_started	Ride - time task started (GMT)			started				

Column B contains the corrected variable labels, column D indicates the value labels to be used for categorical variables, and column I recodes the underlying numbers in those variables. The differences between columns E and A indicate changes to variable names. Typically, it is strongly recommended not to rename variables at the cleaning stage, because it is important to maintain correspondence with the original data set. However, that was not possible in this case, because the same question had inconsistent variable names across multiple transfers of the data from the technology firm managing the mobile application. In fact, this is one of the two cleaning tasks that

(Box continues on next page)

could not be performed directly through `iecodebook` (the other was transforming string variables to a categorical format for increased efficiency). The following code shows a few examples of how these cleaning tasks were carried out directly in the script:

```
1 * Encode crowd rate
2     encode  ride_crowd_rate, gen(RI_crowd_rate)
3
4 * Reconcile different names for compliance variable
5     replace ride_men_present = approx_percent_men if missing(ride_men_present)
6
7 * Encode compliance variable
8     encode  ride_men_present, gen(RI_men_present)
9
10 * Did you look in the cars before you made your choice?
11 * Turn into dummy from string
12     foreach var in sv_choice_pink sv_choice_regular {
13         gen `var'_ = (`var' == "Sim") if (!missing(`var') & `var' != "NA")
14     }
```

To document the contents of the original data, the team published supplemental materials on GitHub, including the description of tasks shown in the app. All of the codebooks and Excel sheets used by the code to clean and correct data were also included in the documentation folder of the reproducibility package.

For the complete do-file for cleaning the ride task, visit the GitHub repository at https://git .io/Jtgqj. For the corresponding codebook, visit the GitHub repository at https://git.io/JtgNS.

Documenting data cleaning

Throughout the data-cleaning process, extensive inputs are often needed from the people responsible for data collection. Sometimes this is the research team, but often it is someone else. For example, it could be a survey team, a government ministry responsible for administrative data systems (for an example, see Fernandes, Hillberry, and Alcántara 2015), or a technology firm that generates remote-sensing data. Regardless of who originally collected the data, it is necessary to acquire and organize all documentation describing how the data were generated. The type of *documentation* available depends on how the data were collected. For original data collection, it should include field protocols, data collection manuals, survey instruments, supervisor notes, and data quality monitoring reports. For secondary data, the same type of information is useful but often not available unless the data source is a

Data documentation is the process of systematically recording information related to research data work. For more details, see the DIME Wiki at https:// dimewiki.worldbank .org/Data_Documentation.

well-managed data publication. Independent of its exact composition, the data documentation should be stored alongside the data dictionary and codebooks. These files will probably be needed during analysis, and they should be published along with the data, so other researchers may use them for their analysis as well.

FIGURE 5.1 **Data-cleaning tasks and outputs**

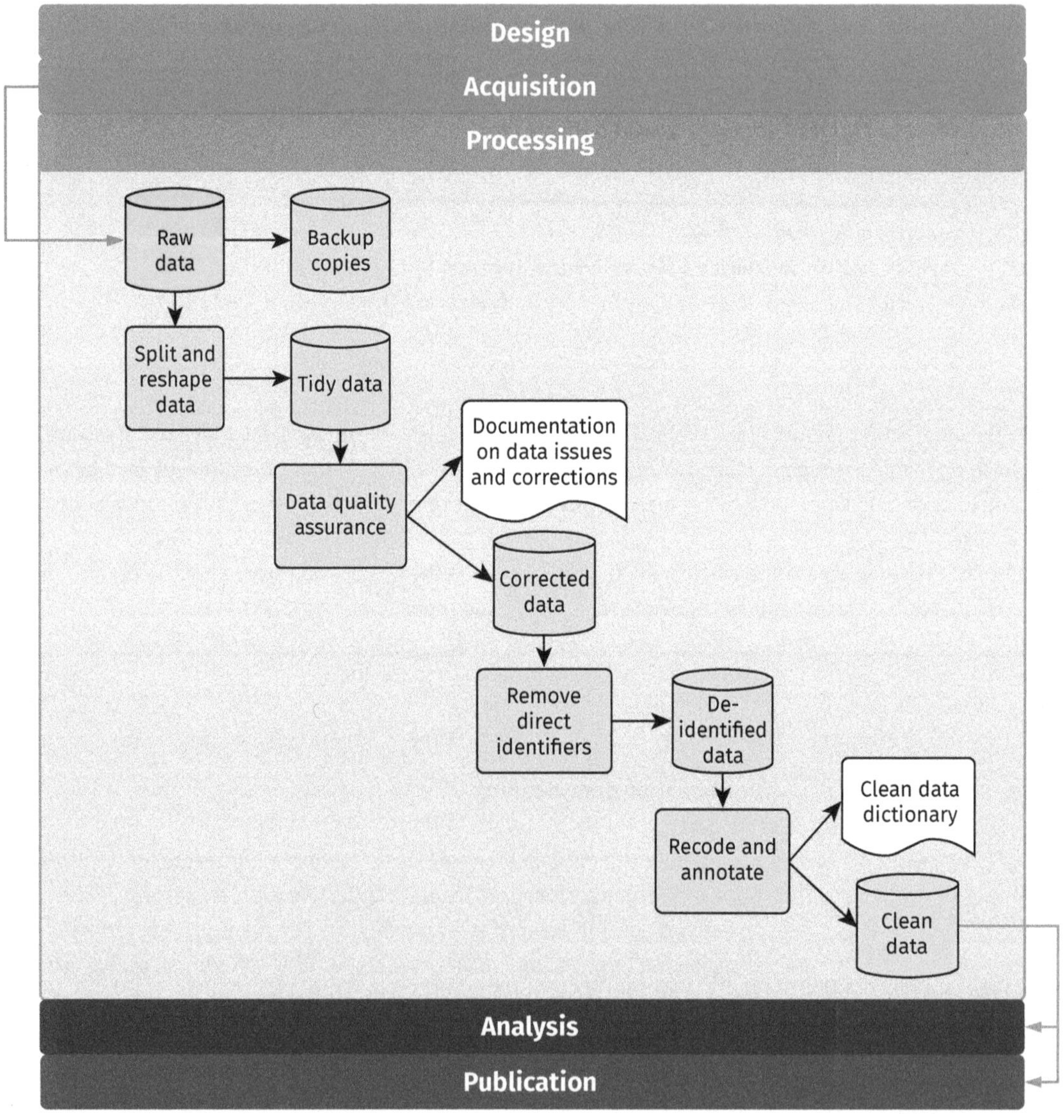

Source: DIME (Development Impact Evaluation), World Bank.

DEVELOPMENT RESEARCH IN PRACTICE: THE DIME ANALYTICS DATA HANDBOOK

Looking ahead

This chapter introduced a workflow for formatting, cleaning, and assuring the quality of original data acquired from the field or from partners, illustrated in figure 5.1. These tasks create the first research output when using original data: a clean data set. This data set is well structured to describe the units of analysis (it is "tidy"), it faithfully represents the measurements it was intended to collect, and it does not expose the identities of the people described by it. The team has taken the time to understand the patterns and structures in the data and has annotated and labeled them for use by the team and by others. Combined with the data map, this data set is the fundamental starting point for all analysis work. Chapter 6 describes the steps needed to run the analyses originally specified in the analysis plan and answer the research question—or perhaps to generate even more questions.

References

Andrade, Luíza, Maria Jones, Sveta Milusheva, Leonardo Viotti. 2021. "How Can We Improve the Quality of Big Data for Development Economics Research? Experiences from Traditional Data Collection Can Help!" *Data Blog* (blog), March 2, 2021. https://blogs.worldbank.org/opendata/how-can-we-improve-quality-big-data-development-economics-research-experiences-traditional.

Banerjee, Abhijit, Eliana La Ferrara, and Victor Orozco. 2019. "Entertainment, Education, and Attitudes toward Domestic Violence." *AEA Papers and Proceedings* 109 (May): 133–37.

Benschop, Thijs, and Matthew Welch. n.d. "Statistical Disclosure Control: A Practice Guide." World Bank, Washington, DC. https://sdcpractice.readthedocs.io/en/latest/.

Fernandes, Ana M., Russell Hillberry, and Alejandra Mendoza Alcántara. 2015. "Trade Effects of Customs Reform: Evidence from Albania." Policy Research Working Paper 7210, World Bank, Washington, DC.

Özler, Berk, Lia C. H. Fernald, Patricia Kariger, Christin McConnell, Michelle Neuman, and Eduardo Fraga. 2016. "Combining Preschool Teacher Training with Parenting Education: A Cluster-Randomized Controlled Trial." Policy Research Working Paper 7817, World Bank, Washington, DC.

Chapter 6

Constructing and analyzing research data

The process of data analysis is typically a back-and-forth discussion between people with differing skill sets. For effective collaboration in a team environment, data, code, and outputs must be well organized and well documented, with a clear system for version control, analysis scripts that all team members can run, and fully automated output creation. Putting in time up front to structure the data analysis workflow in a reproducible manner pays substantial dividends throughout the process. Similarly, documenting research decisions made during data analysis is essential not only for the quality and transparency of research but also for the smooth implementation of a project.

This chapter discusses the steps needed to transform cleaned data into informative outputs such as tables and figures. The suggested work-flow starts where chapter 5 ended, with the outputs of data cleaning. The first section covers variable construction: transforming the cleaned data into meaningful indicators. The second section discusses the analysis code itself. The chapter does not offer instructions on how to conduct specific analyses, because this process is determined by research design, and many excellent guides address this issue. Rather, it discusses how to structure and document data analysis in a fashion that is easy to follow and understand, both for members of the research team and for consumers of research. The third section discusses ways to automate common outputs so that the work is fully reproducible, and the final section discusses tools for incorporating these outputs into fully dynamic documents. Box 6.1 summarizes the main points, lists the responsibilities of different members of the research team, and supplies a list of key tools and resources for implementing the recommended practices.

BOX 6.1 SUMMARY: CONSTRUCTING AND ANALYZING RESEARCH DATA

Moving from raw data to the final data sets used for analysis almost always requires combining and transforming variables into the relevant indicators and indexes. These constructed variables are then used to create analytical outputs, ideally using a dynamic document workflow. Construction and analysis involve three main steps:

1. *Construct variables and purpose-built data sets.* The process of transforming observed data points into abstract or aggregate variables and analyzing them properly requires guidance from theory and is unique to each study. However, it should always follow these protocols:

   - Maintain separate construction and analysis scripts, and put the appropriate code in the corresponding script, even if they are being developed or executed simultaneously.
   - Merge, append, or otherwise combine data from different sources or units of observation, and transform data to appropriate levels of observation or aggregation.
   - Create purpose-built analytical data sets, name and save them appropriately, and use them for the corresponding analytical tasks, rather than building a single analytical data set.
   - Carefully document each of these steps in plain language so that the rationale behind each research decision is clear for any consumer of research.

2. *Generate and export exploratory and final outputs.* Tables and figures are the most common types of analytical outputs. All outputs must be well organized and fully replicable. When creating outputs, the following tasks are required:

   - Name exploratory outputs descriptively, and store them in easily viewed formats.
   - Store final outputs separately from exploratory outputs, and export them using publication-quality formats.
   - Version-control all code required to produce all outputs from analysis data.
   - Archive code when analyses or outputs are not used, with documentation for later recovery.

3. *Set up an efficient workflow for outputs.* Efficient workflow means the following:

   - Exploratory analyses are immediately accessible, ideally created with dynamic documents, and can be reproduced by executing a single script.
   - Code and outputs are version-controlled so it is easy to track where changes originated.
   - Final figures, tables, and other code outputs are exported from the statistical software fully formatted, and the final document is generated in an automated manner, so that no manual workflow is needed to update documents when changes are made to outputs.

Key responsibilities for task team leaders and principal investigators

   - Provide the theoretical framework for and supervise the production of analytical data sets and outputs, reviewing statistical calculations and code functionality.
   - Approve the final list of analytical data sets and their accompanying documentation.
   - Provide rapid review and feedback for exploratory analyses.
   - Advise on file format and design requirements for final outputs, including dynamic documents.

(Box continues on next page)

Creating analysis data sets

This chapter assumes that the analysis is starting from one or multiple well-documented tidy data sets (Wickham and Grolemund 2017). It also assumes that these data sets have gone through quality checks and have incorporated any corrections needed (see chapter 5). The next step is to construct the variables that will be used for analysis—that is, to transform the cleaned data into analysis data. In rare cases, data might be ready for analysis as acquired, but in most cases the information will need to be prepared by integrating different data sets and creating derived variables (dummies, indexes, and interactions, to name a few; for an example, see Adjognon, van Soest, and Guthoff 2019). The derived indicators to be constructed should be planned during research design, with the preanalysis plan serving as a guide. During variable construction, data will typically be reshaped, merged, and aggregated to change the level of the data points from the *unit of observation* in the original data set(s) to the *unit of analysis*.

Each analysis data set is built to answer a specific research question. Because the required subsamples and units of observation often vary for different pieces of the analysis, it will be necessary to create purpose-built analysis data sets for each one. In most cases, it is not good practice to try to create a single "one-size-fits-all"

The **unit of observation** is the type of entity that is described by a given data set. In tidy data sets, each row should represent a distinct entity of that type. For more details, see the DIME Wiki at https://dimewiki.worldbank .org/Unit_of_Observation.

analysis data set. For a concrete example of what this means, think of an agricultural intervention that was randomized across villages and affected only certain plots within each village. The research team may want to run household-level regressions on income, test for plot-level productivity gains, and check to see if village characteristics are balanced. Having three separate data sets for each of these three pieces of analysis will result in cleaner, more efficient, and less error-prone analytical code than starting from a single analysis data set and transforming it repeatedly.

Organizing data analysis workflows

Variable construction is the process of transforming cleaned data into analysis data by creating the derived indicators that will be analyzed. For more details, see the DIME Wiki at https://dimewiki.worldbank.org/Variable_Construction.

Variable construction follows data cleaning and should be treated as a separate task for two reasons. First, doing so helps to differentiate correction of errors (necessary for all data uses) from creation of derived indicators (necessary only for specific analyses). Second, it helps to ensure that variables are defined consistently across data sets. For example, take a project that has a baseline survey and an endline survey. Unless the two data collection instruments are exactly the same, which is preferable but rare, the data cleaning for each of these rounds will require different steps and will therefore need to be done separately. However, the analysis indicators must be constructed in the same way for both rounds so that they are exactly comparable. Doing this all correctly will therefore require at least two separate cleaning scripts and a unified construction script. Maintaining only one construction script guarantees that, if changes are made for observations from one data set, they will also be made for the other.

In the research workflow, variable construction precedes data analysis, because derivative variables need to be created before they are analyzed. In practice, however, during data analysis, it is common to revisit construction scripts continuously and to explore various subsets and transformations of the data. Even if construction and analysis tasks are done concurrently, they should always be coded in separate scripts. If every script that creates a table starts by loading a data set, reorganizing it in subsets, and manipulating variables, any edits to these construction tasks need to be replicated in all analysis scripts. Doing this work separately for each analysis script increases the chances that at least one script will have a different sample or variable definition. Coding all variable construction and data transformation in a unified script, separate from the analysis code, prevents such problems and ensures consistency across different outputs.

Integrating multiple data sources

To create the analysis data set, it is typically necessary to combine information from different data sources. Data sources can be combined by adding more observations, called "appending," or by adding more

A **data flowchart** is the
component of a data map
that lists how the data sets
acquired for the project are
intended to be combined
to create the data sets
used for analysis. For more
details and an example, see
the DIME Wiki at https://
dimewiki.worldbank
.org/Data_Flow_Charts.

The **data linkage table** is
the component of a data
map that lists all the data
sets in a particular project
and explains how they
are linked to each other.
For more details and an
example, see the DIME Wiki at
https://dimewiki.worldbank
.org/Data_Linkage_Table.

iecodebook is a Stata
command to document
and execute repetitive
data-cleaning tasks such
as renaming, recoding, and
labeling variables; to create
codebooks for data sets; and
to harmonize and append
data sets containing similar
variables. It is part of the
iefieldkit package. For
more details, see the DIME
Wiki at https://dimewiki
.worldbank.org/iecodebook.

variables, called "merging." These are also commonly referred to as "data joins." As discussed in chapter 3, any process of combining data sets should be documented using *data flowcharts*, and different data sources should be combined only in accordance with the *data linkage table*. For example, administrative data may be merged with survey data in order to include demographic information in the analysis, geographic information may be integrated in order to include location-specific controls, or baseline and endline data may be appended to create a panel data. To understand how to perform such operations, it is necessary to consider the unit of observation and the identifying variables for each data set.

Appending data sets is the simplest approach because the resulting data set always includes all rows and all columns from each data set involved. In addition to combining data sources from multiple rounds of data acquisition, appends are often used to combine data on the same unit of observation from multiple study contexts, such as different regions or countries, when the different tables to be combined include the same variables but not the same instances of the unit of observation. Most statistical software requires identical variable names across all data sets appended, so that data points measuring the same attribute are placed in a single column in the resulting combined data set. A common source of error in appending data sets is the use of different units of measurement or different codes for categories in the same variables across the data sets. Examples include measuring weights in kilograms and grams, measuring values in different local currencies, and defining the underlying codes in categorical variables differently. These differences must be resolved before appending data sets. The iecodebook append command in the iefieldkit package was designed to facilitate this process.

Merges are more complex operations than appends, with more opportunities for errors that result in incorrect data points. This is because merges do not necessarily retain all the rows and columns of the data sets being combined and are usually not intended to. Merges can also add or overwrite data in existing rows and columns. Whichever statistical software is being used, it is useful to take the time to read through the help file of merge commands to understand their options and outputs. When writing the code to implement merge operations, a few steps can help to avoid mistakes.

The first step is to write pseudocode to understand which types of observations from each data set are expected to be matched and which are expected to be unmatched, as well as the reasons for these patterns. When possible, it is best to predetermine exactly which and how many matched and unmatched observations should result from the merge, especially for merges that combine data from different levels of observation. The best tools for understanding this step are the three components of the data map discussed in chapter 3. The second step is to think carefully about whether the intention is to keep matched and unmatched observations from one or both data sets or to keep only matching observations. The final step is to run the code to merge the data sets, compare the outcome to the expectations, add comments to explain any exceptions, and write validation code so the script will return an error if unexpected results show up in future runs.

Paying close attention to merge results is necessary to avoid unintentional changes to the data. Two issues that require careful scrutiny are missing values and dropped observations. This process entails reading about how each command treats missing observations: Are unmatched observations dropped, or are they kept with missing values? Whenever possible, automated checks should be added in the script to throw an error message if the result is different than what is expected; if this step is skipped, changes in the outcome may appear after running large chunks of code, and these changes will not be flagged. In addition, any changes in the number of observations in the data need to be documented in the comments, including explanations for why they are happening. If subsets of the data are being created, keeping only matched observations, it is helpful to document the reason why the observations differ across data sets as well as why the team is only interested in observations that match. The same applies when adding new observations from the merged data set.

Some merges of data with different units of observation are more conceptually complex. Examples include overlaying road location data with household data using a spatial match; combining school administrative data, such as attendance records and test scores, with student demographic characteristics from a survey; or linking a data set of infrastructure access points, such as water pumps or schools, with a data set of household locations. In these cases, a key contribution of the research is figuring out a useful way to combine the data sets. Because the conceptual constructs that link observations from the two data sources are important and can take many possible forms, it is especially important to ensure that the data integration is documented extensively and separately from other construction tasks (see box 6.2 for an example of merges followed by automated tests from the Demand for Safe Spaces project).

BOX 6.2 INTEGRATING MULTIPLE DATA SOURCES: A CASE STUDY FROM THE DEMAND FOR SAFE SPACES PROJECT

The research team received the raw crowdsourced data acquired for the Demand for Safe Spaces study in a different level of observation than the one relevant for analysis. The unit of analysis was a ride, and each trip was represented in the crowdsourced data set by three rows, one for questions answered before boarding the train, one for those answered during the trip, and one for those answered after leaving the train. The *Tidying data* example in box 5.3 explains how the team created three intermediate data sets for each of these tasks. To create the ride-level data set, the team combined the individual task data sets. The following code shows how the team assured that all observations had merged as expected, showing two different approaches depending on what was expected.

(Box continues on next page)

```
1 /*****************************************************************************
2 *   Merge ride tasks
3 *****************************************************************************/
4
5     use   "${dt_int}/compliance_pilot_ci.dta", clear
6     merge 1:1  session  using "${dt_int}/compliance_pilot_ride.dta", assert(3) nogen
7     merge 1:1  session  using "${dt_int}/compliance_pilot_co.dta"  , assert(3) nogen
```

The first code chunk shows the quality assurance protocol for when the team expected
that all observations would exist in all data sets so that each merge would have only matched
observations. To test that this was the case, the team used the option assert(3). When two
data sets are merged in Stata without updating information, each observation is assigned
the merge code 1, 2, or 3. A merge code of 1 means that the observation existed in the data
set only in memory (called the "master data"), 2 means that the observation existed only
in the other data set (called the "using data"), and 3 means that the observation existed in
both. The option assert(3) tests that all observations existed in both data sets and were
assigned code 3.

When observations that do not match perfectly are merged, the quality assurance protocol
requires the research assistant to document the reasons for mismatches. Stata's merge result code is,
by default, recorded in a variable named _merge. The Demand for Safe Space team used this variable
to count the number of unique riders in each group and used the command assert to throw an error
if the number of observations in any of the categories changed, ensuring that the outcome remained
stable if the code was run multiple times.

```
1 /*****************************************************************************
2 *   Merge demographic survey
3 *****************************************************************************/
4
5     merge m:1  user_uuid  using "${dt_int}/compliance_pilot_demographic.dta"
6
7 * 3 users have rides data, but no demo
8     unique user_uuid if _merge == 1
9     assert r(unique) == 3
10
11 * 49 users have demo data, but no rides: these are dropped
12    unique user_uuid if _merge == 2
13    assert r(unique) == 49
14    drop if _merge == 2
15
16 * 185 users have ride & demo data
17    unique user_uuid if _merge == 3
18    assert r(unique) == 185
```

For the complete do-file, visit the GitHub repository at https://git.io/JtgYf.

Creating analysis variables

After assembling variables from different sources into a single working data set with the desired raw information and observations, it is time to create the derived indicators of interest for analysis. Before constructing new indicators, it is important to check and double-check the units, scales, and value assignments of each variable that will be used. This step is when the knowledge of the data and documentation developed during cleaning will be used the most. The first step is to check that all categorical variables have the same value assignment, such that labels and levels have the same correspondence across variables that use the same options. For example, it is possible that 0 is coded as "No" and 1 as "Yes" in one question, whereas in another question the same answers are coded as 1 and 2. (Coding binary questions either as 1 and 0 or as TRUE and FALSE is recommended, so that they can be used numerically as frequencies in means and as *dummy variables* in regressions. This recommendation often implies recoding categorical variables like gender to create new binary variables like woman.) Second, any numeric variables being compared or combined need to be converted to compatible scales or units of measure: it is impossible to add 1 hectare and 2 acres and get a meaningful number. New derived variables should be given functional names, and the data set should be ordered so that related variables remain together. Attaching notes to each newly constructed variable if the statistical software allows it makes the data set even more user-friendly.

At this point, it is necessary to decide how to handle any outliers or unusual values identified during data cleaning. How to treat outliers is a research question. There are multiple possible approaches, and the best choice for a particular case will depend on the objectives of the analysis. Whatever the team decides, the decision and how it was made should be noted explicitly. Results can be sensitive to the treatment of outliers; keeping both the original and the new modified values for the variable in the data set will make it possible to test how much the modification affects the outputs. All of these points also apply to the imputation of missing values and other distributional patterns. As a general rule, original data should never be overwritten or deleted during the construction process, and derived indicators, including handling of outliers, should always be created with new variable names.

Two features of data create additional complexities when constructing indicators: research designs with multiple units of observation and analysis and research designs with repeated observations of the same units over time. When research involves different units of observation, creating analysis data sets will probably mean combining variables measured at these different levels. To make sure that constructed variables are consistent across data sets, each indicator should be constructed in the data set corresponding to its unit of observation.

Once indicators are constructed at each level of observation, they may be either merged or first aggregated and then merged with data

Dummy variables are categorical variables with exactly two mutually exclusive values, where a value of 1 represents the presence of a characteristic and 0 represents its absence. Common types include yes/no questions, true/false questions, and binary characteristics such as being below the poverty line. This structure allows dummy variables to be used in regressions, summary statistics, and other statistical functions without further transformation.

containing different units of analysis. Take the example of a project that acquired data at both the student and teacher levels. To analyze the performance of students on a test while controlling for teacher characteristics, the teacher-level indicators would be assigned to all students in the corresponding class. Conversely, to include average student test scores in the analysis data set containing teacher-level variables, the analysis data set would start at the student level, the test score of all students taught by the same teacher would be averaged (using commands like `collapse` in Stata and `summarise` from R's `dplyr` package), and this teacher-level aggregate measure would be merged onto the original teacher data set. While performing such operations, two tasks are important to keep in mind: documenting the correspondence between identifying variables at different levels in the data linkage table and applying all of the steps outlined in the previous section because merges are inevitable.

Finally, variable construction with combined data sets involves additional attention. It is common to construct derived indicators soon after receiving each data set. However, constructing variables for each data set separately increases the risk of using different definitions or samples in each of them. Having a well-established definition for each constructed variable helps to prevent that mistake, but the best way to guarantee that it will not happen is to create the indicators for all data sets in the same script after combining the original data sets.

The most common example is panel data with multiple rounds of data collection at different times. Say, for example, that some analysis variables were constructed immediately after an initial round of data collection and that later the same variables will need to be constructed for a subsequent round. When a new round of data is received, best practice is first to create a cleaned panel data set, ignoring the previous constructed version of the initial round, and then to construct the derived indicators using the panel as input. The DIME Analytics team created the `iecodebook append` subcommand in the Stata package `iefieldkit` to make it easier to reconcile and append data into this type of cleaned panel data set, and the command also works well for similar data collected in different contexts (for instructions and details, see the DIME Wiki at https://dimewiki.worldbank.org/iecodebook).

This harmonization and appending process is done by completing an Excel spreadsheet codebook to indicate which changes in names, value assignments, and value labels should be made so the data are consistent across rounds or settings (Bjärkefur, Andrade, and Daniels 2020). Doing so creates helpful documentation about the appending process. Once the data sets have been harmonized and appended, it is necessary to adapt the construction script so that it can be used on the appended data set. In addition to preventing inconsistencies and documenting the work, this process also saves time and provides an opportunity for the team to review the original code (see box 6.3 for an example of variable construction using a combined data set).

The header of the script that created analysis variables for the crowdsourced data in the Demand for Safe Spaces study is shown below. It started from a pooled data set that combined all waves of data collection. The variable was constructed after all waves had been pooled to make sure that all variables were constructed identically across all waves.

```
 1 /*******************************************************************************
 2 *   Demand for "Safe Spaces": Avoiding Harassment and Stigma                  *
 3 *   Construct analysis variables                                             *
 4 *******************************************************************************
 5
 6    REQUIRES:  ${dt_final}/pooled_rider_audit_rides.dta
 7               ${dt_final}/pooled_rider_audit_exit.dta
 8               ${doc_rider}/pooled/codebooks/label-constructed-data.xlsx
 9
10    CREATES:   ${dt_final}/pooled_rider_audit_constructed_full.dta
11               ${dt_final}/pooled_rider_audit_constructed.dta
12
13    WRITTEN BY: Luiza Andrade, Kate Vyborny, Astrid Zwager
14
15    OVERVIEW:  1 Load and merge data
16               2 Construct new variables
17               3 Recode values
18               4 Keep only variables used for analysis
19               5 Save full data set
20               6 Save paper sample
21
22 *******************************************************************************/
```

For the full construction do-file, visit the GitHub repository at https://git.io/JtgY5. For the do-file in which data from all waves are pooled, visit the GitHub repository at https://git.io/JtgYA.

Documenting variable construction

Because variable construction involves translating concrete observed data points into measures of abstract concepts, it is important to document exactly how each variable is derived or calculated. Careful documentation is linked closely to the research principles discussed in chapter 1. It makes research decisions transparent, allowing someone to look up how each variable was defined in the analysis and what the reasoning was behind these decisions. By reading the documentation, persons who are not familiar with the project should be able to understand the contents of the analysis data sets, the steps taken to create them, and the decision-making process. Ideally, they should also be able to reproduce those steps and recreate the constructed variables. Therefore, documentation is an output of construction as important as the code and data, and it is good practice for papers to have an accompanying data appendix listing the analysis variables and their definitions.

The development of construction documentation provides a good opportunity for the team to have a wider discussion about creating protocols for defining variables: such protocols guarantee that indicators are defined consistently across projects. A detailed account of how variables are created is needed and will be implemented in the code, but comments are also needed explaining in human language what is being done and why. This step is crucial both to prevent mistakes and to guarantee transparency. To make sure that these comments can be navigated more easily, it is wise to start writing a variable dictionary as soon as the team begins thinking about making changes to the data (for an example, see Jones et al. 2019). The variable dictionary can be saved in an Excel spreadsheet, a Word document, or even a plain-text file. Whatever format it takes, it should carefully record how specific variables have been transformed, combined, recoded, or rescaled. Whenever relevant, the documentation should point to specific scripts to indicate where the definitions are being implemented in code.

The `iecodebook export` subcommand is a good way to ensure that the project has easy-to-read documentation. When all final indicators have been created, it can be used to list all variables in the data set in an Excel sheet. The variable definitions can be added to that file to create a concise metadata document. This step provides a good opportunity to review the notes and make sure that the code is implementing exactly what is described in the documentation (see box 6.4 for an example of variable construction documentation).

BOX 6.4 DOCUMENTING VARIABLE CONSTRUCTION: A CASE STUDY FROM THE DEMAND FOR SAFE SPACES PROJECT

In an appendix to the working paper, the Demand for Safe Spaces team documented the definition of every variable used to produce the outputs presented in the paper:

Variable definitions for rider audit demographic survey

Variable	Definition
Age	Median age in years of the rider's age category when demographic survey was responded
Employed	= 1 if rider had part-time or full-time job when responded to demographic survey
High self-reported socio-economic status	= 1 if rider reported being a member of classes A or B
Low education (middle school or less)	= 1 if highest degree obtained by the rider at the time the demographic survey was responded was middle school or lower

(Box continues on next page)

Variable	Definition
Number of Supervia rides in a typical week	Number of times rider would normally ride the Supervia in a typical week during which that rider is not taking any app rides
Single	= 1 if rider was not married when responded to demographic survey
Years of schooling	Number of years equivalent to rider's highest level of education when responded to demographic survey
Young (18–25 years old)	= 1 if rider was between 18 and 25 years old when responded to demographic survey

Appendix B in the working paper presents a set of tables with variable definitions in nontechnical language, including variables collected through surveys, variables constructed for analysis, and research variables assigned by random processes.

For the full set of tables, see appendix B of the working paper at https://openknowledge.worldbank .org/handle/10986/33853.

Writing analysis code

After data have been cleaned and indicators constructed, it is time to start analyzing the data. Many resources deal with data analysis and statistical methods, such as *R for Data Science* (Wickham and Grolemund 2017); *A Gentle Introduction to Stata* (Acock 2018); *Mostly Harmless Econometrics* (Angrist and Pischke 2008); *Mastering 'Metrics* (Angrist and Pischke 2014); and *Causal Inference: The Mixtape* (Cunningham 2021). The discussion here focuses on how to structure code and files for data analysis, not how to conduct specific analyses.

Organizing analysis code

The analysis usually starts with a process called *exploratory data analysis*, which is when researchers begin to look for patterns in the data, create descriptive graphs and tables, and try different statistical tests to understand the results. It progresses into *final analysis* when the team starts to decide which are the "main results"— those that will make it into a research output. Code and code outputs for exploratory analysis are different from those for final analysis. During the exploratory stage, the temptation is to write lots of analysis into one big, impressive, start-to-finish script. Although this is fine when writing the research stream of consciousness into code, it leads to poor practices in the final code, such as not clearing the workspace and not loading a fresh data set before each analysis task.

To avoid mistakes, it is important to take time to organize the code that will be kept—that is, the final analysis code. The result is a curated set of polished scripts that will be part of a reproducibility package. A well-organized analysis script starts with a completely fresh workspace and, for each output it creates, explicitly loads data before analyzing them. This setup encourages data manipulation to be done earlier in the workflow (that is, in separate cleaning and construction scripts). It also prevents the common problem of having analysis scripts that depend on other analysis scripts being run before them. Such dependencies tend to require manual instructions so that all necessary chunks of code are run in the right order. Coding each task so that it is completely independent of all other code, except for the master script, is recommended. It is possible to go so far as to code every output in a separate script, but the key is to make sure that it is clear which data sets are used for each output and which code chunks implement each piece of analysis (see box 6.5 for an example of an analysis script structured like this).

BOX 6.5 WRITING ANALYSIS CODE: A CASE STUDY FROM THE DEMAND FOR SAFE SPACES PROJECT

The Demand for Safe Spaces team split the analysis scripts into one script per output and reloaded the analysis data before each output. This process ensured that the final exhibits could be generated independently from the analysis data. No variables were constructed in the analysis scripts: the only transformation performed was to subset the data or aggregate them to a higher unit of observation. This transformation guaranteed that the same data were used across all analysis scripts. The following is an example of a short analysis do-file:

```
1 /*******************************************************************************
2 *    Demand for "Safe Spaces": Avoiding Harassment and Stigma                  *
3 *******************************************************************************
4     OUTLINE:   PART 1: Load data
5               PART 2: Run regressions
6               PART 3: Export table
7     REQUIRES: ${dt_final}/platform_survey_constructed.dta
8     CREATES:  ${out_tables}/priming.tex
9     WRITEN BY:  Luiza Andrade
10
11 *******************************************************************************
12 *    PART 1: Load data
13 *******************************************************************************/
14
15     use "${dt_final}/platform_survey_constructed.dta", clear
16
17 /*******************************************************************************
18 *    PART 2: Run regressions
19 *******************************************************************************/
20
21     reg scorereputation i.q_group, robust
22     est sto priming1
23
```

(Box continues on next page)

```
24      sum scorereputation
25      estadd scalar mean `r(mean)'
26
27      reg scoresecurity i.q_group, robust
28      est sto priming2
29
30      sum scoresecurity
31      estadd scalar mean `r(mean)'
32
33  /***********************************************************************************
34  *   PART 3: Export table
35  ***********************************************************************************/
36
37      esttab priming1 priming2              ///
38          using "${out_tables}/priming.tex", ///
39          ${star}                           ///
40          tex se replace label              ///
41          nomtitles nonotes                 ///
42          drop(1.q_group)                   ///
43          b(%9.3f) se(%9.3f)                ///
44          scalar("mean Sample mean")        ///
45          posthead("\hline \\[-1.8ex]")     ///
46          postfoot("\hline\hline \end{tabular}")
```

For the complete do-file, and to see how the regression results were exported to a table, visit the GitHub repository at https://git.io/JtgOk.

There is nothing wrong with code files being short and simple. In fact, analysis scripts should be as simple as possible, so whoever is reading them can focus on the concepts, not the coding. Research questions and statistical decisions should be incorporated explicitly in the code through comments, and their implementation should be easy to detect from the way the code is written. This process includes clustering, sampling, and controlling for different variables, to name a few. If the team is working with multiple analysis data sets, the name of each data set should describe the sample and unit of observation it contains. As a decision is made about model specification, the team can create functions and globals (or objects) in the master script to use across scripts. The use of functions and globals helps to ensure that specifications are consistent throughout the analysis. It also makes code more dynamic, because it is easy to update specifications and results through a master file without changing every script (see box 6.6 for an example of this from the Demand for Safe Spaces project).

The Demand for Safe Spaces team defined the control variables in globals in the master analysis script. Doing so guaranteed that control variables were used consistently across regressions. It also provided an easy way to update control variables consistently across all regressions when needed. In an analysis script, a regression that includes all demographic controls would then be expressed as `regress y x ${demographics}`.

```
 1  /****************************************************************************
 2  *   Set control variables
 3  ****************************************************************************/
 4
 5      global star              star (* .1 ** .05 *** .01)
 6      global demographics      d_lowed d_young d_single d_employed d_highses
 7      global interactionvars   pink_highcompliance mixed_highcompliance      ///
 8                               pink_lowcompliance mixed_lowcompliance
 9      global interactionvars_oc pos_highcompliance zero_highcompliance       ///
10                               pos_lowcompliance zero_lowcompliance
11      global wellbeing         CO_concern CO_feel_level CO_happy CO_sad      ///
12                               CO_tense CO_relaxed CO_frustrated CO_satisfied ///
13                               CO_feel_compare
14
15      * Balance variables (Table 1)
16      global balancevars1      d_employed age_year educ_year ride_frequency  ///
17                               home_rate_allcrime home_rate_violent          ///
18                               home_rate_theft grope_pink_cont grope_mixed_cont ///
19                               comments_pink_cont comments_mixed_cont
20      global balancevars2      usual_car_cont nocomp_30_cont nocomp_65_cont  ///
21                               fullcomp_30_cont fullcomp_65_cont
22
23      * Other adjustment margins (Table A7)
24      global adjustind         CI_wait_time_min d_against_traffic CO_switch  ///
25                               RI_spot CI_time_AM CI_time_PM
```

For the complete master do-file from which this code is excerpted, visit the GitHub repository at https://git.io/JtgeT.

Creating this setup entails having an effective data management system, including file naming, organization, and version control. Just as for the analysis data sets, each of the individual analysis files needs to have a descriptive name. File names such as `spatial-diff-in-diff.do`, `matching-villages.R`, and `summary-statistics.py` are clear indicators of what each file is doing and make it easy to find code quickly. If the script files will be ordered numerically to correspond to exhibits as they appear in a paper or report, such numbering should be done closer to publication, because script files will be reordered often during data analysis.

Visualizing data

Data visualization is increasingly popular and is becoming a field of expertise in its own right (Healy 2018; Wilke 2019). Although the same principles for coding exploratory and final data analysis apply to visualizations, creating them is usually more involved than the process of running an estimation routine and exporting numerical results into a table. Some of the difficulty of creating good visualizations of data is due to the difficulty of writing code to create them. The amount of customization necessary to create a nice graph can result in quite intricate commands.

Making a visually compelling graph is hard enough without having to go through many rounds of searching and reading help files to understand the graphical options syntax of a particular software. Although getting each specific element of a graph to look exactly as intended can be hard, the solution to such problems is usually a single well-written search away, and it is best to leave these details to the very last. The trickiest and more immediate problem of creating graphical outputs is getting the data into the right format. Although both Stata and R have plotting functions that graph summary statistics, a good rule of thumb is to ensure that each observation in the data set corresponds to one data point in the desired visualization whenever more complex visualizations are desired. This task may seem simple, but it often requires the use of aggregation and reshaping operations discussed earlier in this chapter.

On the basis of DIME's accumulated experience creating visualizations for impact evaluations, the DIME Analytics team has developed a few resources to facilitate this workflow. First of all, DIME Analytics maintains easily searchable data visualization libraries for both Stata (https://worldbank.github.io/stata-visual-library) and R (https://worldbank.github.io/r-econ-visual-library). These libraries feature curated data visualization examples, along with source code and example data sets, that provide a good sense of what data should look like before code is written to create a visualization. (For more tools and links to other data visualization resources, see the DIME Wiki at https://dimewiki.worldbank.org/Data_visualization.)

The `ietoolkit` package also contains two commands to automate common impact evaluation graphs: `iegraph` plots the values of coefficients for treatment dummies, and `iekdensity` displays the distribution of an outcome variable across groups and adds the treatment effect as a note. (For more on how to install and use commands from `ietoolkit`, see the DIME Wiki at https://dimewiki.worldbank.org/ietoolkit.) To create a uniform style for all data visualizations across a project, setting common formatting settings in the master script is recommended (see box 6.7 for an example of this process from the Demand for Safe Spaces project).

iegraph is a Stata command that generates graphs directly from results of regression specifications commonly used in impact evaluation. It is part of the `ietoolkit` package. For more details, see the DIME Wiki at https://dimewiki.worldbank.org/iegraph.

iekdensity is a Stata command that generates plots of the distribution of a variable by treatment group. It is part of the `ietoolkit` package. For more details, see the DIME Wiki at https://dimewiki.worldbank.org/iekdensity.

The Demand for Safe Spaces team defined the settings for graphs in globals in the master analysis script. Using globals created a uniform visual style for all graphs produced by the project. These globals were then used across the project when creating graphs like the following: twoway (bar cum x, color(${col_aux_light})) (lpoly y x, color(${col_mixedcar})) (lpoly z x, color(${col_womencar})), ${plot_options}.

```
1 /*******************************************************************
2 *   Set plot options
3 *******************************************************************/
4
5     set scheme s2color
6
7     global grlabsize        4
8     global col_mixedcar     `" "18 148 144" "'
9     global col_womencar     purple
10    global col_aux_bold     gs6
11    global col_aux_light    gs12
12    global col_highlight    cranberry
13    global col_box          gs15
14    global plot_options     graphregion(color(white))   ///
15                            bgcolor(white)               ///
16                            ylab(, glcolor(${col_box}))  ///
17                            xlab(, noticks)
18    global lab_womencar     Reserved space
19    global lab_mixedcar     Public space
```

For the complete do-file, visit the GitHub repository at https://git.io/JtgeT.

Creating reproducible tables and graphs

Many outputs are created during the course of a project, including both raw outputs, such as tables and graphs, and final products, such as presentations, papers, and reports. During exploratory analysis, the team will consider different approaches to answer research questions and present answers. Although it is best to be transparent about different specifications tried and tests performed, only a few will ultimately be considered "main results." These results will be exported from the statistical software. That is, they will be saved as tables and figures in file formats that the team can interact with more easily. For example, saving graphs as image files allows the team to review them quickly and to add them as exhibits to other documents. When these code outputs are first being created, it is necessary to agree on where to store them, what software and formats to use, and how to keep track of them. This discussion will save time and effort on two fronts: less time will be spent formatting and polishing tables and graphs that will not make their way into final research products, and it will be easier to remember the paths the team has already taken and avoid having to do the same thing twice. This section addresses key elements to keep in mind when making workflow decisions and outputting results.

Managing outputs

Decisions about storage of outputs are limited by technical constraints and dependent on file format. Plain-text file formats like `.tex` and `.csv` can be managed through version-control systems like Git, as discussed in chapter 2. Binary outputs like Excel spreadsheets, `.pdf` files, PowerPoint presentations, or Word documents, by contrast, should be kept in a synced folder. Exporting all raw outputs as plain-text files, which can be done through all statistical software, facilitates the identification of changes in results. When code is rerun from the master script, the outputs will be overwritten, and any changes (for example, in coefficients or numbers of observations) will be flagged automatically. Tracking changes to binary files is more cumbersome, although there may be exceptions, depending on the version-control client used. GitHub Desktop, for example, can display changes in common binary image formats such as `.png` files in an accessible manner.

Knowing how code outputs will be used supports decisions regarding the best format for exporting them. It is often possible to export figures in different formats, such as `.eps`, `.png`, `.pdf`, or `.jpg`. However, the decision between using Office software such as Word and PowerPoint versus LaTeX and other plain-text formats may influence how the code is written, because this choice often necessitates the use of a particular command.

Outputs generally need to be updated frequently, and anyone who has tried to recreate a result after a few months probably knows that it can be hard to remember where the code that created it was saved. File-naming conventions and code organization, including easily searchable filenames and comments, play a key role in not having to rewrite scripts again and again. Maintaining one final analysis folder and one folder with draft code or exploratory analysis is recommended. The latter contains pieces of code that are stored for reference, but not polished or refined to be used in research products.

Once an output presents a result in the clearest manner possible, the corresponding script should be renamed and moved to the final analysis folder. It is typically desirable to link the names of outputs and scripts—for example, the script `factor-analysis.do` creates the graph `factor-analysis.eps`, and so on. Documenting output creation in the master script running the code is necessary so that a few lines of comments appear before the line that runs a particular analysis script; these comments list data sets and functions that are necessary for the script to run and describe all outputs created by that script (see box 6.8 for how this was done in the Demand for Safe Spaces project).

It is important to document which data sets are required as inputs in each script and what data sets or output files are created by each script. The Demand for Safe Spaces team documented this information both in the header of each script and in a comment in the master do-file where the script was called.

The following is a header of an analysis script called `response.do` that requires the file `platform_survey_constructed.dta` and generates the file `response.tex`. Having this information on the header allows people reading the code to check that they have access to all of the necessary files before trying to run a script.

```
1 /******************************************************************************
2 *    Demand for "Safe Spaces": Avoiding Harassment and Stigma              *
3 ******************************************************************************
4     OUTLINE:   PART 1: Load data
5               PART 2: Run regressions
6               PART 3: Export table
7     REQUIRES:  ${dt_final}/platform_survey_constructed.dta
8     CREATES:   ${out_tables}/response.tex
9 ******************************************************************************/
```

To provide an overview of the different subscripts involved in a project, this information was copied into the master do-file where the script above is called, and the same was done for all of the script called from that master, as follows:

```
1 * Appendix tables ==========================================================
2
3 ******************************************************************************
4 *    Table A1: Sample size description                                     *
5 *--------------------------------------------------------------------------*
6 *    REQUIRES: ${dt_final}/pooled_rider_audit_constructed.dta             *
7 *              ${dt_final}/platform_survey_constructed.dta               *
8 *    CREATES:  ${out_tables}/sample_table.tex                            *
9 ******************************************************************************
10
11    do "${do_tables}/sample_table.do"
12
13 ******************************************************************************
14 *    Table A3: Correlation between platform observations data and rider reports *
15 *--------------------------------------------------------------------------*
16 *    REQUIRES: ${dt_final}/pooled_rider_audit_constructed.dta             *
17 *    CREATES:  ${out_tables}/mappingridercorr.tex                        *
18 ******************************************************************************
19
20    do "${do_tables}/mappingridercorr.do"
21
22 ******************************************************************************
```

(Box continues on next page)

Exporting analysis outputs

As discussed briefly in the previous section, it is not necessary to export each and every table and graph created during exploratory analysis. Most statistical software allows results to be viewed interactively, and doing so is often preferred at this stage. Final analysis scripts, in contrast, must export outputs that are ready to be included in a paper or report. No manual edits, including formatting, should be necessary after final outputs are exported. Manual edits are difficult to reproduce; the less they are used, the more reproducible the output is. Writing code to implement a small formatting adjustment in a final output may seem unnecessary, but making changes to the output is inevitable, and completely automating each output will always save time by the end of the project. By contrast, it is important not to spend much time formatting tables and graphs until it has been decided which ones will be included in research products; see Andrade, Daniels, and Kondylis (2020) for details and workflow recommendations. Polishing final outputs can be a time-consuming process and should be done as few times as possible.

It cannot be stressed too much: do not set up a workflow that requires copying and pasting results. Copying results from Excel to Word is error-prone and inefficient. Copying results from a software console is even more inefficient and totally unnecessary. The amount of work needed in a copy-paste workflow increases rapidly with the number of tables and figures included in a research output and so do the chances of having the wrong version of a result in a paper or report.

Numerous commands are available for exporting outputs from both R and Stata. For exporting tables, Stata 17 includes more advanced built-in capabilities. Some currently popular user-written commands are `estout` (Jann 2005), `outreg2` (Wada 2014), and `outwrite` (Daniels 2019). In R, popular tools include `stargazer` (Hlavac 2015), `huxtable` (Hugh-Jones 2021), and `ggsave` (part of `ggplot2`; Wickham 2016). They allow for a wide variety of output formats. Using formats that are accessible and, whenever possible, lightweight is recommended. *Accessible* means that other people can open them easily. For figures in Stata, accessibility means always using `graph export` to save images as `.jpg`, `.png`, `.pdf`, and so forth, instead of `graph save`, which creates a `.gph` file that can only be opened by Stata. Some publications require "lossless" `.tif` or `.eps` files, which are created by specifying the desired extension. Whichever format is used, the file extension must always be specified explicitly.

There are fewer options for formatting table files. Given the recommendation to use dynamic documents, which are discussed in more detail both in the next section and in chapter 7, exporting tables to `.tex` is preferred. Excel `.xlsx` files and `.csv` files are also commonly used, but they often require the extra step of copying the tables into the final output. The `ietoolkit` package includes two commands to export formatted tables, automating the creation of common outputs and saving time for research; for instructions and details, see the DIME Wiki at https://dimewiki.worldbank.org/ietoolkit. The `iebaltab` command creates and exports balance tables to Excel or LaTeX, and the `ieddtab` command does the same for difference-in-differences regressions.

If it is necessary to create a table with a very specific format that is not automated by any known command, the command can be written manually (using Stata's `filewrite` and R's `cat`, for example). Manually writing the file often makes it possible to write a cleaner script that focuses on the econometrics, not on complicated commands to create and append intermediate matrixes. Final outputs should be easy to read and understand with only the information they contain. Labels and notes should include all of the relevant information that is not otherwise visible in the graphical output. Examples of information that should be included in labels and notes are sample descriptions, units of observation, units of measurement, and variable definitions. For a checklist with best practices for generating informative and easy-to-read tables, see the DIME Wiki at https://dimewiki.worldbank.org/Checklist:_Submit_Table.

Increasing efficiency of analysis with dynamic documents

It is strongly recommended to create final products using a software that allows for direct linkage to raw outputs. In this way, final products will be updated in the paper or presentation every time changes are made to the raw outputs. Files that have this feature are called *dynamic documents*. Dynamic documents are a broad class of tools that enable a streamlined, reproducible workflow. The term "dynamic" can refer to any document-creation technology that allows the inclusion of explicitly encoded links to output files. Whenever outputs are updated, and a dynamic document is reloaded or recompiled, it will automatically include all changes made to all outputs without any additional intervention from the user. This is not possible in tools like Microsoft Office, although tools and add-ons can produce similar functionality. In Word, by default, each

iebaltab is a Stata command that generates balance tables in both Excel and `.tex`. It is part of the `ietoolkit` package. For more details, see the DIME Wiki at https://dimewiki.worldbank.org/iebaltab.

ieddtab is a Stata command that generates tables from difference-in-differences regressions in both Excel and `.tex`. It is part of the `ietoolkit` package. For more details, see the DIME Wiki at https://dimewiki.worldbank.org/ieddtab.

Dynamic documents are files that include direct references to exported materials and update them automatically in the output. For more details, see the DIME Wiki at https://dimewiki.worldbank.org/Dynamic_documents.

object has to be copied and pasted individually whenever tables, graphs, or other inputs have to be updated. This workflow becomes more complex as the number of inputs grows, increasing the likelihood that mistakes will be made or updates will be missed. Dynamic documents prevent this from happening by managing the compilation of documents and the inclusion of inputs in a single integrated process so that copying and pasting can be skipped altogether.

Conducting dynamic exploratory analysis

If all team members working on a dynamic document are comfortable using the same statistical software, built-in dynamic document engines are a good option for conducting exploratory analysis. These tools can be used to write both text (often in Markdown; see https://www.markdownguide.org) and code in the script, and the output is usually a `.pdf` or `.html` file including code, text, and outputs. These kinds of complex dynamic document tools are typically best used by team members working most closely with code and can be great for creating exploratory analysis reports or paper appendixes including large chunks of code and dynamically created graphs and tables. RMarkdown (`.Rmd`) is the most widely adopted solution in R; see https://rmarkdown.rstudio.com. Stata offers a built-in package for dynamic documents—`dyndoc`—and user-written commands are also available, such as `markstat` (Rodriguez 2017), `markdoc` (Haghish 2016), `webdoc` (Jann 2017), and `texdoc` (Jann 2016). The advantage of these tools in comparison with LaTeX is that they create full documents from within statistical software scripts, so the task of running the code and compiling the document is reduced to a single step.

Documents called "notebooks" (such as Jupyter Notebook; see https://jupyter.org) work similarly, because they also include the underlying code that created the results in the document. These tools are usually appropriate for short or informal documents because users who are not familiar with them find it difficult to edit the content, and they often do not offer formatting options as extensive as those in Word. Other simple tools for dynamic documents do not require direct operation of the underlying code or software, simply access to the updated outputs. For example, Dropbox Paper is a free online writing tool that can be linked to files in Dropbox, which are updated automatically anytime the file is replaced. These tools have limited functionality in terms of version control and formatting and should never include any references to confidential data, but they do offer extensive features for collaboration and can be useful for working on informal outputs. Markdown files on GitHub can provide similar functionality through the browser and are version-controlled. However, as with other Markdown options, the need to learn a new syntax may discourage take-up among team members who do not work extensively with GitHub.

Whatever software is used, what matters is that a self-updating process is implemented for table and figures. The recommendations given here are best practices, but each team has to find out what works for it. If a team has decided to use Microsoft Office, for example, there are still a few options for avoiding problems with having to copy and paste. The easiest solution may be for the less code-savvy members of the team to develop the text of the final output pointing to exhibits that are not included inline. If all figures and tables are presented at the end of the file, whoever is developing the code can export them into a Word document using Markdown or simply produce a separate `.pdf` file for tables and figures, so at least this part of the manuscript can be updated quickly when the results change. Finally, statistical programming languages can often export directly to binary formats—for example, using the `putexcel` and `putdocx` commands in Stata can update or preserve formatting in Office documents.

Using LaTeX for dynamic research outputs

Although formatted text software such as Word and PowerPoint are still prevalent, researchers are increasingly choosing to prepare final outputs like documents and presentations using LaTeX, a document preparation and typesetting system with a unique code syntax. Despite LaTeX's significant learning curve, its enormous flexibility in terms of operation, collaboration, output formatting, and styling makes it DIME's preferred choice for most large technical outputs. In fact, LaTeX operates behind the scenes of many other dynamic document tools. Therefore, researchers should learn LaTeX as soon as possible; DIME Analytics has developed training materials and resources available on GitHub at https://github .com/worldbank/DIME-LaTeX-Templates.

The main advantage of using LaTeX is that it updates outputs every time the document is compiled, while still allowing for text to be added and formatted extensively to publication-quality standards. Additionally, because of its popularity in the academic community, the cost of entry for a team is often relatively low. Because `.tex` files are plain text, they can be version-controlled using Git. Creating documents in LaTeX using an integrated writing environment such as TeXstudio, TeXmaker, or LyX is great for outputs that focus mainly on text but also include figures and tables that may be updated. It is good for adding small chunks of code into an output. Finally, some publishers make custom LaTeX templates available or accept manuscripts as raw `.tex` files, so research outputs can be formatted more easily into custom layouts.

Looking ahead

This chapter discussed the steps needed to create analysis data sets and outputs from original data. Combining the observed variables of interest for the analysis (measurement variables) with the information in the data map describing the study design (research variables) creates original data sets that are ready for analysis, as shown in figure 6.1. Doing so is difficult, creative work, and it cannot be reproduced by someone who lacks access to the detailed records and explanations of how the data were interpreted and modified. The chapter stressed that code must be well organized and well documented to allow others to understand how research outputs were created and used to answer the research questions. The next chapter of this book provides a guide to assembling the raw findings into publishable work and describes methods for making data, code, documentation, and other research outputs accessible and reusable alongside the primary outputs.

FIGURE 6.1 **Data analysis tasks and outputs**

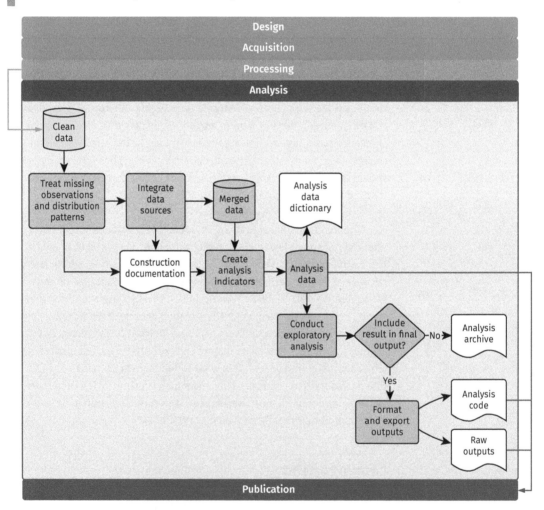

Source: DIME (Development Impact Evaluation), World Bank.

References

Acock, Alan C. 2018. *A Gentle Introduction to Stata,* 6th ed. College Station, TX: Stata Press.

Adjognon, Guigonan Serge, Daan van Soest, and Jonas Guthoff. 2019. "Reducing Hunger with Payments for Ecosystem Services (PES): Experimental Evidence from Burkina Faso." Policy Research Working Paper 8974, World Bank, Washington, DC.

Andrade, Luíza, Benjamin Daniels, and Florence Kondylis. 2020. "Nice and Fast Tables in Stata?" *Development Impact* (blog), May 28, 2020. https://blogs.worldbank.org/impactevaluations/nice-and-fast-tables-stata.

Angrist, Joshua D., and Jörn-Steffen Pischke. 2008. *Mostly Harmless Econometrics: An Empiricist's Companion*. Princeton, NJ: Princeton University Press.

Angrist, Joshua D., and Jörn-Steffen Pischke. 2014. *Mastering 'Metrics: The Path from Cause to Effect*. Princeton, NJ: Princeton University Press.

Bjärkefur, Kristoffer, Luíza Cardoso de Andrade, and Benjamin Daniels. 2020. "iefieldkit: Commands for Primary Data Collection and Cleaning." *Stata Journal* 20 (4): 892–915.

Cunningham, Scott. 2021. *Causal Inference: The Mixtape*. New Haven, CT: Yale University Press.

Daniels, Benjamin. 2019. "outwrite: Stata Module to Consolidate Multiple Regressions and Export the Results to a .xlsx, .xls, .csv, or .tex File." Revised December 7, 2019. Statistical Software Components S458581, Department of Economics, Boston College.

Haghish, E. F. 2016. "markdoc: Literate Programming in Stata." *Stata Journal* 16 (4): 964–88. http://www.stata-journal.com/article.html?article = pr0064.

Healy, Kieran. 2018. *Data Visualization: A Practical Introduction*. Princeton, NJ: Princeton University Press.

Hlavac, Marek. 2015. "stargazer: Beautiful LaTeX, HTML, and ASCII Tables from R Statistical Output." Central European Labour Studies Institute, Bratislava, Slovakia.

Hugh-Jones, David. 2021. "huxtable: Easily Create and Style Tables for LaTeX, HTML and Other Formats." https://hughjonesd.github.io/huxtable/.

Jann, Benn. 2005. "Making Regression Tables from Stored Estimates." *Stata Journal* 5 (3): 288–308. http://www.stata-journal.com/article.html?article = st0085.

Jann, Benn. 2007. "Making Regression Tables Simplified." *Stata Journal* 7 (2): 227–44. http://www.stata-journal.com/article.html?article = st0085_1.

Jann, Benn. 2016. "Creating LaTeX Documents from within Stata Using texdoc." *Stata Journal* 16 (2): 245–63. http://www.stata-journal.com/article.html?article = pr0062.

Jann, Benn 2017. "Creating HTML or Markdown Documents from within Stata Using webdoc." *Stata Journal* 17 (1): 3–38. http://www.stata-journal.com/article.html?article = pr0065.

Jones, Maria Ruth, Florence Kondylis, John Ashton Loeser, and Jeremy Magruder. 2019. "Factor Market Failures and the Adoption of Irrigation in Rwanda." Policy Research Working Paper 9092, World Bank, Washington, DC.

Rodriguez, G. 2017. "Literate Data Analysis with Stata and Markdown." *Stata Journal* 17 (3): 600–18. http://www.stata-journal.com/article.html?article = pr0067.

Wada, Roy. 2014. "outreg2: Stata Module to Arrange Regression Outputs into an Illustrative Table." Revised August 17, 2014. Statistical Software Components S456416, Department of Economics, Boston College, Boston, MA.

Wickham, Hadley. 2016. *ggplot2: Elegant Graphics for Data Analysis.* New York: Springer-Verlag. https://ggplot2.tidyverse.org.

Wickham, Hadley, and Garrett Grolemund. 2017. *R for Data Science: Import, Tidy, Transform, Visualize, and Model Data.* 1st ed. Sebastopol, CA: O'Reilly Media.

Wilke, Claus O. 2019. *Fundamentals of Data Visualization: A Primer on Making Informative and Compelling Figures.* Sebastopol, CA: O'Reilly Media.

Chapter 7

Publishing reproducible research outputs

Publishing research typically involves preparing many iterations of data, code, and code output files, with inputs from multiple collaborators. This process can quickly become unwieldy. It is in nobody's interest for a skilled and busy researcher to spend days renumbering figures, tables, or references when a reasonable amount of up-front effort can automate the task. Similarly, simultaneous collaboration should not involve the repetitive and error-prone task of manually resolving sets of track-change documents with conflicting edits. Furthermore, for most development research projects, a working paper or a policy brief is not the end of the publication stage. Academic journals and research consumers increasingly require reproducibility packages containing the data, code, and supporting materials needed to recreate the results. All working papers resulting from DIME projects are required to produce a reproducibility package and pass a reproducibility check. Replication materials make an intellectual contribution in their own right, because they enable others to learn from the process and better understand the results obtained. If the analysis process is organized according to the general principles outlined in earlier chapters, publication will not require substantial reorganization of the work already done. Hence, publication is the culmination of the system of transparent, reproducible, and credible research introduced in the first chapter of this book.

This chapter recommends tools and workflows for efficiently managing collaboration on research and policy outputs and ensuring reproducible results. The first section discusses how to use dynamic documents to collaborate on writing. The second section covers how to prepare and publish original data, an important research contribution in its own right. The third section provides guidelines for preparing functional and informative reproducibility packages. In all cases, technology is evolving rapidly, and the specific tools noted here may not remain cutting-edge, but the core principles involved in publication and transparency will endure. Box 7.1 summarizes the main points, lists the responsibilities of different members of the research team, and supplies a list of key tools and resources for implementing the recommended practices.

BOX 7.1 SUMMARY: PUBLISHING REPRODUCIBLE RESEARCH OUTPUTS

Whether writing a policy brief or academic article or producing some other kind of research product, it is important to create *three final outputs* that are ready for public release (or internal archiving if not public).

1. *The data publication package.* If the researcher holds the rights to distribute data that have been collected or obtained, this information should be made available to the public as soon as feasible. This release should

   - Contain all nonidentifying variables and observations originally collected in a widely accessible format, with a data codebook describing all variables and values;
   - Contain original documentation about the collection of the data, such as a survey questionnaire, API script, or data license;
   - Be modified or masked only to correct errors and to protect the privacy of people described in the data; and
   - Be appropriately archived and licensed, with clear terms of use.

2. *The research reproducibility package.* Either researchers or their organization will typically have the rights to distribute the code for data analysis, even if access to the data is restricted. This package should

   - Contain all code required to derive analysis data from the published data;
   - Contain all code required to reproduce research outputs from analysis data;
   - Contain a README file with documentation on the use and structure of the code; and
   - Be appropriately archived and licensed, with clear terms of use.

3. *The written research product(s).* These products should be

   - Written and maintained as a dynamic document, such as a LaTeX file;
   - Linked to the locations of all code outputs in the code directory;
   - Recompiled with all final figures, tables, and other code outputs before release; and
   - Authored, licensed, and published in accordance with the policies of the organization or publisher.

Key responsibilities for task team leaders and principal investigators

   - Oversee the production of outputs, and know where to obtain legal or technical support if needed.
   - Have original legal documentation available for all data.
   - Understand the team's rights and responsibilities regarding data, code, and research publication.
   - Decide among potential publication locations and processes for code, data, and written materials.
   - Verify that replication material runs and replicates the outputs in the written research product(s) exactly.

(Box continues on next page)

Key responsibilities for research assistants

- Rework code, data, and documentation to meet the specific technical requirements of archives or publishers.
- Manage the production process for collaborative documents, including technical administration.
- Integrate comments or feedback, and support proofreading, translation, typesetting, and other tasks.

Key resources

- Published data sets in the DIME Microdata Catalog at https://microdata.worldbank.org/index.php/catalog/dime/about
- Access to DIME LaTeX resources and exercises at https://github.com/worldbank/DIME-LaTeX-Templates
- DIME Research Reproducibility Standards at https://github.com/worldbank/dime-standards
- Template README for social science replication packages at https://doi.org/10.5281/zenodo.4319999

Publishing research papers and reports

Development research is increasingly a collaborative effort. This trend reflects changes in the economics discipline overall: the number of sole-authored research outputs is decreasing, and the majority of recent papers in top journals have three or more authors (Kuld and O'Hagan 2017). As a consequence, documents typically pass back and forth between several writers before they are ready for publication or release. As in all other stages of the research process, effective collaboration requires the adoption of tools and practices that enable version control and simultaneous contributions. This book, for example, was written in dynamic document formats (LaTeX and Markdown) and managed on GitHub. All the versions and the history of changes can be viewed at https://github.com/worldbank/dime-data-handbook. As outlined in chapter 6, *dynamic documents* are a way to simplify writing workflows: updates to code outputs that appear in these documents, such as tables and figures, can be passed into the final research output with a single click, rather than being copied and pasted or otherwise handled individually. Managing the writing process in this way improves organization and reduces error, such that there is no risk that materials will be compiled with out-of-date results or that completed work will be lost or redundant.

Using LaTeX for written documents

As discussed in chapter 6, LaTeX is currently the most widely used software for dynamically managing formal manuscripts and policy outputs. It is also becoming more popular for shorter documents, such as policy briefs, with the proliferation of skills and templates for these kinds of products. LaTeX uses explicit references to the file path of each code output (such as tables and figures), which are reloaded from these locations every time the final document is compiled. This is not possible by default in, for example, Microsoft Word. There, you have to copy and paste each object whenever tables, graphs, or other inputs are updated. As time goes on, it becomes increasingly likely that a mistake will be made or something will be missed. In LaTeX, instead of writing in a "what-you-see-is-what-you-get" mode as is done in Word, writing is done in plain text in a `.tex` file, interlaced with coded instructions formatting the document and linking to exhibits (similar to HTML). LaTeX manages tables and figures dynamically and includes commands for simple markup such as font styles, paragraph formatting, section headers, and the like. It includes special controls for footnotes and endnotes, mathematical notation, and bibliography preparation. It also allows publishers to apply global styles and templates to written material, reformatting entire documents in a house style with only a few keystrokes.

Although LaTeX *can* produce complex formatting, such formatting is rarely needed for academic publishing because academic manuscripts are usually reformatted according to the style of the publisher. (Researchers creating policy briefs and other self-produced documents may desire extensive typesetting and investments in custom templates and formatting.) In academia at least, it is rarely worth the investment to go beyond basic LaTeX tools: the title page, sections and subsections, figures and tables, mathematical equations, bolding and italics, footnotes and endnotes, and, last but not least, references and citations. Many of these functionalities, including dynamic updating of some outputs, can be achieved in Microsoft Word through the use of plugins and careful workflows. If it is possible to maintain such a workflow, then this approach is acceptable, but moving toward the adoption of LaTeX is recommended when possible.

One of the most important tools available in LaTeX is the BibTeX citation and bibliography manager (Kopka and Daly 1995). BibTeX keeps all of the references that might be used in a `.bib` file and then references them using a simple command typed directly in the document. Specifically, LaTeX inserts references in text using the `cite` command. Once this is written, LaTeX automatically pulls all the citations into text and creates a complete bibliography based on the citations used to compile the document. The system makes it possible to specify exactly how references should be displayed in text (for example, as superscripts or as inline references) as well as how the bibliography should be styled and in what order (such as Chicago, Modern Language Association, Harvard, or other common styles). The same principles that apply to figures and tables are therefore applied here: references are changed in one place (the `.bib` file), and then everywhere they are used they are updated consistently with a single process. BibTeX is used so widely that it is natively integrated in Google Scholar. Because different publishers have different requirements, it is quite useful to be able to adapt this and other formatting very quickly, including through publisher-supplied templates where available.

Because it follows a standard code format, LaTeX has one more useful trick: the ability to convert raw documents into Word or several other formats using utilities such as `pandoc`, a free and open-source document converter (https://pandoc.org). Even though conversion to Word is required for some academic publishers and can even be preferred for some policy outputs, using LaTeX to prepare these products is still recommended. Exporting to Word should be done only at the final stage, when submitting materials. A `.csl` file (https://github.com /citation-style-language/styles), which styles the citations in a document, can also be applied automatically in this process so references follow the style of nearly any journal desired. Therefore, even if it is necessary to provide `.docx` versions or track-change versions of materials to others, these versions can be created effortlessly from a LaTeX document using external tools like Word's compare feature to generate integrated track-change versions when needed.

Getting started with LaTeX as a team

Although starting to use LaTeX may be challenging, it offers valuable control over the writing process. Because it is written in a plain-text file format, `.tex` can be version-controlled using Git. Contributions and version histories can be managed using the same system recommended for data work. DIME Analytics has created a variety of templates and resources that can be adapted to different needs, available at https:// github.com/worldbank/DIME-LaTeX-Templates. Integrated editing and compiling tools like TeXstudio (https://www.texstudio.org) and `atom-latex` (https://atom.io/packages/atom-latex) offer the most flexibility to work with LaTeX in teams.

Although ultimately worth the effort, setting up LaTeX environments locally is not always simple, particularly for researchers who are new to working with plain-text code and file management. LaTeX requires all formatting to be done in its special code language and is not always informative when something has been done wrong. This situation can be off-putting very quickly for people who simply want to begin writing, and those who are not used to programming may find it difficult to acquire the necessary knowledge.

Cloud-based implementations of LaTeX can make it easier for the team to use LaTeX without all members having to invest in new skills or set up matching software environments; they can be particularly useful for first forays into LaTeX writing. One example of cloud-based implementation is Overleaf (https://www.overleaf.com). Most such sites offer a subscription feature with useful extensions and various sharing permissions, and some offer free-to-use versions with basic tools that are sufficient for a broad variety of applications, up to and including writing a complete academic paper with coauthors.

Cloud-based implementations of LaTeX have several advantageous features for teams compared to classic desktop installations. First, because they are hosted completely online, they avoid the inevitable troubleshooting required to set up a LaTeX installation on various personal computers run by different members of a team. Second, they typically maintain a single, continuously synced copy of the document so that different writers do not create conflicted or out-of-sync copies or need to deal with Git themselves to maintain that sync. Third, they typically allow collaborators to edit documents simultaneously, although different services vary the number of collaborators and documents allowed at each subscription tier. Fourth, some implementations provide a "rich text" editor that behaves similarly to familiar tools like Word, so that collaborators can write text directly into the document without worrying too much about the underlying LaTeX coding. Cloud services usually offer a convenient selection of templates so it is easy to start a project and see results right away without knowing a lot of the code that controls document formatting.

Cloud-based implementations of LaTeX also have disadvantages. Some up-front learning is still required, except when using the rich text editor. Continuous access to the internet is necessary, and updating figures and tables may require a file upload that can be tough to automate. Although some services offer ways to track changes and even to integrate a Git workflow, version control is not as straightforward as using Git locally. Finally, cloud-based services also vary dramatically in their ability to integrate with file systems that store code and code outputs, and it is necessary to practice an integrated workflow depending on what is available. Some teams adopt cloud-based tools as a permanent solution, although DIME recommends shifting eventually to local editing and compiling using tools such as TexStudio, while using Git for version control. See box 7.2 for the workflow adopted by the Demand for Safe Spaces team.

BOX 7.2 PUBLISHING RESEARCH PAPERS AND REPORTS: A CASE STUDY FROM THE DEMAND FOR SAFE SPACES PROJECT

The Demand for Safe Spaces project produced a policy brief and a working paper, among other outputs. The policy brief was produced in accordance with the DIME communications protocols. For its production, the graphs exported by R and Stata were saved in .eps format and shared with a designer who adapted them to fit DIME's visual identity. The research paper was written in LaTeX through the Overleaf platform and was published as World Bank Policy Research Working Paper 9269 (Kondylis et al. 2020).

(Box continues on next page)

See the policy brief at http://pubdocs.worldbank.org/en/223691574448705973/Policy-Brief -Demand-for-Safe-Spaces.pdf. **See the working paper at** https://openknowledge.worldbank.org /handle/10986/33853.

Preparing research data for publication

Data publication is the release of data so they can be located, accessed, and cited. For more details, see the DIME Wiki at https://dimewiki .worldbank.org/Publishing _Data. See also pillar 5 of the DIME Research Standards at https://github.com /worldbank/dime-standards.

Although the focus so far has been on written materials, it is also necessary to consider how to publish the data used in research. The open science community views *data publication* both as a citable output and as a necessary transparency measure. Fortunately, it is a conceptually simple task to produce and catalog the required materials. Two separate collections should be cataloged. First, it is necessary to catalog the clean data with all of the variables corresponding directly to fields in the original data set or data collection instrument (this step is not required if the data are secondary data not produced by the team, but explaining carefully the process of acquiring the data is necessary). At the publication stage, if the steps outlined in chapter 5 have been followed, a cleaned data set and supporting documentation will be ready. Projects that did not follow these steps from the beginning, but still need to organize a data release, will find valuable advice in Dupriez and Greenwell (2007).

Second, it is necessary to catalog separately the analysis data set used for the research output being published. This data set is typically included in the replication package for the research output (for an example, see box 7.3). The package should also include the data construction scripts that created transformed and derived indicators, project-specific information such as treatment assignment, and other indicators generated directly by the research team (constructed record linkages are another example). If the workflow recommended in chapter 6 has been followed, all of the necessary files and documentation will be at hand when the publication stage is reached.

De-identifying data for publication

Before publishing data, it is important to perform a careful *final de-identification*. The objective is to reduce the risk of disclosing confidential information in the published data set. Following the workflow outlined in this book, direct identifiers were removed as a first step after acquiring the data (see the discussion of initial de-identification in chapter 5). For the final de-identification, indirect identifiers are also removed, and the statistical *disclosure risk* of the data is assessed. Unlike direct identifiers, for which a link (or lack thereof) to public information is verifiable, indirect identifiers require an assessment of the likelihood that an individual can be singled out in the data and then linked to public information using combinations of available data. For example, seemingly innocuous variables such as US zip code, gender, and date of birth uniquely identify approximately 87 percent of the US population (Sweeney 2000). In development data, information such as the size of a household, the age and marital status of household members, and the types of work or schooling they engage in may be more than enough to identify a person or family from a sufficiently small group.

> **Disclosure risk** is the likelihood that a released data record can be linked with the individual or organization it describes.

Some tools have been developed to help researchers to de-identify data. For example, the `sdcMicro` package (Benschop and Welch, n.d.) has a useful feature for assessing the uniqueness of records. It produces simple measures of the identifiability of records from the combination of potentially indirectly identifying variables and the application of common information-masking algorithms, such as binning, top-coding, and jittering data before release. At this stage, it is necessary to determine how sensitive the results are to these transformations; it may be that masked data cannot be used for the reproducibility package.

There is almost always a trade-off between accuracy and privacy. For publicly disclosed data, privacy should be favored. Stripping identifying variables from a data set may not be sufficient to protect the privacy of respondents, because of the risk of re-identification. One solution is to add noise to the data, as the US Census Bureau has proposed (Abowd 2018). This solution makes explicit the trade-off between data accuracy and privacy. But there are, as of yet, no established norms for such "differential privacy" approaches: most approaches fundamentally rely on judging "how harmful" information disclosure would be. The fact remains that there is always a balance between the release of information (and therefore transparency) and the protection of privacy, and this balance should be examined actively and explicitly. The best step is to compile a complete record of the steps that have been taken so that the process can be reviewed, revised, and updated as necessary.

Removing variables results in loss of information, so the de-identification process requires careful assessment of the potential risk that could be caused by disclosure of a person's identity or personal information. This risk varies widely, depending on the types of information collected and the overall vulnerability of the population. In extreme cases, such as when the population is highly vulnerable and combinations of information are highly specific, it may not be possible to release any data publicly at all. It is still necessary to catalog and cite the data, even if the information cannot be released publicly. In practice, this situation may mean publishing only a catalog entry providing information about the content of the data sets and how future users might request permission to access them (even if someone else will grant that permission). In some cases, it may be possible to release the data set but to embargo specific variables that are required for the analysis but cannot be released publicly. It may be necessary to grant access to the embargoed data for specific purposes, such as a computational reproducibility check required for publication, if done under careful data security protocols and approved by an institutional review board.

Publishing research data sets

Publicly documenting all original data acquired as part of a research project is an important contribution in its own right. Cataloging or archiving original data sets makes a significant contribution in addition to any publication of analysis results. Publicly releasing data allows other researchers to validate the mechanical construction of results, investigate what other results might be obtained from the same population, and test alternative approaches or answer other questions. It fosters collaboration and may enable researchers to explore variables and questions that the team did not have time to address.

The first step toward data publication is choosing the platform for publication. Various options exist; it is important to choose one that provides a digital object identifier (DOI) for the location of the data—even if its URL changes—and a formal citation for the data so that the information can be cited in other research outputs (https://www.doi.org). Two common platforms for development data are the World Bank's Development Data Hub and Harvard University's Dataverse. The World Bank's Development Data Hub (https://datacatalog.worldbank.org) includes a Microdata Catalog and a Geospatial Catalog, where researchers can publish data and documentation for their projects (the Demand for Safe Spaces data were published in the Microdata Catalog, as detailed in box 7.3). The Harvard Dataverse (https://dataverse.harvard.edu) publishes both data and code, and its Datahub for Field Experiments in Economics and Public Policy (https://dataverse.harvard.edu/dataverse/DFEEP) is especially relevant for publishing impact evaluations. Both the World Bank Microdata Catalog and the Harvard Dataverse create data citations for deposited entries. DIME has its own collection of data sets in the Microdata Catalog, accessible at https://microdata.worldbank.org/catalog/dime, where data from DIME projects are published.

Once a platform has been chosen, it is time to determine exactly what data will be published. As mentioned earlier, there are typically two types of data releases for a research project: complete (de-identified) original data sets and derivative data sets used for specific research outputs. Whether the original data set can be published depends on data ownership and licensing agreements. If the data were acquired through a survey that was contracted by the research team, the data most likely belong to the research team, and therefore the team has publication rights to both the original and the derivative data. If data were acquired from a partner through a licensing agreement, the terms of the license will determine publication rights. These data sets should match the survey instrument or source documentation as closely as possible and should not include indicators constructed by the research team. Releasing constructed data is often more straightforward; depending on data licensing, researchers who do not have rights to publish the original data may be able to publish derivative data sets prepared by the research team. These data sets usually contain only the constructed indicators and associated documentation and should also be included in the replication package.

When data are published, how they may be used and what license will be assigned to them have to be determined. It is essential to understand the rights associated with any data release and to communicate them to future users. Material without a license may never be reused. It is best to offer a license that is explicit and details whether and how specific individuals may access the data. Terms of use available in the World Bank Microdata Catalog include, in order of increasing restrictiveness: open access, direct access, and licensed access. *Open access* data are freely available to anyone and simply require attribution. *Direct access* data are available to registered users who agree to use the data for statistical and scientific research purposes only, to cite the data appropriately, and not to attempt to identify respondents or data providers or link the data to other data sets that could allow for reidentification. *Licensed access* data are restricted to users who submit a documented application detailing how they will use the data and who sign a formal agreement governing data use. The user must be acting on behalf of an organization, which will be held responsible for any misconduct. (See https://microdata.worldbank.org/index.php/terms-of-use for more details.)

Published data should be released in a widely recognized format. Although software-specific data sets are acceptable accompaniments to the code (because those precise materials are probably necessary), releasing data sets in plain-text formats, such as .csv files, with accompanying codebooks should be considered, because any researcher can use these files. Additionally, .pdf or code versions of the data collection instrument or survey questionnaire should be released so that readers can understand which data components are collected directly in the field and which are derived. Together with the analysis data set, the code that constructs any derived measures from the clean data set should be released, so that others can learn from the work and adapt it as they like.

Publishing a reproducible research package

Major journals often require researchers to provide both the data and the code required to recreate the results. Some even require the ability to reproduce the results themselves before they will approve a paper for publication (Vilhuber, Turrito, and Welch 2020). Researchers who are producing a policy output, such as an open policy analysis (Hoces de la Guardia, Grant, and Miguel 2018) or some other type of material (for example, see Andrade et al. 2019; Castaneda Aguilar, Debebe, and de Simone 2020; World Bank 2018) may also want to make their materials publicly reproducible. Even if the work is meant for use only inside the sponsoring organization, having a final set of production materials is still a valuable output. This set of materials, taken together, is often referred to as a *reproducibility package*. If the workflows described in this book have been followed, preparing the replication package will require only a small amount of extra work. If not, creating this package may take time. When the replication package has been completed, anyone who downloads it should be able to understand how the code produces results from the data and be able to reproduce them exactly by executing the included master script.

Organizing code for reproducibility

Before the code is released, it should be edited for content and clarity just as if it were written material. The purpose of releasing code is to allow others to understand exactly what was done to obtain the results and to enable them to apply similar methods in future projects. Other researchers should be able to reproduce individual portions of the analysis by making only small adjustments to the code. In either a scripts folder or the root directory, a master script should be included to allow someone else to run the entire project and recreate all raw code outputs by changing only a single line of code setting the root directory path. The code should be both functional and readable, through the use of a clear structure and extensive commenting. Code is often not written this way when it is first prepared, so it is important to review the content and organization so that a new reader can figure out what the code should do and how it does it. It is necessary to invest sufficient time in making code clean and readable before releasing the reproducibility package.

DIME requires all academic outputs to pass a computational reproducibility check before being submitted for publication. Several practices and requirements have been adopted to support the production of high-quality reproducibility packages. The materials for these practices are publicly available and are useful for checking the reproducibility of work. This reproducibility check is initiated by submitting a reproducibility package checklist, which is available in Pillar 3 of the DIME Standards GitHub repository at https://github.com/worldbank/dime-standards. DIME projects are required to organize code with a master script, to facilitate handovers across team members, and to make the computational reproducibility check a one-click exercise. Compliance with these and other coding standards at DIME is monitored through quarterly rounds of peer code reviews, which allow research assistants to improve their code and documentation as they are written, rather than having to revisit them in a rush near publication time. DIME projects are also expected to use Git and GitHub to document project work and collaboration and to keep the main branch up-to-date as a working edition.

Before a reproducibility package is publicly released, it is essential to make sure that the code runs and produces the same results on the current setup and on a fresh installation of the software. To ensure that code will run completely on a new computer, any required user-written commands in the master script have to be installed. In Stata, the commands `ssc install` or `net install` can be used to install them. In R, options include the base command `install.packages` and functions in the `pacman` package. Remember to indicate the package version if relevant (in R, the `renv` package helps with tracking package versions). In Stata, it may be preferable to provide the underlying code for any user-installed packages needed to ensure forward compatibility. System settings like software version and memory used may also need to be defined when using Stata. The `ieboilstart` command defines and applies these settings for a chosen Stata version.

Finally, code inputs and outputs need to be identified clearly. A new user should, for example, be able to find and quickly recreate any files generated by the code, locate an output in the code, and correspond code to its outputs. Code should be broken into separate scripts as much as possible to minimize the need to search through long files. Someone reading the code should be able to figure out fairly easily what state the

`ieboilstart` is a Stata command to standardize version, memory, and other Stata settings across all users for a project. It is part of the `ietoolkit` package. For more details, see the DIME Wiki at https://dimewiki .worldbank.org/ieboilstart.

program will be in at any point without scrolling through hundreds of lines; similarly, they should not have to look in different files or faraway sections of code to make changes to outputs. Each file should be an understandable, independent selection of related processes. Readers should also be able to map all of the outputs of the code easily to where they appear in the associated published material, so it is necessary to ensure that the raw components of figures or tables are identified. For example, code outputs should correspond by name to an exhibit in the paper and vice versa. Documentation in the master script is often used to indicate this information, and supplying a compiling LaTeX document can also support this task. Code and code outputs not used in the final paper should be removed from the final replication package and archived for transparency.

Releasing a reproducibility package

Once the replication package has been prepared for public release, it is time to find a place to publish the materials. At the time of writing this handbook, there is no consensus on the best solution for publishing code, and different archives and storage providers cater to different needs. The technologies available are likely to change dramatically over the next few years; this section highlights the strengths and weaknesses of some current approaches.

Features to look for in a platform on which to release reproducibility packages include the possibility to store data and documentation as well as code, the creation of a static copy of content that cannot be changed or removed, and the assignment of a permanent DOI. Unlike data, code usually has few external constraints to publication. The research team owns the code in almost all cases, and code is unlikely to contain identifying information (though it is important to verify that it does not). Publishing code also requires assigning a license to it; most code publishers offer permissive licensing options. In the absence of a license, no one can reuse the code. It is common to, at most, require attribution and citation for reuse, without any barriers or restrictions to code access.

GitHub is one option for creating and releasing a reproducibility package. Making a public GitHub repository is free. The repository can hold any type of file; provide a structured, compressed download of the whole project; and allow others to look at alternate versions or histories. It is straightforward to upload a fixed directory to GitHub, apply a sharing license, and obtain a URL for the whole package. There is a strict size restriction of 100 megabytes per file and 100 gigabytes for the repository as a whole, so larger projects will need alternative solutions. However, GitHub is not the ideal platform on which to publish reproducibility packages. It is built to version-control code and to facilitate collaboration on it. It is not an archive, meaning that it does not guarantee the permanence of uploaded materials or the access URL, and it does not manage citations or noncode licenses by default. One suggestion is to combine

GitHub with Zenodo (https://zenodo.org) or the Open Science Framework (OSF; https://osf.io), which can link easily to and import material from GitHub and apply a permanent URL, DOI, formal citation, general license, and archival services to it. Other options include the Harvard Dataverse and ResearchGate (https://www.researchgate.net).

Any of the aforementioned archival services is acceptable—the main requirement is that the system can handle the structured directory being submitted and that it can provide a stable URL for the project and report exactly what, if any, modifications have been made since initial publication. It is even possible to combine more than one tool, as long as the tools clearly reference each other. For example, code and the corresponding license can be published on GitHub, while referring to data published on the World Bank Microdata Catalog. Emerging technologies such as the "containerization" approach of CodeOcean (https://codeocean.com) offer to store both code and data in one repository and also provide an online workspace in which others can execute and modify code without having to download the tools and match the local environment used to create it.

In addition to code and data, an author's copy or preprint of the article itself could be released along with these materials, but it is important to check with the publisher before doing so; not all journals will accept material that has been publicly released before its formal publication date, although, in most development research fields, the release of working papers is a fairly common practice. This release can be done on preprint websites, many of which are topic specific. It is also possible to use GitHub or OSF and link to the PDF file directly through a personal website or whatever medium is sharing the preprint. Using file-sharing services such as Dropbox or Google Drive is not recommended for this purpose, because their access is more restrictive, and organizations often restrict access to such platforms.

Finally, any reproducibility package should include an overview of its contents and instructions on how to recreate outputs. Box 7.4 describes how the Demand for Safe Spaces project released its reproducibility package. This overview is typically provided in the form of a README file. A good README file guides the reader through all of the items included in the package. Fortunately, a consortium of social science data editors offers a very good template for such documents, which can be found at https://doi.org/10.5281/zenodo.4319999.

information for the materials, software and hardware requirements including time needed to run, and instructions for accessing and placing the original data before running the code (which must be downloaded separately). Finally, it has a detailed list of the code files that will run, their data inputs, and the outputs of each process.

List of analysis codes and outputs

The provided code reproduces all numbers provided in text in the paper and all tables and figures in the paper, with the exception of Figure A1. Reproducing figure A1 requires access to identified data on riders home location (bolded dataset below).

All analysis code is stored in `dofiles/analysis/paper`. All outputs are saved to `outputs`. All the code can be run from the `Master.do` script, but the code to recreate each exhibit can also be run independently, as long as the folder globals and custom programs are set using the master.

Exhibit	Input dataset	Program	Output file
Numbers in text	pooled_rider_audit_constructed.dta platform_survey_constructed.dta	Numbers in main text.do	
Figure 2	pooled_rider_audit_constructed.dta	graphs/eventstudy_bypremium.do	graphs/eventstudy_bypremium.png
Figure 3	pooled_rider_audit_constructed.dta	graphs/takeup.do	graphs/takeup_fe.png graphs/takeup_person.png
Figure 4	pooled_rider_audit_constructed.dta	graphs/wtp_harass.do	graphs/wtp_harass.png

README.md

Demand for "Safe Spaces": Avoiding Harassment and Stigma

This repository contains the supplemental material and replication package for the Working Paper "Demand for 'Safe Spaces': Avoiding Harassment and Stigma" by Florence Kondylis, Arianna Legovini, Kate Vyborny, Astrid Zwager, and Luiza Andrade.

Abstract

What are the costs to women of harassment on public transit? We randomize the price of a women-reserved "safe space" in Rio de Janeiro and crowd-source information on 22,000 rides. Women in the public space experience harassment once a week. A fourth of riders are willing to forgo 20% of the fare to ride in the "safe space". Randomly assigning riders to the "safe space" reduces physical harassment by 50%, implying a cost of $1.45 per incident. Implicit Association Tests show that women face a stigma for riding in the public space which may outweigh benefits of the safe space.

Repository Content

- Most recent version of full paper
- Online appendix: Robustness Checks & Supplemental Material
- Reproducibility Package

(Box continues on next page)

README.md

Demand for "Safe Spaces": Avoiding Harassment and Stigma

This folder contains the reproducibility package for the Working Paper "Demand for 'Safe Spaces': Avoiding Harassment and Stigma" by
Florence Kondylis, Arianna Legovini, Kate Vyborny, Astrid Zwager, and Luiza Andrade.

If you run into any troubles running this code or reproducing results, please create an Issue in this repository.

License for Code

The code is licensed under a Creative Commons license. See LICENSE for details.

Computational requirements

Software Requirements

- Stata (code was last run with version 16)
    - estout (3.23)
    - iefieldkit (2.0)
    - ietoolkit (6.3)
    - unique (1.2.4)
    - coefplot (1.8.3)
    - the program " MASTER.do " will install all dependencies locally if the local packages in line 30 is set to 1.

Memory and Runtime Requirements

- The code was last run on a **Windows 10 laptop with 16GB of RAM.**
- Stata analysis code takes apprixmately 5 minutes to run.

Instructions to Replicators

The code to reproduce the results included in the working paper. To recreate the outputs, follow the steps below

1. Click on the green button Clone or download shown above the list of files in this folder to download a local copy of this repository
2. Open the downloaded folder and navigate to rio-safe-space/Reproducibility Package .
3. The data used for this paper is available in the Microdata Catalogue, under the survey ID number BRA_2015-2016_DSS_v01_M. Copy this
   data to the data folder.
4. On the folder rio-safe-space/Reproducibility Package , you will see two scripts called MASTER : one in R, one in Stata.

See the reproducibility package at https://github.com/worldbank/rio-safe-space.

Looking ahead

This chapter described the culmination of all of the efforts involved in
acquiring, cleaning, processing, and analyzing data—the production
of materials to share with the world that answer a scientific or policy
question in a way that has never been done before. Figure 7.1 provides an
overview of the outputs created by this process. Making sure that everything that was discovered and created is as broadly available and as easy
to use as possible is the last step in producing scientific evidence from
original data. This assurance is the purpose of all the rigor, organization,
and documentation that are encouraged and detailed at every step of the
process: because all of the research materials are continuously organized,
shareable, secure, documented, and readable, they are both valuable to
the research team and accessible to others.

FIGURE 7.1 **Publication tasks and outputs**

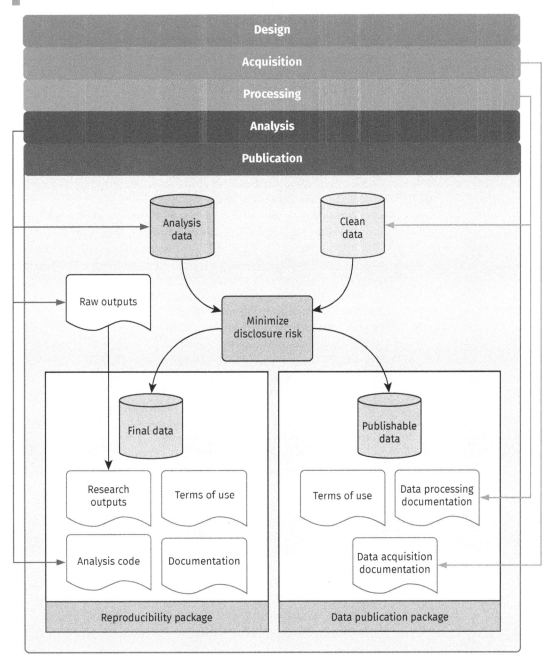

Source: DIME (Development Impact Evaluation), World Bank.

References

Abowd, John M. 2018. "The U.S. Census Bureau Adopts Differential Privacy."
In *KDD '18: Proceedings of the 24th ACM SIGKDD International Conference
on Knowledge Discovery and Data Mining*, 2867. New York: Association for
Computing Machinery.

Andrade, Luíza, Guadalupe Bedoya, Benjamin Daniels, Maria Jones, and Florence
Kondylis. 2019. "What Development Economists Talk about When They
Talk about Reproducibility ..." *Development Impact* (blog), September 16,
2019. https://blogs.worldbank.org/impactevaluations/what-development
-economists-talk-about-when-they-talk-about-reproducibility.

Benschop and Welch. n.d. "Statistical Disclosure Control for Microdata: A Practice
Guide." World Bank, Washington, DC. Retrieved on February 17, 2021. https://
sdcpractice.readthedocs.io/en/latest.

Castaneda Aguilar, R. Andres, Zelalem Yilma Debebe, and Martín de Simone.
2020. "How We Mass-Produced Reproducible Human Capital Project Country
Briefs." *Data Blog*, February 5, 2020. https://blogs.worldbank.org/opendata
/how-we-mass-produced-reproducible-human-capital-project-country-briefs.

Dupriez, Olivier, and Geoffrey Greenwell. 2007. "Quick Reference Guide for Data
Archivists." IHSN Paper, International Household Survey Network. https://guide
-for-data-archivists.readthedocs.io/en/latest/.

Hoces de la Guardia, Fernando, Sean Grant, and Edward Miguel. 2018. "A Framework
for Open Policy Analysis." Berkeley Initiative for Transparency in the Social
Sciences (BITSS), University of California, Berkeley, April 5, 2018.

Kondylis, Florence, Arianna Legovini, Kate Vyborny, Astrid Zwager, and Luíza
Andrade. 2020. "Demand for Safe Spaces: Avoiding Harassment and Stigma."
Policy Research Working Paper 9269, World Bank, Washington, DC.

Kopka, Helmut, and Patrick W. Daly. 1995. "A Guide to LaTeX." *IEEE Multimedia*
2: 473–80.

Kuld, Lukas, and John O'Hagan. 2017. "The Trend of Increasing Co-Authorship in
Economics: New Evidence." *VOX EU CEPR* (blog), December 16, 2017. https://
voxeu.org/article/growth-multi-authored-journal-articles-economics.

Sweeney, Latanya. 2000. "Simple Demographics Often Identify People Uniquely."
Data Privacy Working Paper 3, Data Privacy Lab, Carnegie Mellon University,
Pittsburgh, PA. http://dataprivacylab.org/projects/identifiability/.

Vilhuber, Lars, James Turrito, and Keesler Welch. 2020. "Report by the AEA Data
Editor." *AEA Papers and Proceedings* 110 (May): 764–75.

World Bank. 2018. *Atlas of Sustainable Development Goals 2018: World Development
Indicators (English)*. Washington, DC: World Bank Group. http://documents
.worldbank.org/curated/en/590681527864542864/Atlas-of-Sustainable
-Development-Goals-2018-World-Development-Indicators.

Chapter 8

Conclusion

Development Research in Practice: The DIME Analytics Data Handbook teaches readers to handle data more efficiently, effectively, and ethically at all stages of development research projects. It lays out a start-to-finish vision of the tasks and workflows that a modern development researcher will need to undertake, from planning a project's measurement framework and data strategy to acquiring and analyzing data to publishing the code and data. Each chapter explores key tasks and concepts and provides links to resources and DIME Wiki pages that provide further details and implementation guidance. This structure is intended to allow readers to return to each chapter as they become progressively more familiar with individual topics.

Bringing it all together

Although each chapter is written to stand alone, the recommended workflows detailed in *Development Research in Practice* build on each other. Adopting the best practices from early chapters will allow for easier and more intuitive adoption of workflows and tasks in subsequent chapters. From the design and structure of measurement frameworks and data acquisition to the creation of reproducibility packages and data documentation, this book provides the tools and concepts needed to connect all stages of research coherently rather than undertaking them as discrete tasks. Figure 8.1 offers a visual representation of the interconnections among outputs created over the research data life cycle. It shows how different steps are related, as materials created in one step then feed into the next and eventually create a complete publication package for a research product.

FIGURE 8.1 **Research data work outputs**

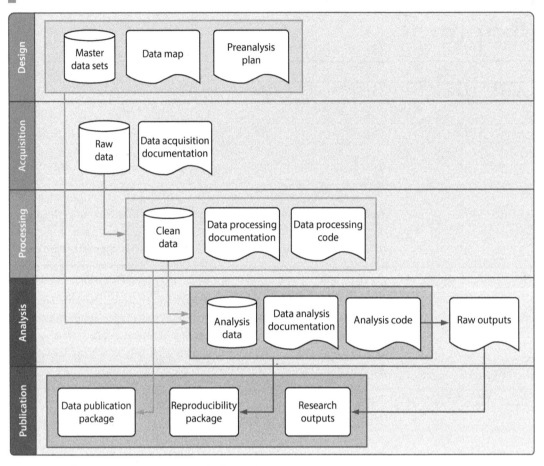

Source: DIME (Development Impact Evaluation), World Bank.

The first chapter begins the book with a discussion of credibility, transparency, and reproducibility in research. The overarching idea is that research should always be accessible and available to others, both within and outside the research team. The handbook treats data work as a "social process" involving multiple team members with different roles and technical abilities. The fundamental theme of accessible open science research provides structure for all subsequent tasks and offers both private and public benefits: data work that is intentionally designed for others to interact with will also be easier for teams to collaborate on and maintain over time.

This idea is carried through to the second chapter, which introduces the reader to the technical tools and concepts needed to develop a work environment conducive to accessible research. An open science approach necessitates cooperation with a diverse group of collaborators using modern approaches to computing technology. It requires collective agreement on specific tools and methods of collaboration and record keeping as well as on technical approaches like version control, file sharing, and directory organization.

The third chapter translates research design into a specific measurement framework and data map. The perspective of reproducible research emphasizes the need to clarify and document how data will describe the research design and record scientific measurements. The documentation-centric data map approach ensures that a research team agrees how multiple data sources are intended to be linked without error and how the structure of those data corresponds to the research design. It also describes how to use these concepts to implement research design through reproducible routines for sampling and randomization and discusses how to analyze and document statistical power.

The fourth chapter turns to modern data acquisition methods and governance frameworks, including data licensing, data ownership, electronic data collection, and data security. Establishing clear data ownership and publication rights at this stage is essential to creating open, reproducible outputs at publication. For researchers undertaking primary data collection, the chapter details how to prepare for and implement high-quality electronic surveys and how to document data structure and data quality. Finally, the chapter describes how to ensure that all data sets are stored properly and securely to protect the privacy of research participants and prevent data loss.

The fifth chapter provides a detailed workflow for data cleaning and processing, emphasizing tidy data, quality control, privacy protection, and documentation. The workflow calls upon outputs created in previous stages, relying on the data map and survey documentation to guide the creation of analysis-ready data sets. The chapter offers specific consideration of how to structure data sets at the correct units of observation, connecting each unit to the project's overarching measurement framework through appropriate identification variables. By the end of the data-cleaning process, all data points are corrected, variables and values are labeled, duplicates are resolved, and identifying information is removed from working copies of the data sets so they can be processed more rapidly in the analytical stage that follows in the workflow.

The sixth chapter details how to construct data sets that are deliberately structured for analysis, analyze them effectively and efficiently, and generate reproducible outputs. The chapter separates data construction, exploratory analysis, and final analysis—in code as well as in human-readable dynamic documents—so that final outputs can be incorporated easily into research outputs for publication. Separating out the final analysis also has the advantage of producing code that is nearly ready for publication and reproducibility as written, usually requiring only minor modifications for release.

The seventh chapter provides an overview of the workflow required to move research results to publication—no matter the format of the output—as well as the tools and practices for making research publicly accessible. It becomes clear that following recommended practices at all stages of the research life cycle greatly simplifies the final publication process. The chapter gives extensive attention to the collaborative preparation of research outputs, bringing together technical outputs like figures and tables with versatile formatting, collaboration, and version-control tools in LaTeX documents. It then provides guidelines both for releasing and licensing data in a way that balances the twin responsibilities of privacy and access and for structuring code so that it is accessible and useful to other readers. The final output is a reproducibility package that brings together all of the final materials from the project in a single location, fulfilling the goals laid out in the first chapter.

Where to go from here

Throughout *Development Research in Practice*, the narrative provides enough detail for readers to understand the purpose and function of each of the core research steps and how they link together. For readability, the number of technical details and implementation guidelines provided directly in the text is limited. Instead, this book provides a wide variety of resources for readers to continue building their knowledge and skills. Sidenotes throughout the book link to DIME Wiki pages detailing specific protocols, code conventions, and field procedures that DIME considers best practices. References to theoretical papers are included to help researchers to figure out how to handle the unique cases that will undoubtedly arise, and references to examples of various techniques and situations are also provided throughout.

The book includes case studies from the Demand for Safe Spaces project, which are used to show how the research tasks described are implemented in practice and eventually prepared and released to the public. By accessing the various repositories and resources linked from the Demand for Safe Spaces case study, readers can examine the original materials and research outputs from a completed DIME project in detail, including the code and data used to produce them.

This edition of *Development Research in Practice* also has three appendixes covering important topics that do not fall within the research workflow at any particular point. Appendix A, the DIME Analytics Coding Guide, includes a general discussion of considerations for writing good code as part of a research team and instructions for accessing the code examples throughout the book, and the style guide that DIME uses for coding in Stata. Appendix B, the DIME Analytics Resource Directory, provides pointers and descriptions for the materials, trainings, code tools, and other public goods produced by DIME Analytics to improve the quality of development research. Appendix C, which focuses on research design for impact evaluation, provides an overview of modern methods for work in causal inference and program evaluation, with extensive links to the DIME Wiki and references to the literature.

This diverse set of resources is intended to allow readers to continue learning at the level of detail that is appropriate to their role. It provides accessible and useful approaches for everyone seeking to improve their understanding of the research process or its practical considerations—from project managers and principal investigators to research assistants and field staff to students as well as to research partners and consumers. The introduction to each chapter includes key responsibilities for different members of a typical research team. A useful first task for a research team after reading this book would be to discuss these key responsibilities in the context of the team's research projects.

The DIME Analytics team hopes that this book, its appendixes, and the wide range of resources and examples highlighted throughout will serve as a useful guide for anyone who participates in or interacts with development research. The book is also a living document, with a live version available online at https://worldbank.github.io/dime-data-handbook and a GitHub repository for inputs, discussions, and revisions at https://github.com/worldbank/dime-data-handbook. Both are publicly available, and readers are invited to participate in the active improvement of this book and all of the related resources that DIME Analytics maintains, especially the DIME Wiki (https://dimewiki.worldbank.org).

Appendix A

The DIME Analytics Coding Guide

Most academic programs that prepare students for a career in the type of work discussed in this book spend a disproportionately small amount of time teaching students coding skills in relation to the share of professional time those students will spend writing code in their first few years after graduation. Recent masters-level graduates joining the DIME team have demonstrated very good theoretical knowledge but require a lot of training in practical skills. This is like an architecture graduate having learned how to sketch, describe, and discuss the concepts and requirements of a new building very well, but lacking the technical ability to contribute to a blueprint following professional standards that others can use and understand. The reasons for this disconnect are a topic for another book, but, in today's data-driven world, people working in quantitative development research must be proficient collaborative programmers, which requires more than being able to compute correct numbers.

This appendix starts by offering general and language-agnostic principles on how to write "good" code. Good code not only generates correct results *but also* is easily read and adapted by other professionals. The second section contains instructions on how to access and use the code examples provided in this book. The last section presents the DIME Analytics Stata Style Guide. Widely accepted and used style guides are common in most programming languages, but, as yet, there is no sufficiently encompassing style guide for Stata. The DIME Analytics Stata Style Guide is intended to increase the emphasis given to using, improving, sharing, and standardizing code style among the Stata community. It shares practices that greatly improve the quality of research projects coded in Stata. By applying the guidance provided in this appendix, readers will learn to write code that, like an architect's blueprint, can be understood and used by everyone in the trade.

Writing good code

Good code has two elements: (1) it is correct, in that it does not produce any errors and its outputs are the objects intended, and (2) it is useful and comprehensible to someone who has not seen it before (or even someone who sees it again weeks, months, or years later). Many researchers have only been trained to code correctly. However, when code runs on a computer and obtains the desired results, the job of writing *good* code is only half done. Good code is easy to read and replicate, making it easier to spot mistakes. Good code reduces sampling, randomization, and cleaning errors. Good code can be reviewed easily by others before it is published and can be reused afterward. The best code is written as if a stranger will be reading it.

Good code has three major elements: structure, syntax, and style. The *structure* is the environment and file organization in which the code lives: good structure means that it is easy to find individual pieces of code, within and across files, that correspond to specific tasks and outputs. It also means that functional code blocks are sufficiently independent from each other such that they can be shuffled around, repurposed, and even deleted without affecting the execution of other portions. The *syntax* is the literal language of code. Good syntax means that the code is readable in terms of how its mechanics implement ideas; it should not require arcane reverse-engineering to figure out what a code chunk is trying to do. It should use common commands in a generally accepted way so that others can easily follow and reconstruct the researcher's intentions. Finally, *style* is the way that the nonfunctional elements of code convey its purpose. Elements like spacing, indentation, and naming conventions (or lack thereof) can make code much more (or much less) accessible to someone who is reading it for the first time and needs to understand it quickly and accurately.

One key tool for writing good code is using help documentation. Regardless of how much experience a person has with a particular programming language—Stata, R, Python, or one of the many others—it is helpful to revisit help files frequently. It is impossible to overemphasize how important it is to get into the habit of reading help files. Even for the most common commands, there is always something new to learn. A help file window should be open at all times, making it easy to look up commands or uses of commands that are unfamiliar or whose functionality has been forgotten. The belief that help files are only for beginners could not be further from the truth. The only way to get better at a programming language is to read help files often. Stata help files can be accessed by writing `help [command]` whenever necessary. For example, to learn about `isid`, writing `help isid` will open the help file for that command.

Using the code examples in this book

This book provides code boxes throughout the chapters that offer examples of good code execution of some of the most common tasks in quantitative development research. Stata is one of several programming languages used at DIME, but this book focuses on Stata for the code boxes because few high-quality resources exist relative to Stata's frequency of use in development research. The code examples in each of the code boxes and most of the code in this appendix rely on preinstalled data sets as often as possible, so that they will run independently of any other materials. (By contrast, the Demand for Safe Spaces case study code examples can only be run together with the rest of the reproducibility package). The code boxes also demonstrate best-practice coding style for researchers, such as the generous use of comments. In the book, code examples are presented like the following:

```
1    * Load the auto dataset
2    sysuse auto.dta, clear
3
4    * Run a simple regression
5    reg price mpg rep78 headroom, coefl
6
7    * Transpose and store the output
8    matrix results = r(table)'
9
10   * Load the results into memory
11   clear
12   svmat results, n(col)
```

To access this code in do-file format, visit the GitHub repository at https://github.com/worldbank /dime-data-handbook/tree/main/code.

The raw code used in examples in this book can be accessed in several ways. DIME uses GitHub to version-control all of the content of this book, including the code boxes. To see the examples from the code boxes, go to https://github.com/worldbank/dime-data-handbook/tree /master/code. There is no need to download any data, because the examples use Stata's built-in data sets. If Stata is installed on the computer, then it already has the data files used in the code.

For readers not familiar with GitHub, the simplest way to access the code is to click the individual file in the GitHub link provided previously and then click the button labeled "Raw." Doing so will load a page that looks like the one at https://raw.githubusercontent.com/worldbank /dime-data-handbook/master/code/code.do. There, the code can be copied from the browser window into the do-file editor with the formatting intact. This method is practical for only a single file at a time. To download all code used in this book, instead go to https://github.com/worldbank /dime-data-handbook/archive/main.zip. That link downloads a .zip file with all of the content used in writing this book, including the plain-text files used for the book itself. After extracting the .zip file, all of the code will be in a folder called /code/.

The code boxes use built-in commands as much as possible, but user-written commands are also used when they provide important

ietoolkit is a Stata package containing several commands to routinize tasks in impact evaluation. It can be installed through the Boston College Statistical Software Components (SSC) archive (https://ideas.repec .org/c/boc/bocode/s458137 .html), and the code is available at https://github .com/worldbank/ietoolkit. To learn more, see the DIME Wiki at https://dimewiki .worldbank.org/ietoolkit.

iefieldkit is a Stata package containing several commands to routinize tasks related to primary data collection. It can be installed through SSC (https://ideas .repec.org/c/boc/bocode /s458600.html), and the code is available at https://github .com/worldbank/iefieldkit. To learn more, see the DIME Wiki at https://dimewiki .worldbank.org/iefieldkit.

new functionality. In particular, the book points to two suites of Stata commands developed by DIME Analytics, `ietoolkit` and `iefieldkit`, which were written to standardize core data collection, management, and analysis workflows.

To run the code box examples that include user-written commands, it is necessary to install the commands first. The most common place to distribute user-written commands for Stata is the Boston College Statistical Software Components (SSC) archive (https://ideas.repec.org/s/boc /bocode.html). The user-written commands in this book are all available from the SSC archive. Installation of commands from the SSC archive is straightforward, simply type `ssc install randtreat`.

Some commands on SSC are distributed in packages, in which case it is necessary to download the whole package to access the included commands. This is the case, for example, of `ieboilstart`, which is part of the `ietoolkit` package. Commands that are distributed in packages cannot be installed on their own; it will not work to type `ssc install ieboilstart`. Instead, Stata will suggest using `findit ieboilstart`, which will search SSC (among other places) for a package containing a command called `ieboilstart`. Stata will find `ieboilstart` in the package `ietoolkit` and suggest installing it by typing `ssc install ietoolkit` in Stata instead.

Although it can be confusing to work with packages for the first time, doing so is the best way to set up a Stata installation and to benefit from the publicly available work of others. After learning how to install commands like this, it will not be confusing at all. When writing code that relies on user-written commands, it is best practice to install such commands at the beginning of the master do-file, so that the user does not have to search for packages manually.

The DIME Analytics Stata Style Guide

The programming languages used in computer science always have associated style guides. Sometimes they are official, universally agreed-upon style guides, such as PEP8 for Python (van Rossum, Warsaw, and Coghlan 2013). More commonly, they are well-recognized but unofficial style guides like Hadley Wickham's *Tidyverse Style Guide* for R (Wickham, n.d.) or the JavaScript Standard Style for JavaScript (https://standardjs .com/#the-rules). It is also common for large software companies to maintain their own style guides for all languages used in their projects. However, these are not always made public.

Aesthetics are an important part of style guides, but not the main reason for their existence. Rather, style guides allow programmers who are likely to work together to share conventions and understandings of how to execute various common intentions using mutually understandable code language. They also help to improve the quality of the code produced by all programmers using that language. By using a shared style, newer programmers can learn from more experienced programmers how certain coding practices are more or less prone to errors.

The best style guide is the one that is adopted the most widely. Broadly accepted style conventions make it easier for coders to borrow solutions from each other and from examples online without causing bugs that might be found too late. Similarly, globally standardized style guides make it easier for programmers to collaborate on each other's problems and to move from project to project and from team to team.

There is room for personal preference when using style guides, but style guides are first and foremost about quality and standardization, especially when collaborating on code. DIME Analytics created this Stata style guide to improve the quality of all code written in Stata. It is not necessary to follow the style guide precisely. All style rules introduced in this section follow the DIME Analytics suggestion for how to code, but the most important recommendation is to make sure that the style used for code is *consistent*. This guide allows the DIME team to have a consistent code style.

Commenting code

Comments do not change the output of code or how it runs, but without them code will not be accessible to other readers. It will also take much longer to update or edit code written in the past if it does not have adequate comments explaining its intent and functionality. It is important to comment a lot: not only about *what* the code is doing but also about *why* it was written the way it was. In general, writing simpler code that needs less explanation is preferrable to using an elegant and complex method in less space, unless the advanced method is widely accepted.

There are three types of comments in Stata, and they have different purposes.

Commenting multiple lines

```
1 /*
2     This is a do-file with examples of comments in Stata.
3     This type of comment is used to document all of the do-file or a large
4     section of it
5 */
```

Commenting a single line

```
1     * Standardize settings, explicitly set version, and clear memory
2     * (This comment is used to document a task covering at maximum a few lines of code)
3     ieboilstart, version(13.1)
4     `r(version)'
```

(Continues on next page)

Abbreviating commands

Stata commands can often be abbreviated in the code. A command can be abbreviated if the help file indicates an abbreviation by under-lining part of the name in the syntax section at the top. Only built-in commands can be abbreviated; user-written commands cannot. Although Stata allows some commands to be abbreviated to one or two characters, doing so can be confusing—two-letter abbreviations can rarely be "pronounced" in an obvious way that connects them to the functionality of the full command. Therefore, command abbreviations in code should not be shorter than three characters, with the exception of tw for twoway and di for display, and abbreviations should be used only when a widely accepted abbreviation exists. (Many commands also allow options to be abbreviated: these abbreviations are always acceptable at the shortest allowed abbreviation.) The frequently used commands local, global, save, merge, append, or sort should never be abbreviated. The table below lists accepted abbreviations of common Stata commands.

Accepted abbreviations of common Stata commands

Abbreviation	Command
tw	twoway
di	display
gen	generate
mat	matrix
reg	regress
lab	label
sum	summarize
tab	tabulate
bys	bysort
qui	quietly
noi	noisily
cap	capture
forv	forvalues
prog	program
hist	histogram

Abbreviating variable names

Variable names should never be abbreviated; they should be written out completely. Code may change if a variable is introduced later that makes the abbreviation no longer unique. `ieboilstart` executes the command `set varabbrev off` by default and will therefore break any code using variable abbreviations.

Using wildcards and lists in Stata for variable lists (`*`, `?`, and `-`) is also discouraged, because the functionality of the code may change if the data set is changed or even simply reordered. To capture all variables of a certain type, it is better to use `unab` or `lookfor` to build that list in a local macro, which can then be checked so that the right variables are in the right order.

Writing loops

In example code in Stata and other languages, it is common for the name of the local generated by `foreach` or `forvalues` to be something as simple as `i` or `j`. It is preferable, however, to name that index descriptively. One-letter indexes are acceptable only for general examples, for looping through *iterations* with `i`, and for looping across matrices with `i` and `j`. Best practice is for index names to describe what the code is looping over—for example, household members, crops, or medicines. Even counters should be named explicitly. Doing so makes code much more readable, particularly in nested loops.

```
GOOD:

1    * Loop over crops
2    foreach crop in potato cassava maize {
3        * do something to `crop'
4    }


GOOD:

1    * Loop over crops
2    local crops potato cassava maize
3    foreach crop of local crops {
4        * Loop over plot number
5        forvalues plot_num = 1/10 {
6            * do something to `crop' in `plot_num'
7        } // End plot loop
8    } // End crop loop
```

(Continues on next page)

```
1    * Loop over crops
2    foreach i in potato cassava maize {
3        * do something to `i'
4    }
```

To access this code in do-file format, visit the GitHub repository at https://github.com/worldbank /dime-data-handbook/tree/main/code.

Using white space

In Stata, adding one or many spaces does not change the execution of code and can make the code much more readable. Most researchers are well trained in using white space in software like PowerPoint and Excel: a PowerPoint presentation would not have text that does not align, and an Excel table would not have unstructured rows and columns. The same principles apply to coding. In the example below, the exact same code is written twice, but in the better example white space is used to signal that the central object of this segment of code is the variable employed. Organizing the code in this way makes it much quicker to read, and small typos stand out more, making them easier to spot.

```
1    * Create dummy for being employed
2    gen employed = 1
3    replace employed = 0 if (_merge == 2)
4    lab var employed "Person exists in employment data"
5    lab def yesno 1 "Yes" 0 "No"
6    lab val employed yesno
```

```
1    * Create dummy for being employed
2    gen        employed = 1
3    replace    employed = 0 if (_merge == 2)
4    lab var    employed "Person exists in employment data"
5    lab def              yesno 1 "Yes" 0 "No"
6    lab val    employed yesno
```

To access this code in do-file format, visit the GitHub repository at https://github.com/worldbank /dime-data-handbook/tree/main/code.

Indentation is another type of white space that makes code more readable. Any segment of code that is repeated in a loop or conditional on an `if`-statement should be indented four spaces relative to either the loop or the condition as well as the closing curly brace. Similarly, continuing lines of code should be indented under the initial command. If a segment is in a loop inside a loop, then it should be indented another four spaces, making it eight spaces more indented than the main code. In some code editors, this indentation can be achieved by using the tab button. However, the type of tab used in the Stata do-file editor does not always display the same across platforms, such as when publishing code on GitHub. Therefore, inserting four spaces manually is recommended instead of using a tab.

```
GOOD:

1     * Loop over crops
2     foreach crop in potato cassava maize {
3         * Loop over plot number
4         forvalues plot_num = 1/10 {
5             gen crop_`crop'_`plot_num' = "`crop'"
6         }
7     }
8
9     * or
10    local sampleSize = `c(N)'
11    if (`sampleSize' <= 100) {
12        gen use_sample = 0
13    }
14    else {
15        gen use_sample = 1
16    }

BAD:

1     * Loop over crops
2     foreach crop in potato cassava maize {
3     * Loop over plot number
4     forvalues plot_num = 1/10 {
5     gen crop_`crop'_`plot_num' = "`crop'"
6     }
7     }
8
9     * or
10    local sampleSize = `c(N)'
11    if (`sampleSize' <= 100) {
```

(Continues on next page)

```
12      gen use_sample = 0
13      }
14      else {
15      gen use_sample = 1
16      }
```

To access this code in do-file format, visit the GitHub repository at https://github.com/worldbank /dime-data-handbook/tree/main/code.

Writing conditional expressions

All conditional (true/false) expressions should be within at least one set of parentheses. The negation of logical expressions should use bang (!) and not tilde (~). Explicit truth checks should be used (if `value' == 1) rather than implicit ones (if `value'). The missing(`var') function should be used instead of arguments like (if `var' >= .). It is important always to consider whether missing values will affect the evaluation of conditional expressions and modify them appropriately.

```
GOOD:

1      replace gender_string = "Woman" if (gender == 1)
2      replace gender_string = "Man"   if ((gender != 1) & !missing(gender))


BAD:

1      replace gender_string = "Woman" if  gender == 1
2      replace gender_string = "Man"   if (gender ~= 1)
```

To access this code in do-file format, visit the GitHub repository at https://github.com/worldbank /dime-data-handbook/tree/main/code.

When applicable, if-else statements should be used even if the same thing can be expressed with two separate if statements. The use of if-else statements communicates that the two cases are mutually exclusive, which makes code more readable. It is also less error-prone and easier to update if the conditional statement needs to be modified.

GOOD:

```
1    if (`sampleSize' <= 100) {
2        * do something
3    }
4    else {
5        * do something else
6    }
```

BAD:

```
1    if (`sampleSize' <= 100) {
2        * do something
3    }
4    if (`sampleSize' > 100) {
5        * do something else
6    }
```

To access this code in do-file format, visit the GitHub repository at https://github.com/worldbank /dime-data-handbook/tree/main/code.

Writing file paths

All file paths should always be enclosed in double quotes and should always use forward slashes for folder hierarchies (/). Mac and Linux computers cannot read file paths with back slashes, and back slashes cannot be removed easily with find-and-replace because the character has other functional uses in code. File names should be written in lowercase with dashes (my-file.dta). File paths should always include the file extension (.dta, .do, .csv, and so forth). Omitting the extension causes ambiguity if another file with the same name is created, even if there is a default file type.

File paths should also be absolute and dynamic. *Absolute* means that all file paths start at the root folder of the computer, often C:/ in Windows or /Users/ in macOS. Doing so ensures that the correct file is always in the correct folder. The cd command should not be used unless a command specifically requires it. When using cd, it is easy to overwrite a file in another project folder, because many Stata commands implicitly use cd, and therefore the working directory in Stata often changes without warning. Relative file paths are common in many other programming languages, but, unless they are relative to the location of the file running the code, using them is a risky practice. In Stata, relative file paths are relative to the working directory, not to the code file being run.

Dynamic file paths use global macros for the location of the root folder. These globals should be set in a central master do-file. Using the root folder path stored in a global makes it possible to write file paths in Stata that work very similarly to relative paths. It also achieves the functionality that setting cd is often intended to achieve: executing the code on a new system only requires updating file path globals in one location. If global names are unique, there is no risk that files will be saved in the incorrect project folder. Multiple folder globals can be created as needed, and this practice is encouraged.

```
GOOD: Absolute and dynamic paths

1    global myDocs    = "C:/Users/username/Documents"
2    global myProject = "${myDocs}/MyProject"
3    use "${myProject}/my-dataset.dta", clear


BAD: Relative paths

1    cd "C:/Users/username/Documents/MyProject"
2    use MyDataset.dta


BAD: Static paths

1    use "C:/Users/username/Documents/MyProject/MyDataset.dta"
```

To access this code in do-file format, visit the GitHub repository at https://github.com/worldbank /dime-data-handbook/tree/main/code.

Using line breaks

Long lines of code are difficult to read, making it necessary to scroll left and right to see the full line of code. When a line of code is wider than text on a regular paper, a line break is needed. A common line-breaking length is around 80 characters. Stata's do-file editor and other code editors provide a visible guideline. Around that length, using /// breaks the line in the code editor, while telling Stata that the same line of code continues on the next line. Recent versions of the Stata do-file editor—and many other code editors—automatically wrap code lines that are too long. We do not recommend relying on this functionality; instead, actively using /// to wrap lines is recommended to ensure that line breaks are placed such that the code remains the most readable. The /// breaks do not need to be aligned vertically in code, although doing so may help to align comments and improve readability, because indentations should reflect that the command continues to a new line. Lines should be broken where it makes functional sense. Writing comments after /// just as with // usually is a good idea, especially if it is being used to separate functional parts of a single command for clarity.

The #delimit command should be used only for advanced function programming and is officially discouraged in analytical code (Cox 2005). Typing /* */ should never be used to wrap a line: it is distracting and difficult to follow, and those characters should be used only to write regular comments. Line breaks and indentations may be used to highlight the placement of the option comma or other functional syntax in Stata commands.

```
GOOD:

1    graph hbar invil      /// Proportion in village
2        if (priv == 1)    /// Private facilities only
3    , over(statename, sort(1) descending)     /// Order states by values
4        blabel(bar, format(%9.0f))            /// Label the bars
5        ylab(0 "0%" 25 "25%" 50 "50%" 75 "75%" 100 "100%") ///
6        ytit("Share of private primary care visits made in own village")

BAD:

1    #delimit ;
2    graph hbar
3        invil if (priv == 1)
4    , over(statename, sort(1) descending) blabel(bar, format(%9.0f))
5        ylab(0 "0%" 25 "25%" 50 "50%" 75 "75%" 100 "100%")
6        ytit("Share of private primary care visits made in own village");
7    #delimit cr

UGLY:

1    graph hbar /*
2    */    invil if (priv == 1)
```

To access this code in do-file format, visit the GitHub repository at https://github.com/worldbank/dime-data-handbook/tree/main/code.

Using boilerplate code

Boilerplate code consists of a few lines of code that always appear at the top of the code file, and its purpose is to harmonize settings across users running the same code to the greatest degree possible. There is no way in Stata to guarantee that any two installations will always run code in exactly the same way. In the vast majority of cases, they do, but not always, and boilerplate code can mitigate that risk. DIME Analytics developed the `ieboilstart` command to implement many commonly used boilerplate settings that are optimized given a particular installation of Stata. It requires two lines of code to execute the `version` setting, which avoids differences in results due to different versions of Stata. Among other things, it turns the `more` flag off so that code never hangs while waiting to display more output; it turns `varabbrev` off so that abbreviated variable names are rejected; and it maximizes the allowed memory usage and matrix size so that other machines do not reject code for violating system limits. (For example, Stata/SE and Stata/IC allow for different maximum numbers of variables, and the same happens with Stata 14 and Stata 15, so code written in one of these versions may not be able to run in another.) Finally, it clears all stored information in Stata memory, such as noninstalled programs and globals, getting as close as possible to opening a fresh Stata session.

GOOD:

```
1    ieboilstart, version(13.1)
2    `r(version)'
```

ACCEPTABLE:

```
1    set more off, perm
2    clear all
3    set maxvar 10000
4    version 13.1
```

To access this code in do-file format, visit the GitHub repository at https://github.com/worldbank/dime-data-handbook/tree/main/code.

Miscellaneous notes

Multiple graphs should be written as `tw (xx)(xx)(xx)`, not `tw xx||xx||xx`.

In simple expressions, spaces are needed around each binary operator except `^`, writing `gen z = x + y` and `gen z = x^2`.

When the order of operations applies, spacing and parentheses may be adjusted: write `hours + (minutes/60) + (seconds/3600)`, not `hours + minutes / 60 + seconds / 3600`. For long expressions, `+` and `-` operators should start the new line, but `*` and `/` should be used inline. For example:

```
1     gen newvar = x ///
2               - (y/2) ///
3               + a * (b - c)
```

To access this code in do-file format, visit the GitHub repository at https://github.com/worldbank
/dime-data-handbook/tree/main/code.

Instead of printing code to the results window, which is slow, it is better to use `qui` whenever possible and to use `run file.do` rather than `do file.do` in master scripts. To minimize output printed to the command window, commands like `sum` and `tab` should be used sparingly in do-files, unless they are for the purpose of storing r-class statistics. In that case, using the `qui` prefix will prevent printing output. It is also faster to get outputs from commands like `reg` using the `qui` prefix.

References

Cox, Nicholas J. 2005. "Suggestions on Stata Programming Style." *The Stata Journal* 5 (4): 560–66.

van Rossum, Guido, Barry Warsaw, and Nick Coghlan. 2013. "PEP8: Style Guide for Python Code." Python. https://www.python.org/dev/peps/pep-0008/.

Wickham, Hadley. n.d. *The Tidyverse Style Guide.* Tydyverse. https://style.tidyverse .org/index.html.

Appendix B

DIME Analytics resource directory

The resources listed in this appendix are mentioned throughout this book. This appendix provides them in one place for easy reference. All of these resources are made public under generous open-source licenses. This means that they are free to use, reuse, and adapt for any purpose, so long as they are cited appropriately.

Public resources and tools

DIME Wiki. One-stop shop for impact evaluation research solutions. The DIME Wiki is a resource focused on practical implementation guidelines rather than theory, open to the public, easily searchable, suitable for users of varying levels of expertise, up-to-date with the latest technological advances in electronic data collection, and curated by a vibrant network of editors with expertise in the field. Hosted at https://dimewiki.worldbank.org.

Stata Visual Library. A curated, easy-to-browse selection of graphs created in Stata. Clicking on each graph reveals the source code, allowing for easy replication. Hosted at https://worldbank.github.io/stata-visual-library.

R Econ Visual Library. A curated, easy-to-browse selection of graphs created in R. Clicking on each graph reveals the source code, allowing for easy replication. Hosted at https://worldbank.github.io/r-econ-visual-library.

DIME Analytics Research Standards. A repository outlining DIME's public commitments to research ethics, transparency, reproducibility, data security, and data publication, along with supporting tools and resources. Hosted at https://github.com/worldbank/dime-standards.

Flagship training courses

Manage Successful Impact Evaluations (MSIE). The flagship training of DIME Analytics. MSIE is a week-long annual course, held in person in Washington, DC. MSIE is intended to improve the skills and knowledge of impact evaluation practitioners, familiarizing them with critical issues in impact evaluation implementation, recurring challenges, and cutting-edge technologies. The course consists of lectures and hands-on sessions. Through small group discussions and interactive computer lab sessions, participants work together to apply what they have learned and have an opportunity to develop their skills. Hands-on sessions are offered in parallel tracks, with different options based on software preferences and skill level. Course materials available at https://osf.io/h4d8y.

Manage Successful Impact Evaluation Surveys (MSIES). A fully virtual course in which participants learn the workflow for primary data collection. The course covers best practices at all stages of the survey workflow, from planning to piloting instruments and monitoring data quality once fieldwork begins. There is a strong focus throughout on research ethics and reproducible workflows. The course uses a combination of virtual lectures, case studies, readings, and hands-on exercises. Course materials available at https://osf.io/resya.

Research Assistant Onboarding Course. A course designed to familiarize research assistants and research analysts with DIME's standards for data work. By the end of the course's six sessions, participants have the tools and knowledge to implement best practices for transparent and reproducible research. The course focuses on how to set up a collaborative workflow for code, data sets, and research outputs. Most content is platform-independent and software-agnostic, but participants are expected to be familiar with statistical software. The course materials are available at https://osf.io/qtmdp.

Introduction to R for Advanced Stata Users. An introduction to the R programming language, building on knowledge of Stata. The course focuses on common tasks in development research related to descriptive analysis, data visualization, data processing, and geospatial data work. Materials available at https://osf.io/nj6bf.

DIME Analytics Trainings. The DIME Analytics homepage on the Open Science Framework includes links to materials for all past courses and technical trainings. Materials available at https://osf.io/wzjtk.

Software tools and trainings

`ietoolkit`. A suite of Stata commands to routinize common tasks for data management and impact evaluation analysis. Developed at https://github.com/worldbank/ietoolkit.

`iefieldkit`. A suite of Stata commands to routinize and document common tasks in primary data collection. Developed at https://github .com/worldbank/iefieldkit.

DIME Analytics GitHub Trainings and Resources. A GitHub repository containing all the GitHub training materials and resources developed by DIME Analytics. The trainings follow DIME's model for organizing research teams on GitHub and are designed for face-to-face delivery, but materials are shared so that they may be used and adapted by others. Hosted at https://github.com/worldbank/dime-github-trainings.

DIME Analytics LaTeX Training. A user-friendly guide to getting started with LaTeX. Exercises provide opportunities to practice creating appendixes, exporting tables from R or Stata to LaTeX, and formatting tables in LaTeX. Available at https://github.com/worldbank/DIME-LaTeX-Templates.

Appendix C

Research design for impact evaluation

Development Research in Practice focuses on tools, workflows, and practical guidance for implementing research projects. All research team members, including field staff and research assistants, also need to understand research design and specifically how research design choices affect data work. Without going into too much technical detail, because there are many excellent resources on how to design impact evaluations, this appendix presents a brief overview of the most common methods of causal inference, focusing on their implications for data structure and analysis. This appendix is intended to be a reference, especially for junior team members, for understanding how treatment and control groups are constructed for common methods of causal inference, the data structures needed to estimate the corresponding effects, and specific code tools designed for each method.

Research team members who will do the data work need to understand the study design for several reasons. First, if team members do not know how to calculate the correct estimator for the study, they will not be able to assess the statistical power of the research design. This negatively affects their ability to make real-time decisions in the field, where trade-offs about allocating scarce resources between tasks are inevitable, such as deciding between increasing sample size or increasing response rates. Second, understanding how data need to be organized to produce meaningful analytics will save time throughout a project. Third, being familiar with the various approaches to causal inference will make it easier to recognize research opportunities: many of the most interesting projects occur because people in the field recognize the opportunity to implement one of these methods in response to an unexpected event.

This appendix is divided into two sections. The first covers methods of causal inference in experimental and quasi-experimental research designs. The second discusses how to measure treatment effects and structure data for specific methods, including cross-sectional randomized control trials, difference-in-differences designs, regression discontinuity, instrumental variables, matching, and synthetic controls.

Understanding causality, inference, and identification

The types of inputs that impact evaluations are typically concerned with—usually called "treatments"—are also commonly referred to as "programs" or "interventions." Treatments are observed and measured in order to obtain estimates of study-specific *treatment effects*, which are the changes in outcomes attributable to the treatment (Abadie and Cattaneo 2018). The primary goal of research design is to establish causal identification for a treatment effect. *Causal identification* means establishing that a change in an input directly altered an outcome. When a study is well identified, it is possible to say with confidence that the estimate of the treatment effect would, with an infinite amount of data, be precise.

Under this condition, it is possible to draw evidence from the limited samples that are actually accessible, using statistical techniques to express the uncertainty due to not having infinite data. Without identification, it is not possible to say whether the estimate would be accurate, even with unlimited data; therefore, changes in outcomes cannot be attributed to the treatment in the small samples to which researchers typically have access. Having more data is, therefore, not a substitute for having a well-identified experimental design, so it is important to understand how a study identifies its estimate of treatment effects. This understanding allows estimates to be calculated and interpreted appropriately.

All of the study designs discussed here use the potential outcomes framework (Athey and Imbens 2017b) to compare a group that received some treatment to another, counterfactual, group. Each of these approaches can be used in two types of designs: experimental designs, in which the research team is directly responsible for creating the variation in treatment, and quasi-experimental designs, in which the team identifies a "natural" source of variation and uses it for identification. Neither type is implicitly better or worse, and both types are capable of achieving causal identification in different contexts.

Estimating treatment effects using control groups

The key assumption behind estimating treatment effects is that every person, facility, village, or whatever the unit of intervention is, has two possible states: their outcomes if they do not receive some treatment and their outcomes if they do receive that treatment. Each unit's treatment effect is the individual difference between the outcomes that would be realized in the treated state and those that would be realized in the untreated state, and the *average treatment effect* (ATE) is the average of these individual differences across the potentially treated population. Most research designs attempt to estimate this parameter by establishing a counterfactual. A *counterfactual* is a statistical description of what would have happened to specific individuals in an alternative scenario—for example, a different treatment assignment outcome. Several resources provide more or less mathematically intensive approaches to under-standing how various methods do this. *Impact Evaluation in Practice* (Gertler et al. 2016) is a strong general guide to these methods. *Causal Inference* (Hernán and Robins 2010) and *Causal Inference: The Mixtape* (Cunningham 2021) provide more detailed approaches to the tools. *Mostly Harmless Econometrics* (Angrist and Pischke 2008) and *Mastering 'Metrics* (Angrist and Pischke 2014) are excellent resources on the statistical principles behind all econometric approaches.

Intuitively, the problem of causal inference is as follows: it is not possible to observe the same unit in both its treated and untreated states simultaneously, so measuring and averaging these effects directly is impossible (Rubin 2003). Instead, researchers typically make inferences from samples. Causal inference methods are those in which it is possible to identify and estimate an average treatment effect (or, in some designs, other types of treatment effects) by comparing averages between groups. Every research design is based on a way of comparing the outcomes of treated groups against those of another set of "control" observations. These designs all serve to establish that the outcomes in the control group would have been identical on average to those of the treated group in the absence of the treatment. Then, the mathematical properties of averages imply that the calculated difference in averages is equivalent to the average difference, which is the parameter of interest. In this frame-work, almost all causal inference methods can be described as a series of between-group comparisons.

Most of the methods encountered in impact evaluation research rely on some variant of this approach, which is designed to maximize the ability to estimate the effect of the treatment to be evaluated. The focus on identifying treatment effects, however, means that several essential features of causal identification methods are not common in other types of statistical and data science work. First, the econometric models and estimating equations used here do not attempt to create a predictive or comprehensive model of how outcomes are generated. Typically, causal inference designs are not interested in predictive accuracy, so the estimates and predictions that they produce are not as good at predicting outcomes or fitting the data as those of other data science approaches.

Second, when control variables or other variables are included in estimating equations, there is no guarantee that the parameters obtained for those variables are marginal effects in the same way that parameters for the treatment effect(s) are. They can be interpreted only as correl-ative averages, unless there are additional sources of identification. The models that will be constructed and estimated are intended to do exactly one thing: to express the intention of a project's research design and to estimate accurately the effect of the treatment it is evaluating. In other words, these models tell the story of the research design in a way that clarifies the exact comparison being made between control and treatment groups.

Designing experimental and quasi-experimental research

Experimental research designs explicitly allow the research team to change the condition of the populations being studied, often in the form of government programs, nongovernmental organization projects, new regulations, information campaigns, and many more types of interventions (Banerjee and Duflo 2009; see the DIME Wiki at https://dimewiki .worldbank.org/Experimental_Methods). The classic experimental causal inference method is the *randomized control trial* (RCT; see the DIME Wiki at https://dimewiki.worldbank.org/Randomized_Control_Trials). In RCTs, the treatment group is randomized. That is, from an eligible population, a random group of units is placed in the treatment state. Another way to think about these designs is how they establish the control group: a random subset of units is *not* placed in the treatment state, so that it may serve as a counterfactual for the subset that is.

A randomized control group, intuitively, is meant to measure how things would have turned out for the treatment group if its members had not been treated. The RCT approach is particularly effective at doing this, as evidenced by its broad credibility in fields ranging from clinical medicine to development. As a result, RCTs are very popular tools for determining the causal impact of specific programs or policy interventions, as evidenced by the awarding of the 2019 Nobel Prize in Economics to Abhijit Banerjee, Esther Duflo, and Michael Kremer "for their experimental approach to alleviating global poverty" (Royal Swedish Academy of Sciences 2019). However, many types of interventions are impractical or unethical to approach effectively using an experimental strategy; for this reason, the ability to access "big questions" through RCT approaches is sometimes limited (Deaton 2009).

Randomized designs all share several major statistical concerns. The first is the fact that it is always possible to select, by chance, a control group that is not in fact very similar to the treatment group. This risk is called randomization noise, and all RCTs need to assess how randomization noise affects the estimates that are obtained. Second, take-up and implementation fidelity (how closely work carried out in the field corresponds to its planning and intention) are extremely important because programs will, by definition, have no effect if the population intended to be treated does not accept or does not receive the treatment (for an example, see Jung and Hasan 2016). Loss of statistical power occurs quickly and is highly nonlinear: 70 percent take-up or efficacy doubles the required sample, and 50 percent quadruples it (McKenzie 2011). Such effects are also very hard to correct ex post, because they require strong assumptions about the randomness or lack of randomness of take-up and fidelity. Therefore, field time and descriptive work must be dedicated to understanding how these effects play out in a given study.

Quasi-experimental research designs, by contrast, use causal inference methods based on events not controlled by the research team (see the DIME Wiki at https://dimewiki.worldbank.org/Quasi-Experimental_Methods). Instead, they rely on "experiments of nature," in which natural variation can be argued to approximate the type of exogenous variation in treatment availability that a researcher would attempt to create with an experiment (DiNardo 2016). Unlike carefully planned experimental designs, quasi-experimental designs typically require the extra luck of having access to data collected at the right times and places to exploit events that occurred in the past or having the ability to collect data in a time and place where an event that produces causal identification occurred or will occur. Therefore, these methods often use secondary data, or they use primary data in a cross-sectional retrospective method, including administrative data or other new classes of routinely collected information.

Quasi-experimental designs therefore can sometimes access a much broader range of questions than experimental designs, and much less effort is required to produce the treatment and control groups. However, these designs require in-depth understanding of the precise events the researcher wishes to use in order to know what data to acquire and how to model the corresponding experimental design. Additionally, because the population exposed to such events is limited by the scale of the event, quasi-experimental designs are often power-constrained. Because the research team cannot change the population of the study or the treatment assignment, statistical power is typically maximized by ensuring that sampling for data collection is designed to match the study objectives and that attrition from the sampled groups is minimized.

Obtaining treatment effects from specific research designs

Cross-sectional designs

A *cross-sectional* research design is any type of study that observes data in only one time period and directly compares treatment and control groups. Such data are easy to collect and handle because it is not necessary to track units across time. If the time period is after a treatment has been fully delivered, then the outcome values at that time already reflect the effect of the treatment. If the study is experimental, the treatment and control groups are randomly constructed from the population eligible to receive each treatment. By construction, each unit's receipt of the treatment is unrelated to any of its other characteristics, and the ordinary least squares regression of outcome on treatment, without any control variables or adjustments other than for the design (such as clustering and stratification), produces an unbiased estimate of the ATE.

Cross-sectional designs can also exploit variations in nonexperimental data to argue that observed correlations do in fact represent causal effects. This causation can be true unconditionally, which is to say that some random event, such as winning the lottery, is a truly random process and can provide information about the effect of receiving a large amount of money (Imbens, Rubin, and Sacerdote 2001). It can also be true conditionally, which is to say that, once the characteristics that would affect both the likelihood of exposure to a treatment and the outcome of interest are controlled for, the process is as good as random. For example, a study could argue that, once risk preferences are taken into account, exposure to an earthquake is unpredictable (among people with the same risk preferences), and any excess differences after the event (after accounting for differences caused by risk preferences) are caused by the event itself (Callen 2015).

For cross-sectional designs, what must be carefully maintained in data are the research design variables describing the treatment randomization process itself (whether experimental or not) as well as detailed information about differences in data quality and attrition across groups (Athey and Imbens 2017a). Only design controls for the randomization process are needed to construct the appropriate estimator. Clustering of the standard errors is required at the level at which the treatment is assigned to observations, and variables that were used to stratify the treatment must be included as controls in the form of strata fixed effects (Barrios 2014). *Randomization inference* can be used to estimate the underlying variability in the randomization process. *Balance checks*—statistical tests of the similarity of treatment and control groups—are often reported as evidence of an effective randomization and are particularly important when the design is quasi-experimental, because then the randomization process cannot be simulated explicitly. However, controls for balance variables are usually superfluous in experimental designs, because it is certain that the treatment and the balance factors are not correlated in the data-generating process (McKenzie 2017).

Analysis of randomization is typically straightforward and well understood. A typical analysis will include a description of the sampling and randomization results, with analyses such as summary statistics for the eligible population and balance checks for randomization and sample selection. The main results will usually be primary regression specifications for outcomes of interest, with appropriate adjustments for multiple hypothesis testing (for an example, see Armand et al. 2017). These will be followed by additional specifications with adjustments for nonresponse, imbalance, and other potential contaminations. Robustness checks might include randomization-inference analysis or other placebo regression approaches. Various user-written code tools are available to help with the complete process of data analysis, including analyzing balance (iebaltab; see the DIME Wiki at https://dimewiki.worldbank.org /iebaltab) and visualizing treatment effects (iegraph; see the DIME Wiki at https://dimewiki.worldbank.org/iegraph). Extensive tools and methods are available for analyzing selective nonresponse (Özler 2017).

Difference-in-differences

Whereas cross-sectional designs draw their estimates of treatment effects from differences in outcome levels in a single measurement, *difference-in-differences* designs (abbreviated as DD, DiD, diff-in-diff, and other variants; see the DIME Wiki at https://dimewiki.worldbank.org/Difference-in-Differences) estimate treatment effects from *changes* in outcomes between two or more rounds of measurement. In the simplest form of these designs, three control group averages are used to compute effect estimates—the baseline level of treatment units, the baseline level of nontreatment units, and the endline level of nontreatment units (Torres-Reyna 2015). The estimated treatment effect is the excess growth of units that receive the treatment in the period they receive it: calculating that value is equivalent to taking the difference in means between treatment and nontreatment units at endline and subtracting the difference in means at baseline (McKenzie 2012). The regression model includes a control variable for treatment assignment and a control variable for time period, and the treatment effect estimate corresponds to an interaction variable for treatment and time: it indicates the group of observations for which the treatment is active.

This "two-way fixed effects" design depends on the assumption that, in the absence of the treatment, the outcome of the two groups would have changed at the same rate over time, typically referred to as the *parallel trends* assumption (Friedman 2013). Experimental approaches satisfy this requirement in expectation, but a given randomization should still be checked for pretrends as an extension of balance checking (McKenzie 2020). More complex designs with multiple treatment groups or multiple time periods require correspondingly adjusted models (Baker, Larcker, and Wang 2021).

There are two main types of data structures for difference-in-differences: repeated cross-sectional and panel data. In *repeated cross-sectional* designs, each successive round of data collection contains a random sample of observations from the treated and untreated groups; as in cross-sectional designs, both the randomization and sampling processes are critically important to maintain alongside the data. *Panel* data structures are used to observe the exact same units at different times, so that the same units can be analyzed both before and after they have (or have not) received treatment (Jakiela 2019). This structure allows each unit's baseline outcome (the outcome before the intervention) to be used as an additional control for its endline outcome, which can provide increases in power and robustness (McKenzie 2015). When tracking individuals over time for this purpose, maintaining sampling and tracking records is especially important because attrition will remove that unit's information from all time periods, not just the one in which they are unobserved. Panel-style experiments therefore require more effort in fieldwork for studies using original data (Torres-Reyna 2007). Because the baseline and endline may be far apart in time, creating careful records during the first round makes it possible to follow up with the same subjects and to account properly for attrition across rounds (Özler 2017).

As with cross-sectional designs, difference-in-differences designs are widespread. Therefore, many standardized tools are available for analysis. DIME's `ietoolkit` Stata package includes the `ieddtab` command, which produces standardized tables for reporting results (see https://dimewiki .worldbank.org/ieddtab). For more complicated versions of the model (and they can get quite complicated quite quickly), an online dashboard can be used to simulate counterfactual results (Kondylis and Loeser 2019a). As in cross-sectional designs, these main specifications will always be accompanied by balance checks (using baseline values) as well as by randomization, selection, and attrition analysis. In trials of this type, reporting experimental design and execution using the CONSORT style is common in many disciplines and is useful for tracking data over time (Schulz, Altman, and Moher 2010).

Regression discontinuity

Regression discontinuity (RD) designs exploit sharp breaks or limits in policy designs to separate a single group of potentially eligible recipients into comparable groups of individuals who do and do not receive a treatment (see the DIME Wiki at https://dimewiki.worldbank .org/Regression_Discontinuity). These designs differ from cross-sectional and difference-in-differences designs in that the group eligible to receive treatment is not defined directly but instead is created during the treatment implementation. In an RD design, there is typically some program or event that has limited availability because of practical considerations or policy choices and is therefore made available only to individuals who meet a certain threshold requirement.

The intuition of this design is that an underlying *running variable* serves as the sole determinant of access to the program, and a strict cutoff determines the value of this variable at which eligibility stops (Imbens and Lemieux 2008). Common examples are test score thresholds and income thresholds (Evans 2013). The intuition is that individuals who are just above the threshold are very nearly indistinguishable from those who are just below it, and their outcomes after treatment are therefore directly comparable (Lee and Lemieux 2010). The key assumption here is that the running variable cannot be manipulated directly by the potential recipients. If the running variable is time (what is commonly called an "event study"), there are special considerations (Hausman and Rapson 2018). Similarly, spatial discontinuity designs are handled differently because of their multidimensionality (Kondylis and Loeser 2019b).

RD designs are, once implemented, similar in analysis to cross-sectional or difference-in-differences designs. Depending on the available data, the analytical approach will compare individuals who are narrowly on the inclusion side of the discontinuity with those who are narrowly on the exclusion side (Cattaneo, Idrobo, and Titiunik 2019). The regression model will be identical to the corresponding research designs—that is, contingent on whether data have one or more time periods and whether the same units are known to be observed repeatedly.

The treatment effect will be identified by the addition of a control for the running variable—meaning that the treatment effect estimate will be automatically valid only for a subset of observations in a window around the cutoff. In many cases, the treatment effects estimated will be "local" rather than "average" when they cannot be assumed to hold for the entire sample. In the RD model, the functional form of the running variable control and the size of that window, often referred to as the choice of *bandwidth* for the design, are the critical parameters for the result (Calonico et al. 2019). Therefore, RD analysis often includes extensive robustness checks using a variety of both functional forms and bandwidths as well as placebo tests for nonrealized locations of the cutoff.

In the analytical stage, RD designs often include a substantial component of visual evidence. These visual presentations help to suggest both the functional form of the underlying relationship and the type of change observed at the discontinuity; they also help to avoid pitfalls in modeling that are difficult to detect with parameterized hypothesis tests (Pischke 2018). Because these designs are more flexible than others, an extensive set of commands helps to assess the efficacy and results from these designs under various assumptions (Calonico, Cattaneo, and Titiunik 2014). These packages support the testing and reporting of robust plotting and estimation procedures, tests for manipulation of the running variable, and tests for power, sample size, and randomization inference approaches that will complement the main regression approach used for point estimates.

Instrumental variables

Instrumental variables (IV) designs, unlike the previous approaches, begin by assuming that the treatment delivered in the study in question is linked to the outcome in a pattern such that its effect is not directly identifiable. Instead, similar to RD designs, IV designs attempt to focus on a subset of the variation in treatment take-up and assess a limited window of variation that can be argued to be unrelated to other factors (Angrist and Krueger 2001). To do so, the IV approach selects an *instrument* for the treatment status—an otherwise-unrelated predictor of exposure to treatment that affects the take-up status of an individual (see the DIME Wiki at https://dimewiki.worldbank.org/Instrumental_Variables). Whereas RD designs are "sharp"—treatment status is strictly determined by which side of a cutoff an individual is on—IV designs are "fuzzy," meaning that the values of the instrument(s) do not strictly determine the treatment status but instead influence the probability of treatment.

As in RD designs, the fundamental form of the regression is similar to either cross-sectional or difference-in-differences designs. However, instead of controlling for the instrument directly, the IV approach typically uses the *two-stage-least-squares* estimator (Bond 2020). This estimator first forms a prediction of the probability that each unit receives treatment using a regression of treatment status against the instrumental variable(s). That prediction will, by assumption, be the portion of the actual treatment that is due to the instrument and not to any other source; because the instrument is unrelated to all other factors, this portion of the treatment variation can be used to estimate relevant effect sizes.

IV estimators are known to have very high variances relative to other methods, particularly when the relationship between the instrument and the treatment is weak (Andrews, Stock, and Sun 2019). IV designs furthermore rely on strong but untestable assumptions about the relationship between the instrument and the outcome (Bound, Jaeger, and Baker 1995). Therefore, IV designs face scrutiny on the strength and exogeneity of the instrument, and tests for sensitivity to alternative specifications and samples are usually required. However, the method has special experimental cases that are significantly easier to assess: for example, a randomized treatment *assignment* can be used as an instrument for the eventual take-up of the treatment itself (for an example, see Iacovone, Maloney, and McKenzie 2019), especially in cases when take-up is expected to be low or in circumstances when the treatment is available to those who are not specifically assigned to it ("encouragement designs").

In practice, various packages can be used to analyze data and report results from IV designs. Although the built-in Stata command `ivregress` is often used to create the final results, the built-in packages are not sufficient on their own. The first stage of the design should be tested extensively to demonstrate the strength of the relationship between the instrument and the treatment variable being instrumented (Stock and Yogo 2005). This testing can be done using the `weakiv` and `weakivtest` commands (Pflueger and Wang 2015). Additionally, tests should be run that identify and exclude individual observations or clusters that have extreme effects on the estimator, using customized bootstrap or leave-one-out approaches (Young 2019). Finally, bounds can be constructed allowing for imperfections in the exogeneity of the instrument using loosened assumptions, particularly when the underlying instrument is not directly randomized (Clarke and Matta 2018).

Matching

Matching methods use observable characteristics of individuals to construct treatment and control groups that are as similar as possible to each other, either before a randomization process or after the collection of nonrandomized data (see the DIME Wiki at https://dimewiki .worldbank.org/Matching). Matching groups of observations within a data set may result in one-to-one matches or the creation of mutually matched groups; the result of a matching process is similar in concept to the use of randomization strata. In this way, the method can be conceptualized as averaging across the results of a large number of "micro-experiments" in which the units in each potential treatment group are verifiably similar except for their treatment status.

When matching is performed before a randomization process, it can be done on any observable characteristics, including baseline outcomes, if they are available. The randomization should record an indicator identifier for each matching set, as these sets become equivalent to randomization strata and require controls in analysis. This approach reduces the number of potential randomizations dramatically from the possible number that would be available if the matching was not conducted and therefore reduces the variance caused by the study design.

When matching is done ex post in order to substitute for randomization, it is based on the assertion that, within the matched groups, the assignment of treatment is as good as random. However, because many matching models rely on a specific linear model, such as *propensity score matching* (PSM), they are open to the criticism of "specification searching," meaning that researchers can try different models of matching until one, by chance, leads to the desired result. Analytical approaches have shown that the better the fit of the matching model, the more likely it is to have arisen by chance and therefore to be biased (King and Nielsen 2019). Newer methods, such as *coarsened exact matching* (Iacus, King, and Porro 2012), are designed to remove some of the dependence on functional form. In all ex post cases, prespecification of the exact matching model can prevent some of the potential criticisms on this front, but ex post matching in general is not regarded as a strong identification strategy.

Analysis of data from matching designs is relatively straightforward; the simplest design only requires using controls (indicator variables) for each group or, in the case of propensity scoring and similar approaches, weighting the data appropriately in order to balance the analytical samples on the selected variables. The `teffects` suite in Stata provides a wide variety of estimators and analytical tools for various designs (SSCC 2015). The coarsened exact matching (`cem`) package applies the nonparametric approach (Blackwell et al. 2009). The `iematch` command in the `ietoolkit` package produces matchings based on a single continuous matching variable (see the DIME Wiki at https://dimewiki.worldbank.org /iematch). In any of these cases, detailed reporting of the matching model is required, including the resulting effective weights of observations, because in some cases the lack of overlapping supports for treatment and control means that a large number of observations will be weighted near zero and the estimated effect will be generated using a subset of the data.

Synthetic control

Synthetic control is a relatively new method for the case when appropriate counterfactual units do not exist for a treatment of interest, and often there are very few (or only one) treatment units (Abadie, Diamond, and Hainmueller 2015). For example, finding valid comparators for state- or national-level policy changes that can be analyzed only as a single unit is typically very difficult because the set of potential comparators is usually small and diverse with no close matches for the treated unit. Intuitively, the synthetic control method works by constructing a counterfactual version of the treated unit using an average of the other units available (Abadie, Diamond, and Hainmueller 2010). This approach is particularly effective when the lower-level components of the units would be directly comparable: people, households, businesses, and so on in the case of states and countries or passengers or cargo shipments in the case of transport corridors, for example (Gobillon and Magnac 2016). In those situations, the average of the untreated units can be thought of as balancing because it matches the composition of the treated unit.

To construct this estimator, the synthetic control method requires retrospective data on the treatment unit and possible comparators, including historical data on the outcome of interest for all units (for an example, see Fernandes, Hillberry, and Berg 2016). The counterfactual blend is chosen by optimizing the prediction of past outcomes on the basis of potential input characteristics and typically selects a small set of comparators to weight into the final analysis. These data sets therefore may not have a large number of variables or observations, but the extent of the time series both before and after implementation of the treatment are key sources of power for the estimate, as are the number of counterfactual units available. Visualizations are often excellent demonstrations of these results. The synth package provides functionality for use in Stata and R; however, because the number of possible parameters and implementations of the design is large, the package can be complex to operate (Abadie, Diamond, and Hainmueller 2014).

References

Abadie, Alberto, and Matias D. Cattaneo. 2018. "Econometric Methods for Program Evaluation." *Annual Review of Economics* 10 (1): 465–503.

Abadie, Alberto, Alexis Diamond, and Jens Hainmueller. 2010. "Synthetic Control Methods for Comparative Case Studies: Estimating the Effect of California's Tobacco Control Program." *Journal of the American Statistical Association* 105 (490): 493–505.

Abadie, Alberto, Alexis Diamond, and Jens Hainmueller. 2014. "Synth: Stata Module to Implement Synthetic Control Methods for Comparative Case Studies." Statistical Software Components S457334, Department of Economics, Boston College, Boston, MA.

Abadie, Alberto, Alexis Diamond, and Jens Hainmueller. 2015. "Comparative Politics and the Synthetic Control Method." *American Journal of Political Science* 59 (2): 495–510.

Andrews, Isaiah, James H. Stock, and Liyang Sun. 2019. "Weak instruments in instrumental variables regression: Theory and practice." *Annual Review of Economics* 11: 727–53.

Angrist, Joshua D., and Alan B. Krueger. 2001. "Instrumental Variables and the Search for Identification: From Supply and Demand to Natural Experiments." *Journal of Economic Perspectives* 15 (4): 69–85.

Angrist, Joshua D., and Jörn-Steffen Pischke. 2008. *Mostly Harmless Econometrics: An Empiricist's Companion*. Princeton, NJ: Princeton University Press.

Angrist, Joshua D., and Jörn-Steffen Pischke. 2014. *Mastering Metrics: The Path from Cause to Effect*. Princeton, NJ: Princeton University Press.

Armand, Alex, Pedro Carneiro, Andrea Locatelli, Selam Mihreteab, and Joseph Keating. 2017. "Do Public Health Interventions Crowd Out Private Health Investments? Malaria Control Policies in Eritrea." *Labour Economics* 45 (April): 107–15.

Athey, Susan, and Guido W. Imbens. 2017a. "The Econometrics of Randomized Experiments." In *Handbook of Economic Field Experiments.* Vol. 1, edited by Abhijit Vinayak Banerjee and Esther Duflo, 73–140. Amsterdam: North Holland.

Athey, Susan, and Guido W. Imbens. 2017b. "The State of Applied Econometrics: Causality and Policy Evaluation." *Journal of Economic Perspectives* 31 (2): 3–32.

Baker, Andrew, David F. Larcker, and Charles C. Y. Wang. 2021. "How Much Should We Trust Staggered Difference-In-Differences Estimates?" Finance Working Paper No. 736/2021, European Corporate Governance Institute, Brussels, Belgium; Working Paper No. 246, Rock Center for Corporate Governance at Stanford University, Stanford, California. http://dx.doi.org/10.2139/ssrn.3794018.

Banerjee, Abhijit V., and Esther Duflo. 2009. "The Experimental Approach to Development Economics." *Annual Review of Economics* 1 (1): 151–78.

Barrios, Thomas. 2014. "How to Randomize Using Many Baseline Variables." *Development Impact* (blog), January 13. 2014. https://blogs.worldbank.org /impactevaluations/how-randomize-using-many-baseline-variables-guest-post -thomas-barrios.

Blackwell, Matthew, Stefano Iacus, Gary King, and Giuseppe Porro. 2009. "CEM: Coarsened Exact Matching in Stata." *Stata Journal* 9 (4): 524–46.

Bond, Steve. 2020. "IV Estimation Using Stata—A Very Basic Introduction." Nuffield College, Oxford. https://www.nuffield.ox.ac.uk/media/3905/iv-estimation -using-stata.pdf.

Bound, John, David A. Jaeger, and Regina M. Baker. 1995. "Problems with Instrumental Variables Estimation When the Correlation between the Instruments and the Endogenous Explanatory Variable Is Weak." *Journal of the American Statistical Association* 90 (430): 443–50.

Callen, Michael. 2015. "Catastrophes and Time Preference: Evidence from the Indian Ocean Earthquake." *Journal of Economic Behavior & Organization* 118 (October): 199–214.

Calonico, Sebastian, Matias D. Cattaneo, Max H. Farrell, and Rocio Titiunik. 2019. "Regression Discontinuity Designs Using Covariates." *Review of Economics and Statistics* 101 (3): 442–51.

Calonico, Sebastian, Matias D. Cattaneo, and Rocio Titiunik. 2014. "Robust Data-Driven Inference in the Regression-Discontinuity Design." *Stata Journal* 14 (4): 909–46.

Cattaneo, Matias D., Nicolás Idrobo, and Rocío Titiunik. 2019. *A Practical Introduction to Regression Discontinuity Designs: Foundations.* New York: Cambridge University Press.

Clarke, Damian, and Benjamín Matta. 2018. "Practical Considerations for Questionable IVs." *Stata Journal* 18 (3): 663–91.

Cunningham, Scott. 2021. *Causal Inference: The Mixtape.* New Haven, CT: Yale University Press.

Deaton, Angus S. 2009. "Instruments of Development: Randomization in the Tropics and the Search for the Elusive Keys to Economic Development." NBER Working Paper 14690, National Bureau of Economic Research, Cambridge, MA.

DiNardo, John. 2016. "Natural Experiments and Quasi-Natural Experiments." In *The New Palgrave Dictionary of Economics*, 2d ed. New York: Palgrave Macmillan.

Evans, David. 2013. "Regression Discontinuity Porn." *Development Impact* (blog), November 16, 2013. https://blogs.worldbank.org/impactevaluations /regression-discontinuity-porn.

Fernandes, Ana M., Russell Hillberry, and Claudia Berg. 2016. "Expediting Trade: Impact Evaluation of an in-House Clearance Program." Policy Research Working Paper 7708, World Bank, Washington, DC.

Friedman, Jed. 2013. "The Often (Unspoken) Assumptions behind the Difference-in -Difference Estimator in Practice." *Development Impact* (blog), November 21, 2013. https://blogs.worldbank.org/impactevaluations/often-unspoken-assumptions-behind -difference-difference-estimator-practice.

Gertler, Paul J., Sebastian Martinez, Patrick Premand, Laura B. Rawlings, and Christel M. J. Vermeersch. 2016. *Impact Evaluation in Practice*. 2d ed. Washington, DC: World Bank.

Gobillon, Laurent, and Thierry Magnac. 2016. "Regional Policy Evaluation: Interactive Fixed Effects and Synthetic Controls." *Review of Economics and Statistics* 98 (3): 535–51.

Hausman, Catherine, and David S. Rapson. 2018. "Regression Discontinuity in Time: Considerations for Empirical Applications." *Annual Review of Resource Economics* 10 (1): 533–52.

Hernán, Miguel A., and James M. Robins. 2010. *Causal Inference: What If.* Boca Raton, FL: CRC Press.

Iacovone, Leonardo, William F. Maloney, and David J. McKenzie. 2019. "Improving Management with Individual and Group-Based Consulting: Results from a Randomized Experiment in Colombia." Policy Research Working Paper 8854, World Bank, Washington, DC.

Iacus, Stefano M., Gary King, and Giuseppe Porro. 2012. "Causal Inference without Balance Checking: Coarsened Exact Matching." *Political Analysis* 20 (1): 1–24.

Imbens, Guido W., and Thomas Lemieux. 2008. "Regression Discontinuity Designs: A Guide to Practice." *Journal of Econometrics* 142 (2): 615–35.

Imbens, Guido W., Donald B. Rubin, and Bruce I. Sacerdote. 2001. "Estimating the Effect of Unearned Income on Labor Earnings, Savings, and Consumption: Evidence from a Survey of Lottery Players." *American Economic Review* 91 (4): 778–94.

Jakiela, Pamela. 2019. "What Are We Estimating When We Estimate Difference-in-Differences?" *Development Impact* (blog), September 30, 2019. https://blogs .worldbank.org/impactevaluations/what-are-we-estimating-when-we-estimate -difference-differences.

Jung, Haeil, and Amer Hasan. 2016. "The Impact of Early Childhood Education on Early Achievement Gaps in Indonesia." *Journal of Development Effectiveness* 8 (2): 216–33.

King, Gary, and Richard Nielsen. 2019. "Why Propensity Scores Should Not Be Used for Matching." *Political Analysis* 27 (4): 435–54.

Kondylis, Florence, and John Loeser. 2019a. "Econometrics Sandbox: Event Study Designs & Co." *Development Impact* (blog), October 16, 2019. https://blogs .worldbank.org/impactevaluations/econometrics-sandbox-event-study-designs-co.

Kondylis, Florence, and John Loeser. 2019b. "Spatial Jumps." *Development Impact* (blog), March 13, 2019. https://blogs.worldbank.org/impactevaluations /spatial-jumps.

Lee, David S., and Thomas Lemieux. 2010. "Regression Discontinuity Designs in Economics." *Journal of Economic Literature* 48 (2): 281–355.

McKenzie, David. 2011. "Power Calculations 101: Dealing with Incomplete Take-up." *Development Impact* (blog), May 23, 2011.

McKenzie, David. 2012. "Beyond Baseline and Follow-up: The Case for More T in Experiments." *Journal of Development Economics* 99 (2): 210–21.

McKenzie, David. 2015. "Another Reason to Prefer Ancova: Dealing with Changes in Measurement between Baseline and Follow-up." *Development Impact* (blog), June 22, 2015. https://blogs.worldbank.org/impactevaluations/another-reason-prefer-ancova-dealing-changes-measurement-between-baseline-and-follow.

McKenzie, David. 2017. "Should We Require Balance T-Tests of Baseline Observables in Randomized Experiments?" *Development Impact* (blog), June 26, 2017. https://blogs.worldbank.org/impactevaluations/should-we-require-balance-t-tests-baseline-observables-randomized-experiments.

McKenzie, David. 2020. "Revisiting the Difference-in-Differences Parallel Trends Assumption: Part I Pre-Trend Testing." *Development Impact* (blog), January 21, 2020. https://blogs.worldbank.org/impactevaluations/revisiting-difference-differences-parallel-trends-assumption-part-i-pre-trend.

Özler, Berk. 2017. "Dealing with Attrition in Field Experiments." *Development Impact* (blog), September 24, 2017. https://blogs.worldbank.org/impactevaluations/dealing-attrition-field-experiments.

Pflueger, Carolin E., and Su Wang. 2015. "A Robust Test for Weak Instruments in Stata." *Stata Journal* 15 (1): 216–25. https://doi.org/10.1177/1536867X1501500113.

Pischke, Jorn-Steffen. 2018. "Regression Discontinuity Design." London School of Economics, London. https://econ.lse.ac.uk/staff/spischke/ec533/RD.pdf.

Royal Swedish Academy of Sciences. 2019. "The Prize in Economic Sciences 2019." Royal Swedish Academy of Sciences, Stockholm, October 14. 2019. https://www.nobelprize.org/prizes/economic-sciences/2019/summary/.

Rubin, Donald B. 2003. "Basic Concepts of Statistical Inference for Causal Effects in Experiments and Observational Studies." Summary of course material used in Quantitative Reasoning 33, Harvard University, Cambridge, MA.

Schulz, Kenneth F., Douglas G. Altman, and David Moher. 2010. "CONSORT 2010 Statement: Updated Guidelines for Reporting Parallel Group Randomised Trials." *BMC Medicine* 8 (1): 18.

SSCC (Social Science Computing Cooperative). 2015. "Propensity Score Matching in Stata Using Teffects." University of Wisconsin, Madison, WI. https://www.ssc.wisc.edu/sscc/pubs/stata_psmatch.htm.

Stock, James, and Motohiro Yogo. 2005. "Testing for Weak Instruments in Linear IV Regression." In *Identification and Inference for Econometric Models*, edited by Donald W. K. Andrews, 80–108. New York: Cambridge University Press. https://scholar.harvard.edu/files/stock/files/testing_for_weak_instruments_in_linear_iv_regression.pdf.

Torres-Reyna, Oscar. 2007. "Panel Data Analysis Fixed and Random Effects Using Stata (V. 4.2)." Data and Statistical Services, Princeton University, Princeton, NJ.

Torres-Reyna, Oscar. 2015. "Differences-in-Differences (Using Stata)." Data and Statistical Services, Princeton University, Princeton, NJ. http://dss.princeton.edu/training/.

Young, Alwyn. 2019. "Consistency without Inference: Instrumental Variables in Practical Application." London School of Economics, London.